Sud Ingle

IN SEARCH OF PERFECTION
How to Create/Maintain/Improve Quality

A SPECTRUM BOOK

Prentice-Hall, Inc., Englewood Cliffs, New Jersey 07632

Library of Congress Cataloging in Publication Data

Ingle, Sud.
   In search of perfection.

   "A Spectrum Book."
   Bibliography: p.
   Includes index.
   1. Organizational change. 2. Organizational effectiveness. 3. Quality control. 4. Quality circles. I. Title.
HD58.8.154   1985   658.5'62   84-26202
ISBN 0-13-467556-8
ISBN 0-13-467523-1 (pbk.)

Figures 2-1, 2-3, 3-1, 4-1, 4-2, 4-3, 4-4, 5-3, 18-17, 18-18, 18-19, 18-20, 18-21, 19-1, A-1, and B-1 courtesy of Organizational Quality Improvement slide/cassette programs, published by BNA Communications, Rockville, MD 20850.
Figures 7-2 and 13-4 courtesy of Ricoh Corporation, 5 Dedrick Place, West Caldwell, NJ 07006.
Figure 8-3 courtesy of Precision Metal, 614 Superior Avenue West, Cleveland, OH 44113.

© 1985 by Prentice-Hall, Inc., Englewood Cliffs, New Jersey 07632.
All rights reserved. No part of this book may be reproduced in any form or by any means without permission in writing from the publisher.
A Spectrum Book. Printed in the United States of America.

10 9 8 7 6 5 4 3 2

ISBN 0-13-467556-8

ISBN 0-13-467523-1 {PBK.}

Editorial/production supervision: Marlys Lehmann
Cover design ©1985 by Jeannette Jacobs
Manufacturing buyer: Gary Orso

This book is available at a special discount when ordered in bulk quantities. Contact Prentice-Hall, Inc., General Publishing Division, Special Sales, Englewood Cliffs, N.J. 07632.

Prentice-Hall International, Inc., *London*
Prentice-Hall of Australia Pty. Limited, *Sydney*
Prentice-Hall Canada Inc., *Toronto*
Prentice-Hall Hispanoamericana, S.A., *Mexico*
Prentice-Hall of India Private Limited, *New Delhi*
Prentice-Hall of Japan, Inc., *Tokyo*
Prentice-Hall of Southeast Asia Pte. Ltd., *Singapore*
Whitehall Books Limited, *Wellington, New Zealand*
Editora Prentice-Hall do Brasil Ltda., *Rio de Janeiro*

To
IAQC (International Association of Quality Circles), which strengthens my belief in a people-building philosophy, ASQC (American Society of Quality Control), which taught me the basics of quality control, and other societies around the world that are engaged in promoting quality improvement activities contributing to the betterment of the world

CONTENTS

Preface vii

Chapter One In Search of Perfection 1

Part One

Chapter Two Basics of OQI 19
Chapter Three Managing for OQI 32
Chapter Four Statistical Problem-Solving Methods 42
Chapter Five Quality Planning 51
Chapter Six Quality Deployment 69
Chapter Seven New Product Introduction: Quality of Design 82
Chapter Eight Vendor Quality Control 110
Chapter Nine Manufacturing Quality 125
Chapter Ten Computer-Aided Quality Information Systems 146
Chapter Eleven Service Quality 162
Chapter Twelve Quality Audits 170
Chapter Thirteen Quality Circles: Improving Quality Through People Involvement 188

Chapter Fourteen	Recommended Training Programs for OQI 218
Chapter Fifteen	OQI in Service Industries 229
Chapter Sixteen	Nationwide Quality Improvement 245
Chapter Seventeen	Why Japan Is Ahead 254

Part Two

Chapter Eighteen	Basic Industrial Statistics for Nonstatisticians (SPC) 269

Part Three

Chapter Nineteen	Conclusion: Who Will Survive? 299

Appendix A: Sources for Statistical and OQI Training 303

Appendix B: Quality Costs 309

Appendix C: Statistical Process Control (SPC) 318

Appendix D: Design of Experiments 329

Appendix E: Quality Assurance Manual 332

Appendix F: Organizational Quality Performance Evaluation 337

Index 339

PREFACE

This book is for everyone connected with an organization. It is said that "Quality is everyone's job." However, one cannot find a system or a method to make it happen that easily. I have tried to put together in this book my experiences in various organizations where the quality improvement process is being implemented as a way of life. The experience indicates that one cannot make total organizational quality improvement unless everybody is involved in the quality improvement system.

Today we are entering a new quality era. One cannot rest on one's past laurels and enjoy their fruits forever. The world is getting smaller and the competition is getting tougher day by day. Hence, one needs to search constantly for new methods to improve quality, productivity, and efficiency, and to reduce cost. Japan has shown to the rest of the world that if everyone is involved in building high-quality products or offering high-quality services, the rest of the improvement follows automatically. One must remember that ongoing quality improvement is a necessity to keep customers satisfied, and happy customers are a key to success.

This book is intended to show you how to implement the organizational improvement process using systematic statistical problem-solving methods.

The first three chapters explain the basics of the organizational quality improvement process. Chapter Five stresses the importance of quality planning and quality policy. This is also the first reference to our Quality Wheel, and I discuss the various spokes of the Quality Wheel in the next several chapters. In studying the Quality Wheel concept, you should get a thorough idea of what is involved in improving various functions of the organization. Chapter Thirteen describes an exciting participative management technique called Quality Circles, and the next few chapters describe at length the various strategies needed for nationwide quality improvement.

It is important that we begin a quality movement on a nationwide basis so that organizations can help each other in quality improvement. This gives the quality improvement process a global perspective. I conclude the first part with a brief review of Japanese manufacturing and quality control techniques.

In Part II, the basic statistical techniques are explained in simple language for use by nonstatisticians. This section is intended to offer nonstatisticians the ability to use and effectively apply simple industrial statistical techniques.

The final part of the book describes essential ingredients that one should know in implementing the OQI process. Quality costs, SPC, design of experiments, and other key elements are described in the six Appendixes.

The questions at the end of many of the chapters are intended for the evaluation of the reader's own organization. The self-analysis of quality evaluation (Appendix F) is intended to help each organization to find out its weak areas for the quality improvement process. I have used this technique (plus 300 more questions) in evaluating various organizations. I hope that you use this system effectively and get others in the organization to participate in the self-analysis as it is essential that many members of your management personnel take part so as to cooperatively solve quality problems. This team spirit is healthy for an organization.

Acknowledgments

I express my heartfelt gratitude to the following people without whose constant support this manuscript would have been impossible:

At Mercury Marine: R. J. Jordan, president; D. True, vice president, Quality; J. Anthony, vice president, Manufacturing; Dr. E. J. Morgan, director, Advance Research; L. Torriello, director, Advance Planning; R. Curtis, Quality Circle manager; J. Holstein, Q. C. facilitator; and J. Christensen, Q. C. facilitator, all of whom constantly supported my efforts in promoting Quality Circles and the quality improvement process.

I also thank Robert Gerhke, president, B.N.A. Communications; and Jules Eitington and Judy Knight, who helped me in putting my ideas on OQI in slide/casssette form.

I thank especially my wife, Neelima, who worked many hours in rewriting the manuscript. I also thank my daughters, Geeta and Vinita, for giving up their leisure hours to let me work on the manuscript.

Special thanks go to T. Lewis, manager, quality training, Mercury Marine; A. M. Salvekar, assistant administrator, St. Cloud Hospital, St. Cloud, Minnesota; and Anil Ingle; Rosemary Warren; Sharron Pollom; Sherry Tietz; Marie Black; and Joanne Acheson, without whose timely help I would never have finished this book.

Chapter One
IN SEARCH OF PERFECTION

Japan, Japan, Japan! That's all we hear about, all we read about these days—that the quality of the products churned out by the Japanese industry has no peer. Today, we see in every field the phenomenal success of this little country that was almost nonexistent 30 years back. Whether we like it or not, we are going to hear about Japan for the rest of the century, and most likely the twentieth century is going to go down in history as the Japanese era.

The first wave of industrialization happened when Eli Whitney invented the cotton gin. The second wave came when Henry Ford and others started to use mass-production techniques, marking the beginning of standardization in the United States. The third wave of industrialization has taken place in Japan, to improve quality and production through statistical thinking, which no one else can copy that easily today.

Many facts about Japan are published in magazines, newspapers, and trade journals. A recent article published in the *Harvard Business Review* (September–October 1983) described a study made on air-conditioning units. Even though the United States does not directly face Japanese competition in air-conditioning markets today, the article compared the quality and productivity of the companies in the two countries. The results were startling to many executives and management personnel.

Some of the observations given in this study are as follows:

1. Japanese manufacturers, in general, produce products that are far superior to their American rivals because of worker participation in quality control and intense attention to quality problems by top executives in Japan—not because of any technological advances.
2. The companies with the best quality records also have the highest productivity per worker.
3. The extra cost involved in making higher-quality Japanese goods is about half of what American manufacturers spend on fixing defective products.
4. The failure rates of air conditioners made by the worst producers, which are all American, are between 500 and 1000 times greater than those made by the best producers, all of which were Japanese.

One can add to the list many other findings from the automobile, electronic, and steel industries that are published in *Business Week, The New York Times, The Wall Street Journal,* and so on. When we hear and read all this, one wonders where we went wrong. What happened to good old American quality and American pride in building good-quality products? What is happening to our image as a world leader? Let us analyze briefly the problems and convictions we experienced in the last decade in improving our quality in manufacturing and service industries.

Factors Contributing to Low Quality Standards in the Last Decade

1. Emphasis on Quantity Instead of Quality

Our industries are manufacturing products in large quantities nowadays, so that they can be sold in the marketplace at competitive rates. However, this quantity-oriented philosophy has deteriorated the quality of the product. It has been observed many times, that several batches of the product have to be rejected due to unsatisfactory quality. In Japan, a similar phenomenon was taking place after World War II. In those days, the products from western countries, particularly from the United States and from European countries such as Germany and Great Britain, were superior in quality to those from Japan. After the 1950s, the trend slowly changed. According to the director of a Japanese firm, "The change has not taken place overnight. We worked hard for the last twenty-five years to achieve the 'quality image' that you see today."

2. Myth—"We are No. 1— No Need for Improvement"

During the last decade, it has been observed that several of our industries have boasted about their enormous increase in production, particularly in the chemical, automobile, and plastics industries, as well as some others. In several instances the remark was made, "We are number one as far as production is concerned. We produce goods at competitive cost and can easily sell our goods in the marketplace with reasonable profit; there is no need to improve any further." This has encouraged a sort of lethargy among workers and management, and the quality of the product has gone down.

3. "We Know What Consumers Need"

There is a trend in all American industries to believe that they have worked out all difficulties with customers, and that they are thoroughly familiar with the customers' needs and wants. This belief, as everyone is aware, is always short-lived. It is well known that no customer will be one hundred percent satisfied at any time. Even the quality product which the producer believes is totally good will have some drawbacks in the eyes of the customers.

4. Always Working on "Short Fixes"— Poor Introduction of New Products or Services

Most organizations will introduce products and services in a rush to beat the competition. Many times customers are used to test the products and services. Later on, when it becomes evident that certain changes are essential, companies will implement short fixes instead of looking for long-range fixes. Consumers have experienced this type of problem with many organizations in the United States. We need to change our attitude toward new products and our corrective actions in fixing products.

5. Doors Closed to Worldwide Competition

After World War II the industries in European countries, as well as Japan, had their greatest setbacks; most of the industrial field has been captured by the United States. The tremendous capacity of the United States to manufacture goods in enormous quantities has resulted in the economical production of those goods. Up to 1970 it was observed that no other country could compete with the United States in the manufacture of any product. It was thought that the U.S. could supply any product—cars, machinery, chemicals, pharmaceuticals, drugs, and dyes, to name a few—to all the world at a competitive rate and that no country could survive this competition. However, due to technical developments and several techniques that have been introduced in industry, other countries such as Japan have risen. By the end of 1980, Japan had become the foremost manufacturing country in the world. In this way, doors closed to worldwide competition and negligence to adopt modified techniques and novel methods, such as use of Quality Circles and statistics, have resulted in deterioration of the image of our industry in the world market.

6. No Long-Term Goals

Several companies that were involved in long-term research progress over the last decade are now planning programs running for two to three years. This policy has obliged the companies to make drastic changes in daily work. People working on one project are being shifted to other projects, and in certain cases, the training given to staff in one area has already been lost forever. For example, during the Carter presidency emphasis was placed on conducting basic research in solar energy; about $40 million was spent on the project. However, the Reagan administration gave this project low priority and cut it to a large extent. Hence, the basic observations and trained manpower in this field have been already lost. They are already outdated; it will be hard for them to catch up once they are out of the race. It is essential for any company to have at least a few long-range projects in which trained manpower is utilized and the basic results will be reviewed now and then, with a view toward adopting them for industrial utilization.

7. Not Enough Investment in New Equipment

The industrial approach to a problem started in a big way in the United States after the Second World War. Companies started to manufacture goods in a big way and to compete with the world market. As the products were sold at a profit, there was no need to review either the technology or the process. Hence, in almost all industries, the old methodology still exists. The old equipment is still utilized. However, in small countries like Japan and Germany, the same product is manufactured by new technology, and several innovations in both analytical and quality-assurance methods have taken place. It has become the need of the day to invest a sizable amount in funds for installing new equipment in industry. Many industries are reluctant to do so because as science becomes more sophisticated, the cost of equipment rises, and more staff and technicians must be hired. However, this is essential to improve the quality of the product.

8. Not Enough Basic Research

There are two opposing views represented in the debate over basic university research. Edward E. David, Jr., president of Exxon Research and Engineering Company, remarked, "There is a fine science and technique created in academia which is not effectively coupled with the nation's commercial innovated system, and research as an autonomous function will tend to fade."

Equally outspoken on the same subject is California Institute and Technology Provost and President, John D. Roberts. He advocates, "State universities are regarded as tools of people, and they have to respond where people want something. But there is a need to have scientists. We have to have scientists who are free to look at the future without being battered by the hurly-burly of current events."

In general, although there is very little input, it is usually thought that basic research is not useful for industries. Funds allotted to basic research are utilized to maintain the R & D lab. However, it is now well established that basic research is a must for industry to improve the quality of a product, and it pays a large dividend in the long run.

9. No Quality Plans or Strategies

If we make a survey of our companies, it is evident that they have few plans to improve the quality of their product or the quality of their work. It is shocking to note that while Japan has planned for nationwide quality control for ten years, we have not even thought about consolidating our efforts and planning strategies to improve quality.

10. No Identification of Quality Costs

Organizations are familiar with cost-benefit analysis or profit-and-loss statements. However, few organizations really try hard to understand and collect information on quality costs. Quality costs, in general, are of four types: prevention costs, appraisal costs, internal failures costs, and external failure costs. Most of the time, accounting departments will give the excuse that they do not understand the details of quality costs and don't know how to go about it. It is about time we change our philosophy and do something in this area. Once we know how to walk, we can learn to run later on!

11. No National Emphasis or Help for Quality Improvement

Any nation interested in improving its quality and productivity needs to understand that there must be a total nationwide commitment toward that end. It is of very little use for a few to try organizing to build up quality when major industries are working in the old-fashioned way. By working in a haphazard manner, national quality does not improve. It is similar to a few farmers spraying pesticides on their crops to eradicate pests. This experiment does not yield results because the neighboring farms are not participating in the program. Emphasis should be given on the *national level,* with a specific commitment from the government to nationwide quality improvement.

12. Need for JIT (Just in Time) Purchasing

"A stitch in time saves nine." This is the case when purchasing materials required for industries. From an industry's inventory and a look at its last year, the annual requirements of raw materials should be evident. It is always beneficial to plan ahead and then purchase these materials "just in time" (JIT), so the production schedule will not be hampered. This philosophy is well known and is accepted in principle by every company. However, the practical experience is altogether different. It has been observed that the purchase of raw materials is conducted at the eleventh hour, when it is badly required by the production department. Due to immediate need, the material has to be purchased at a higher cost—and many times the material of required specification is not available in the required quantity. A small quantity available in the market can be obtained only at an exorbitant premium. The overall effect is an increase in the production cost. Hence, there is always a need for JIT purchasing.

13. Need for (JIT) Production

Observations cited in the case of purchase are equally applicable in the case of production. The company should be well equipped to produce the required product at a definite time. The work schedule should be arranged so that there is no delay in delivering the goods at the specified time. Prompt service and quick delivery at the right time are the essence of business. This type of production also helps in eliminating unnecessary inventory. However, one of its greatest advantages is in locating and fixing quality problems immediately. It is just like large rocks under the water in a lake: If the water level is too high, one cannot see these rocks and avoid the danger. Similarly, if the inventory is small, the defects are spotted and corrected immediately. There is less scrap and rework, and quality improves dramatically.

14. No Constant Revision of Present Production Methods

In industries, the technology of the products introduced a decade ago is still used for production. At that time, it was novel and really made an impact on the market. However, the methods adopted at that time are slowly becoming obsolete; there is always a need to revise production methods now and then. An R & D organization should study the various methods adopted for production and think about new innovative processes or methods that would make the product in a cheaper and more economical way. This constant revision of the method becomes one of the essential factors of the product's quality. However, this factor is usually neglected in industry, and the same old technology is used as long as the product can be sold in the marketplace at a reasonable profit.

15. No Customer-Based Measurements

In large industries, both production and the product are enormous, and it is difficult to produce material according to the specifications of the customer. Many times a customer needs the same product with slight modification. This is hard to do, as the production is on such a large scale. For any company that wants to sell its product to a large number of consumers, a polished public image is important.

16. Cooperation Between Management, Unions, and the Government

In the management of any organization or company, decision making is always in the hands of a few executives. The common worker cannot challenge whether decisions are right or wrong. Many times, decisions taken at the managerial level are harmful to the operation of the company. However, workers cannot raise their voices and point out the pros and cons of the decision. This kind of management style many times brings conflict between management and the workers.

As we are aware, in many countries unions have a very strong hold on industries. If there is conflict between management and the union, the union leaders can organize strikes or create several other difficulties to show their strength. Such situations lead to discomfort in the industrial atmosphere and hamper the progress of the work. Several man-days are wasted and the nation loses large amounts of revenue. It is astonishing to note that a loss of manpower in the United States for only 30 minutes makes the country lose about $10 million.

Thus, you can see how important it is to have mutual cooperation between the government, the management of the company, and the union leaders.

17. Relationship between Vendor and Vendee

Vendors in most organizations are regarded as outsiders; they are not considered part of the organization. They are involved in product development or service development early in the game. Similarly, when problems occur, they are generally left to the vendors to fix. It is their problem. We need to change the working relationship; we need to understand each other and work closely for future quality improvement.

18. Management Styles—Participative Versus Top Down

At its inception, a company will usually consist of a proprietor and subordinates. As the company grows, the proprietor becomes the executive manager. He is responsible for the development of the company and obviously holds the top-ranking position. Other assistants will be graded according to the work allocated to them. This type of management style is known as *top-down management*. In such a management style, decisions are made only by a few people, while the majority of people are left out. Decisions are generally made in a short time, but their implementation takes a long time.

Another type of management style is *participative management*. In this type, various committees are formed to get maximum participation from the employees to manage the business more effectively. Such committees consist of members from the ranking executive to the ground-level worker. These members are either selected by the administration or elected by the workers in their field. In this way, the management committee becomes a cross section of the complete company. The decisions taken by the committee are accepted as the decision taken by the company as a whole. In this way, every worker feels that he or she is responsible for the ups and downs in the company. A worker is always alert to see that the company should be benefited by his or her attitude toward the work. It is found that in many companies such participative management has produced marvelous results.

19. Emphasis on Quality Training in Colleges and Schools

For the last ten years, education in America has become more liberal. Mathematics and science are neglected in high schools as well as in colleges. One can graduate from an educational institution without learning math or statistics. This affects many organizations due to the lack of skilled personnel in these areas. There are very few colleges or schools in our country that train students in statistical quality control or other quality aspects. In Japan, all these subjects are mandatory in schools and colleges.

20. No Use of Statistical Methods in Industries

The main interest of our industries is to get maximum production, even at the cost of quality. For that reason, old-fashioned methods are often used instead of newer methods developed by statistical approaches. These newer methods are essential for accurate testing and strict quality standards. In order to get reliable information to come up with new viable testing methods, Quality Circles are of immense importance.

21. Improvement in "Quality Costs Money" Attitude

"Quality costs money" is a myth. In the long range, quality building does not cost money, but rather makes money. It is a strong belief of the management of industry that improvement in quality costs money. Management believes that there should be minimum change in the daily routine of the company, because even a small change in technology or method will cause the company heavy expenditure. They believe it is doubtful whether the change will improve the quality of the product or not. Hence, improvement in quality is always considered to be a heavy financial risk. They believe companies should strive to minimize the total quality costs in an organization, even though these costs would increase the market share of products and services.

22. Workers Make All the Mistakes

"We are always right" is usually the philosophy of the management of any industry. If any success is achieved, the credit is taken by the administration; however, failures are attributed to the behavior of the employees. Obviously, as we are aware, this is not true. However, mistakes are made in an organization due to poor planning, poor communication, and unclear practices that have existed for years.

23. Less Importance to Worker Participation and Worker's Role in Building Quality Products

Products are produced in industry by utilizing the work force and well-set-up technology. When the optimization of conditions to prepare the required product is achieved, there appears to be no need to pay constant attention to the workers. The product obtained is usually a quality product having certain specifications, and it can be sold in the market like a hotcake. The management does not think to improve the quality any further. Under these circumstances, the order of the day is for workers to attend to their duties and carry out the assigned work sincerely. After eight hours, they usually forget what they have done; they do not get involved in their job.

This type of attitude creates an unhealthy atmosphere in the company. Workers do not regard the job as their responsibility; they do not put their heart and soul into it. They do not concentrate on their work, nor do they try to find out how they can make the product still better. Because of these factors, the quality of the product remains always at a low level.

It is essential that importance should be given to the workers' participation in a project. They should be convinced that their work and ideas are well appreciated by the management and that they play an important role in building quality products. Such an atmosphere can be created in the company by new techniques such as starting Quality Circles.

24. Necessity of Ongoing Training Programs in Various Skills

As science progresses, new equipment, methods, and technologies are being introduced into various industries, and the technologies that had been followed become more obsolete day by day. Due to this rapid progress in the scientific field, workers face tremendous pressure. They are usually trained to a specific job, remaining content with the methods and techniques they learned in their high school and college days. The workers are not usually exposed to new methods or to instrumentational techniques; hence, they are reluctant to work in technologies equipped with modern methods. It becomes of prime importance to expose the worker in various skills to modern techniques every now and then. Hence, ongoing training programs in various skills should be conducted in every company as far as possible. There should at least be workshops conducted that last a week or so, giving the worker the confidence to handle new techniques.

25. Poor Image of Quality-Control Department

It is said that we created problems in this country when we created the quality-control department. The image of the quality-control department has been low for the past decade. Generally, it is thought that the quality-control department creates problems. Quality-control personnel are considered troublemakers; on the other hand, in some cases, the quality-control department is supposed to fix all problems at all times. In reality, the quality-control department neither creates nor fixes problems all by itself. The quality-control department should be regarded as a liaison that collects, analyzes, and solves problems that are created due to poor-quality decisions made by other departments in an organization.

Time is Running Out

None of the problems mentioned above are new. Most of us have been aware of them for a long time. However, it seems that very few of us have taken action to correct them. *Business Week* in July 1983 revealed the vivid story of the steel industry and its fate in the United States, painting a sad picture! But steel industries are not alone. Many other industries—electronic, recreational, air-conditioning, shipbuilding, automobile—are facing similar problems. It is essential for management to act so as to survive in this "new-quality era."

There are four courses of action that can be taken to tackle these problems. They are as follows:

1. Institute major changes in the company, as described in this book.
2. Change gradually when one faces the problems, as is being done in many industries.
3. Ignore the problems and do nothing.
4. Start learning a new language (preferably Japanese), since more and more companies in this country are being run by Japanese management. (Source: Japan Economic Institute of America, *United States of America Today*.) The companies that are run by Japanese management are doing very well; employees of these firms do not mind the changes brought by Japanese management at all. (See "Quasar," story from *People & Productivity* an educational film released by Encyclopaedia Britannica in 1981.)

Management Responsibilities for the Future

Improvements in the quality and productivity of an organization depend on effective management. It is the responsibility of the management to realize the challenge and arrange necessary programs to cope with future changes. One should also remember that quality improvement is a never-ending job.

Today, America and many other countries are changing. The world is getting smaller. To maintain high quality and productivity standards, management must realize and be responsible for the following:

1. We have a quality problem today and need to address it properly. Just understanding that the problem exists will help solve half of it.
2. Improvement in quality is the key to high productivity.
3. Quality is a changing target. It is not only fitness for use or conformity to specifications—the customer needs to be satisfied. It is the customer who is going to decide the quality of products and services in the future.
4. We need to manage the "Five M's" effectively: Man, machines, materials, methods, and money have to be managed properly. However, in each case, quality also has to be looked into and watched closely.
5. We need to promote quality improvements organizationwide and nationwide. One cannot improve quality by introducing quality-improvement programs in bits and pieces. Achieving quality is everybody's job, and it will happen when everyone from top to bottom gets involved actively in the quality-improvement process.

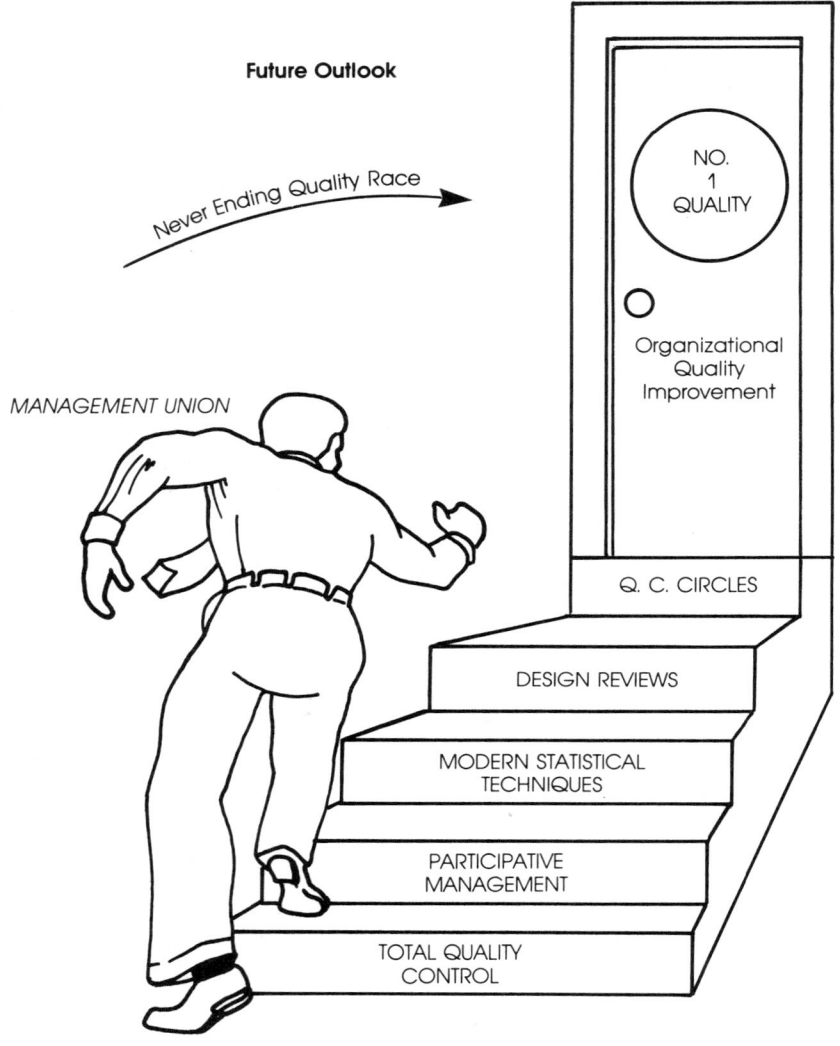

OUR VITAL NEED FOR SURVIVAL
"QUALITY FROM WOMB TO TOMB"

FIGURE 1-1

6. Use of statistical techniques is a must. We cannot overlook the value of statistics and its use in improving quality. Japan makes statistics an integral part of making quality products. I recommend the following training in statistics for various personnel in an organization:

   a. Basic statistics
   b. Statistical process control

c. Design of experiments
   d. Quality Circle techniques

7. Organization must also remember that training plays an important role in improving quality. Training makes people more skillful and more knowledgeable, and when people are knowledgeable, they do quality work.

I do not want to imply in any way that the above list is a complete one. One can add many more responsibilities that management should possess, and ten years from now they may be different. However, for the next decade or so, I feel that the issues described here will play an important role in improving the quality of products and services in an organization.

WHERE ARE YOU TODAY? (A QUALITY QUIZ)

The following questions will help you to analyze your organization, where it stands, and your knowledge of the organization in quality readiness.

1. What is your perception of the quality of products and services of your organization?

0		10
Don't know	OK	Excellent

2. Do you feel your organization is threatened due to poor quality and high cost of services?

0		10
Don't know	Maybe	Yes (100%)

3. Does your organization have total quality commitment from management, and does the organization use the Quality Wheel? (See p. 25.)

0		10
Don't know	Maybe	Yes (100%)

4. Does your organization understand new quality era (use of SPC (Statistical Process Control), TQA (Total Quality Assurance), product deployment, etc.)?

0		10
Don't know	Maybe	Yes (100%)

5. Does your organization respect human brain power and try timely participative management philosophy through employee involvement or participative management system?

0		10
Don't know	Maybe	Yes (100%)

These basic questions are intended to give the readers ideas about the organizational quality-improvement analysis. In the next chapter we will discuss, in detail, this analysis and its use by using one of the most powerful tools, self-analysis. This technique will help you to analyze your organization more effectively and will help you to establish various key projects for organizational quality improvement. These projects will serve as a sound base to improve the quality of the organization for a long time to come.

How to Use this Book Effectively

This book is intended to serve the following purposes:

1. Increase General Knowledge of the Executives in New Quality Era

It is not enough to say that we have a quality-control department or quality products. Ongoing involvement and ongoing quality-control audits must be an essential part of the executive's job. We hope to convey this message and show management how to get involved in carrying out their quality management effectively. Gone are the days when short-term profits were important and financial performance was looked on as a key to the organizational improvement. One needs to value quality as a key issue at all times in order to have a successful organization.

2. Implement Effective Organizational Quality Improvement

This book is also intended for the middle-management personnel who are the doers in an organization's quality-improvement process. Even though top management is involved in quality functions, our experience indicates that most of the carrying out of the quality work, such as training employees, follow-up, and analysis of the projects, has to be done by the middle management. This book shows the reader many methods and offers suggestions in this regard.

3. Statistics for Nonstatisticians

My experience with various organizations indicates that statistical knowledge and the use of it in our organizations is far behind many other countries. One of the major reasons is the fear of statistics and lack of training offered by our educational institutions. In Part Two of this book we describe statistical methods and their use for nonstatisticians.

4. Sustaining the Quality Circle Process in the Organization

Even though Quality Circles have been in existence in Japan for the last 20 years, very little was known about them until 1975. Then the explosion of Quality Circles took place from 1977-80. The author has seen Quality Circles in many countries around the world. However, it seems that the honeymoon is over; many organizations are facing problems in sustaining Quality Circle growth. The author hopes to show how to integrate Quality Circles with total quality commitment for the organization.

5. Eliminate "Burnout Phenomena" for Facilitators and Trainers

Quality Circle facilitators and trainers in various organizations are facing a new challenge. Basic Quality Circle techniques training alone is not enough for a long-term commitment to quality. The book will show these personnel how to expand their duties, how to train, how to get middle management involved, and eventually how to get rid of the burnout problem.

What surprised me the most was that everybody in Japan was so much better than everybody in the United States. Most American companies saw defects and breakdowns as just another cost of doing business. Now that is a serious competitive problem.

David A. Garrin,
assistant professor,
Harvard Business School,
author of "Quality on the Line,"
Harvard Business Review,
September-October 1983

Part One

Chapter Two
BASICS OF OQI

When the market was smaller and life was slower, quality could be assured. A single person could craft a product from start to finish. One pair of hands was in control of quality. But the need for higher productivity challenged quality. Productivity wars were waged. For a period of time, it was thought that quality could never regain its former importance in the consumer's mind. This happened until consumers found that they could have it both ways. Consumers found that certain products from other countries worked better and lasted longer and also were priced reasonably. Consumers found that foreign-made products—automobiles, television sets, motorcycles, electronic goods—were of noticeably higher quality. By the time western industries woke up to what was happening in Japan and Germany, we had won the production war, but had taken a beating in the quality war. Our national economy was a hostage to foreign quality. But we have not surrendered. We have instead rediscovered the need for our own strategy. Now many companies are implementing the very strategy that we exported thirty years ago. It is called Organizational Quality Improvement. OQI gives us back the ability to make products and offer services efficiently, economically, and with quality.

What Is OQI?

OQI is a systematic way of analyzing the performance of an organization in order to improve the quality and productivity of that organization through the use of techniques called self-analysis of the Quality Wheel, quality costs, quality audits, and statistical thinking.

Key Features of OQI

As mentioned above, OQI encompasses mainly three kinds of activities:

- Activities that *create* quality
- Activities that *maintain* quality
- Activities that *improve* quality

These activities are carried out using the following key features of the OQI process:

1. Quality Wheel
2. Self-analysis
3. Quality costs
4. Quality audits
5. Statistical thinking

Let us review these features in more detail.

1. Quality wheel. Figure 2-1 shows the Quality Wheel that every organization should look to for future quality improvement. Designing and adopting a Quality Wheel is the first step in the OQI process. The first section of

FIGURE 2-1

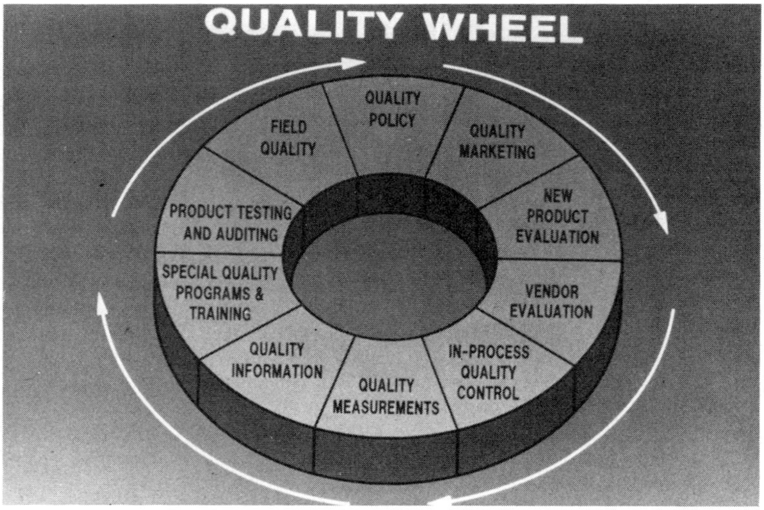

QUALITY WHEEL

the Quality Wheel is *quality planning and policy*. Any organization truly interested in improving quality must have a written quality policy. Everyone in the organization should know what is expected of them during each year and should plan their actions to accomplish company objectives.

The next part of the Quality Wheel is an *evaluation of new products and services*. This guarantees that products undergo a quality review before they are released to full-scale production. In the rush to get a new product on the market, quality is often overlooked. Thus, a thorough analysis of a product should be made before it reaches the point of no return. Any untested product can cause unhappy surprises.

Our Quality Wheel continues with *vendor evaluation*. Your product is only as good as the parts that make it up. Do your vendors have sound quality systems and reliable quality programs? Since most manufacturers purchase between 30 and 50 percent of their parts from outside, an evaluation of vendor quality is essential.

The next section of the wheel involves *in-process quality control*. Parts and subassemblies built in your own plant also need quality checks. This kind of quality control is getting a lot of attention in industry today. Quality begins at home.

Vital to the Quality Wheel are *quality measurements*. Data collection is needed at all times. But equipment and measurement systems must be accurate. Reliable on-line information can be obtained from gauges and various computers.

Quality information must be made available to all key personnel. The collection of data means nothing unless it is disseminated to those who can make judgments and decisions. Computer outputs can supply facts on scrap, rework, and warranties, and are important in making information reports uniform within the company.

Quality training is the most essential and overlooked aspect of the Quality Wheel. Few Western companies offer employee training to the degree required in Japanese industry.

Ongoing training programs are also included in the Quality Wheel. All employees need to get involved in building good products. The Quality Circle process offers this opportunity. Thousands of companies have adopted this exciting method and millions of workers have contributed their brainpower to the problem-solving process.

Product testing and auditing is also included in the Quality Wheel. Products built in-plant need to be checked periodically to see that their quality is upheld. The Volkswagen Company, for example, periodically destroys one car to check for weld quality. This helps to eliminate high warranty costs.

The last section of our wheel is called *field quality*. The after-sale aspects of quality should not be overlooked.

Customers expect quality services. Companies must provide efficient after-sale servicing to protect the integrity of their products.

It's important to remember that the Quality Wheel is dynamic. That is, it rotates continually and its sections are subject to change. A dynamic wheel allows for performance improvement.

2. Self-Analysis. It is essential for an organization to get its own management personnel involved in analyzing and improving the quality of the organization. One of the best ways to involve the personnel is through self-analysis of the situation in the organization. In future chapters of this book we will show how to analyze the organization using the Quality Wheel as a base and going through questions for each section. Management personnel should answer these questions individually and collectively and help to prepare quality projects for future improvement. For example:

Do you think Quality Circles are used effectively in your organization?

```
    0           5           10
Not at all   Sometimes    Always
```

3. Statistical Thinking. The use of statistics has played a very important role in improving quality in Japan. We will discuss this in detail in later chapters. In general, all the people in the organization must learn statistics and use it religiously in daily operation. There are several techniques that are effective and useful. We will discuss them in three groups:

1. Basic statistics, recommended for solving problems through Quality Circles.
2. Intermediate statistics, useful in OQI teams.
3. Advanced statistical techniques for QC engineers and other engineers.

There is no end to the use of statistics in any organization. (More details are discussed in Part Two.)

4. Quality costs. Everything costs money. However, money that is wasted is not profitable to the organization. Quality costs are generally collected to show both the unnecessary wastage in the organization and ways to minimize total quality costs. There are four types of quality costs, namely:

1. Prevention costs
2. Appraisal costs
3. Internal failures
4. External failures

Items 1 and 2 are really investments; items 3 and 4 are waste. Our objective is to minimize the total quality costs. (More details are given in Appendix B.)

5. Quality audits. Quality audits are generally like IRS audits. They are conducted to evaluate the performance of products and services as well as the quality of procedures and administrative operations. Quality audits are performed with the view toward improving the long-range quality of the organization. Audits are conducted externally by independent agencies and internally by plant managers and quality control managers. We will discuss more details in Chapter 12.

WHAT DOES OQI DO?

It is essential in any organization that all the people (management as well as operators) get involved in improving quality and productivity of the organization. The OQI process works toward long-range achievement of this philosophy.

As we see in Figure 2-2, top management acts as a quality council, following all quality activities through quarterly council meetings. Responsibilities of the quality council, quality chairmen, and quality teams are discussed later.

The quality or productivity improvement teams shown in Figure 2-2 are formed with the help of middle-management personnel (department

FIGURE 2-2
ORGANIZATIONAL QUALITY IMPROVEMENT

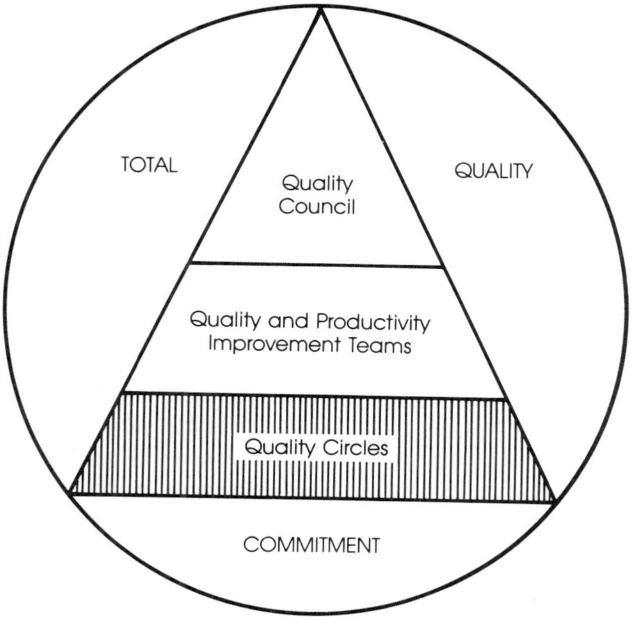

heads, supervisors, and foremen) and given specific tasks to improve quality and productivity. However, projects are selected with the aid of Quality Wheel analysis, which helps to look at the total organization and then improve the quality through teamwork, which is critical for any success.

Finally, Quality Circles, which are generally effective and useful at operators' levels, are also integrated in the OQI process. Organizations that follow the process properly will enjoy a number of benefits for a long time; we will list only a few here. The OQI process:

1. Helps to get top management involved in improving quality.
2. Helps to get middle management actively involved in improving quality.
3. Helps to maintain and expand Quality Circles.
4. Helps an organization compete with foreign industries.
5. Helps an organization to get more market share.
6. Helps to improve quality of products and services.
7. Helps to establish where your organization is today.
8. Helps to organize quality products.
9. Helps to train everyone in an organization in statistical thinking, which eliminates guesswork and improves accuracy.
10. Helps to establish teamwork and job satisfaction in the company.

Difference Between Quality Circles And Quality Improvement Teams

What is the difference between the well-publicized Quality Circles and Organizational Quality Improvement teams? The key differences between the two processes are listed below:

Quality Circles	Organizational Quality Improvement Teams
1. QCs are voluntary.	1. OQI teams are appointed.
2. They use basic statistics.	2. They use high-level statistics.
3. They are generally effective and operational in the shop area.	3. They are generally used with management and supervisors.
4. Their objectives can be diverse.	4. Their key objectives are quality, productivity, and cost reduction.
5. The group is generally homogeneous.	5. OQI teams are mixed.
6. ROI—2:1 to 6:1	6. ROI—10:1 to 20:1

FIGURE 2-3

Quality Circles (continued)

7. A QC's projects are simple and short-term.
8. A QC's projects are presented as they are completed, through management presentation.
9. Generally 10–20% of shop-related problems are solved through QC.

Quality Improvement Teams (continued)

7. OQI's projects are complex and long-term.
8. Projects are followed each quarter and reports are given to the quality council.
9. OQI has a high level (60–70%) of critical problems.

OQI Process

OQI process generally involves four major areas. These are as follows:

1. Planning and preparation.
2. Training
3. Implementation
4. Ongoing training

The *planning and preparation* phase of OQI includes endorsement of the program by top management, selection of a quality council and chairperson, and establishment of a quality policy. The quality-council chairperson also plans for training material and selects management members who should be trained for OQI process. In the *training and self-analysis* phase, training is conducted for the first group and then people are directed to perform self-analysis of the organization. Generally, people are trained in statistical problem-solving methods. In the *implementation* phase, the teams are organized and start functioning for the company. Periodic reviews are done to make sure everything is working and to help get rid of stumbling blocks. Finally, in the *ongoing* phase, the organization establishes an OQI process in which are incorporated a yearly quality plan, OQI training recognition, project review, and many other facets that are necessary to carry on OQI activities effectively.

OQI Organization and Responsibilities

In order to implement the OQI process successfully, it is necessary that the OQI organization should be established in one's company. Figure 2-4 shows the OQI organization.

Let us discuss the key sections and their responsibilities:

1. Quality Council

The quality council is generally formed at the top-management level. Generally, the president and vice-president are involved in the quality council. The major objectives of quality councils are: (a) to get involved in the OQI process in selecting quality-improvement teams, and (b) to provide direction to quality-improvement teams.

Some of the major responsibilities of the council are as follows:

1. To form company quality policy
2. To select the members for OQI training of OQI teams
3. To select training vehicles
4. To provide guidance of the OQI teams
5. To review and approve team work
6. To accept a project implementation schedule
7. To coordinate work (if required)
8. To find and approve financial commitment
9. To work on short-range and long-range objectives of the organization team
10. To key Quality Wheel rotations

One should establish and fix schedules for quality council meetings and preplan the agenda to ensure good results.

O.Q.I. ORGANIZATION

```
                    ┌──────────┐
                    │ Quality  │
                    │ Council  │
                    └────┬─────┘
                         ↓
                    ┌──────────┐
                    │ Quality  │
                    │ Council  │──────────────────────┐
                    │Chairperson│                     │
                    └────┬─────┘                      │
                         ↓                            │
                    ┌──────────┐                      │
                    │ Quality  │                      │
                    │  Action  │   (optional)         │
                    │Committee │                      │
                    └────┬─────┘                      │
      ┌──────────────────┼──────────────────┐         │
      │  QUALITY or PRODUCTIVITY IMPROVEMENT TEAMS    │
      └──┬──────────────┬──────────────┬──┘           │
         ↓              ↓              ↓              │
```

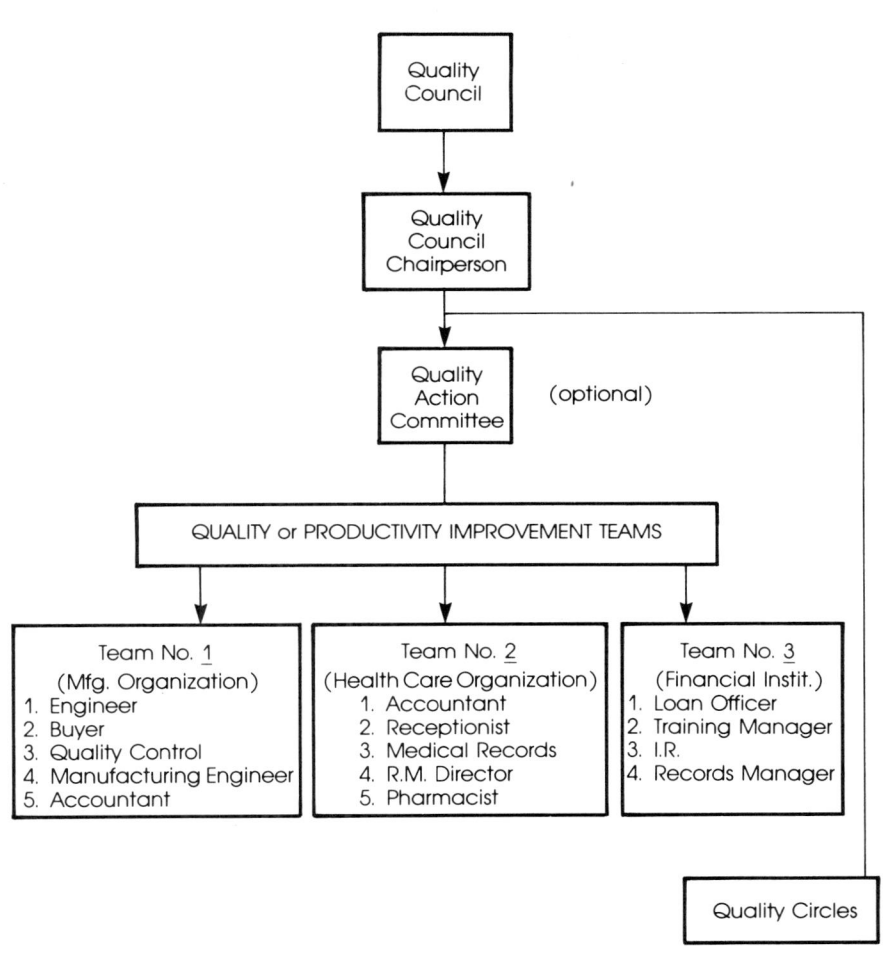

Team No. 1 (Mfg. Organization)	Team No. 2 (Health Care Organization)	Team No. 3 (Financial Instit.)
1. Engineer	1. Accountant	1. Loan Officer
2. Buyer	2. Receptionist	2. Training Manager
3. Quality Control	3. Medical Records	3. I.R.
4. Manufacturing Engineer	4. R.M. Director	4. Records Manager
5. Accountant	5. Pharmacist	

Quality Circles

FIGURE 2-4

Quality-Council Chairperson

This is a very important position and the success of the OQI process depends on the person who fills it; hence it is necessary that an organization choose the proper person for this job. Generally, the quality-control manager or vice-president is appointed to carry out this function. The quality-council chairperson should be enthusiastic and must be a driving force behind the process. He or she should be ready to do the legwork for planning, arranging, and implementing OQI in the organization. He or she must also sell the process to the organization, to management personnel, and to OQI teams. Many times the chairperson may also have to do part of the training.

Some of the key responsibilities for the quality-council chairperson are listed here:

1. To form a quality council and prepare the meeting schedule
2. To conduct council meetings
3. To write for quality policy and get it approved
4. To act as a liaison between the quality council and quality-improvement teams
5. To organize and conduct OQI reviews, meetings, and presentations
6. To organize yearly banquets and recognition programs
7. To organize yearly presentations

Quality-Action Committee

In large-size companies, it is not easy for the quality council to get involved in day-to-day activities. In this case, many organizations form a committee called the quality-action committee, which works in-plant or by location to guide the quality-improvement teams. The responsibilities are already discussed above. In this case, the quality council works on long-range objectives; quality-action committees work on short-range objectives at each location.

Quality-Improvement Teams

Quality-improvement teams are generally formed by the management personnel from the engineering, purchasing, and manufacturing departments. In the service organizations the team could consist of a mixture of different department heads. The major responsibilities of the teams are listed below:

1. To receive the OQI training
2. To participate actively in Quality Wheel self-analysis
3. To gather and analyze data
4. To prepare a list of the key quality projects
5. To propose solutions to the projects
6. To provide cost/benefit analysis
7. To present the proposal to the quality council
8. To work on projects and implement them
9. To participate in banquets
10. To help in future training of new members

Once the organization implements the OQI process, it is not easy to stop working. It has a snowball effect; ongoing training becomes an integral part of the system. Quarterly quality-project review meetings held by the quality council become a way of doing business.

However, you must remember that all of this needs top-management involvement and commitment. It is not enough to say that we have a quality-control department or a quality-control manager that is responsible for the quality of an organization. Quality is everyone's job. It will happen if and only if everyone participates honestly and performs his or her work sincerely.

WHERE IS YOUR ORGANIZATION TODAY? (QUALITY WHEEL QUIZ)

Before we start explaining and describing the OQI process, we would like you to review the current conditions that exist today within your organization. The following questions will help to analyze this condition.

Please answer the questions to the best of your knowledge:

Questions:

1. Our organization has a written quality policy in existence.

0	5	10
Nothing in existence	Maybe in existence	Yes, definitely

2. Our organization has a yearly quality-improvement plan.

0	5	10
Nothing in existence	Maybe in existence	Yes, definitely

3. Our organization knows and uses quality costs.

0	5	10
Nothing in existence	Maybe in existence	Yes, definitely

4. Our organization has customer surveys and customer-based quality deployment.

0	5	10
Nothing in existence	Maybe in existence	Yes, definitely

5. Our organization uses statistical techniques to solve problems.

0	5	10
Nothing in existence	Maybe in existence	Yes, definitely

6. In our organization, employees are involved in small teams solving problems.

0	5	10
Nothing in existence	Maybe in existence	Yes, definitely

7. In our organization, quality audits are performed by top managers and middle management.

0	5	10
Nothing in existence	Maybe in existence	Yes, definitely

BASICS OF OQI

WHERE IS YOUR ORGANIZATION TODAY? (QUALITY WHEEL QUIZ) (continued)

Questions:

Question	0	5	10
8. In our organization, new products and services are introduced after they are thoroughly tested and almost all the bugs are eliminated.	Nothing in existence	Maybe in existence	Yes, definitely
9. In our organization, basic concepts of the Quality Wheel and its segments are used effectively.	Nothing in existence	Maybe in existence	Yes, definitely
10. In our organization, top management emphasizes quality first and quantity second.	Nothing in existence	Maybe in existence	Yes, definitely
11. In our organization, statistical training is followed and used religiously.	Nothing in existence	Maybe in existence	Yes, definitely
12. In our organization, employees' brains are recognized and appreciated.	Nothing in existence	Maybe in existence	Yes, definitely
13. In our organization, cost-benefit analysis is used widely in selecting projects.	Nothing in existence	Maybe in existence	Yes, definitely
14. In our organization, ongoing training is offered to employees to improve their skills.	Nothing in existence	Maybe in existence	Yes, definitely
15. In our organization, statistical process control is used effectively to solve problems.	Nothing in existence	Maybe in existence	Yes, definitely
16. In our organization, quality means merely conforming to specifications.	Nothing in existence	Maybe in existence	Yes, definitely
17. Quality is a serious problem in our industry.	Nothing in existence	Maybe in existence	Yes, definitely
18. Our management should become more democratic and less autocratic.	Nothing in existence	Maybe in existence	Yes, definitely

WHERE IS YOUR ORGANIZATION TODAY? (QUALITY WHEEL QUIZ) (continued)

Questions:

19. Our organization is ready to try a major change in organizational relationships.

0	5	10
Nothing in existence	Maybe in existence	Yes, definitely

20. Our organization has a good communication system from the top down, from down up, and unilaterally.

0	5	10
Nothing in existence	Maybe in existence	Yes, definitely

Total points: _____

Analysis of your answers (based on our experience): Add the total number of points of all answers.

Maximum Total Points: 200

150–200	You are on the right track. (Keep up the good work.)
100–150	Good work, but you need improvement.
50–100	Chances are the competition is way ahead!
0– 50	It's a good idea to learn a new language.

Quality faces a variety of challenges and everyone must pitch in to help overcome them.

Richard J. Frank,
vice-president,
Caterpillar Tractor Company, Peoria, Illinois.
Quality Progress, July 1977

Chapter Three
MANAGING FOR OQI

Many quality-oriented organizations in Japan are already using the OQI concept. These companies are constantly engaged in improving quality and productivity. Organizational Quality Improvement has already been defined as a statistical system under which people in every department of the company cooperate in promoting and improving the quality of products and services from a companywide point of view. Ongoing self-analysis of the Quality Wheel constantly helps to improve quality. The major goal of OQI is to build quality products and offer quality services at reasonable costs and to satisfy customers' expectations and needs. This goal cannot be achieved unless the whole company works together as a team. In general, OQI enhances the quality of products and services and also achieves cost reduction. It also brings intangible benefits such as better management, better communication, and better human relationships.

If OQI is so beneficial, then why aren't organizations eager to implement it; why aren't many more companies adopting this exciting philosophy? One of the key reasons is that there are no systematic training programs that exist today to train management as well as operators. Second, there was no keen competition in the past for quality products and services as there is today. Customers are demanding better quality, and other countries are satisfying their needs. Hence, many products face tougher competition today. Similarly, production costs are increasing tremendously, and we must concentrate our attention on cost reduction, for customers are not going to buy expensive products when they can get the same quality at a cheaper price. Many organizations are also losing their market share around the world; they feel the pinch of poor quality.

As described in Chapter 2, the OQI process mainly involves four broad areas:

1. Planning and preparation
2. Training and self-analysis
3. Implementation
4. Ongoing use of the OQI process

These four areas can be divided into ten phases. Let us describe these ten phases in detail.

Phase   I   – Introduction
Phase   II   – Preparation
Phase   III – Basic OQI Training
Phase   IV   – Management Review
Phase   V   – Advanced OQI Training
Phase   VI   – Approval
Phase   VII – Update
Phase   VIII – Yearly Presentation
Phase   IX   – Recognition Program
Phase   X   – Ongoing OQI

FIGURE 3-1

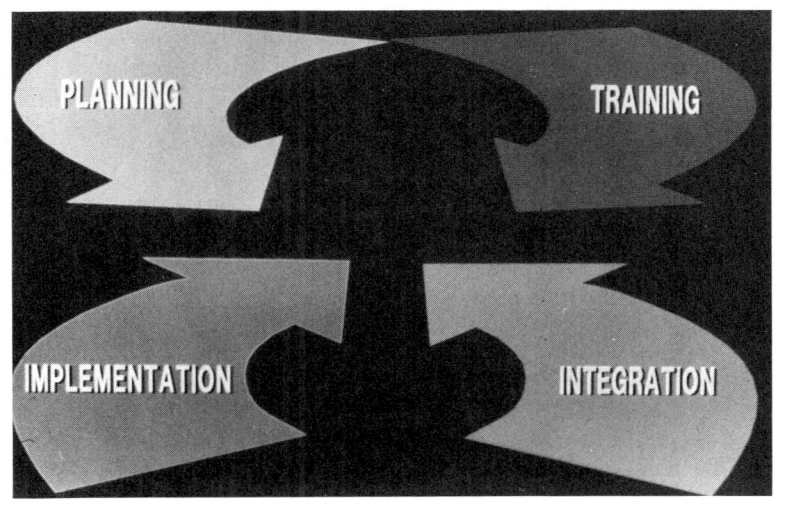

O.Q.I. PROCESS

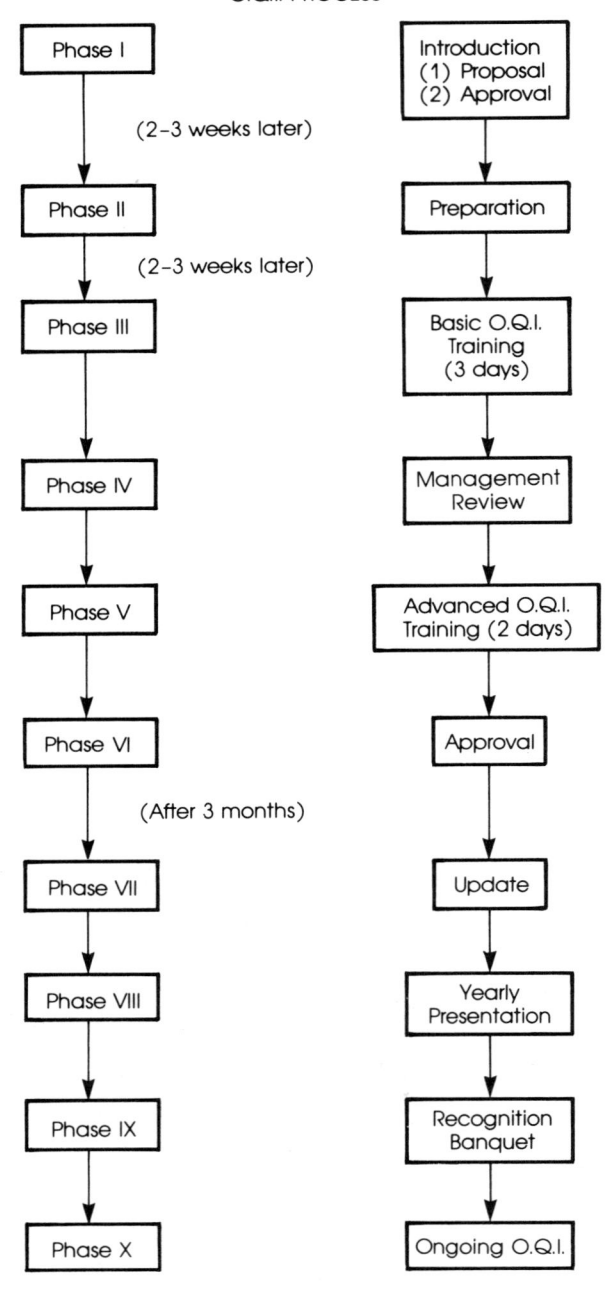

```
     Phase I                    Introduction
        |                       (1) Proposal
        | (2-3 weeks later)     (2) Approval
        v                            |
     Phase II                        v
        |                        Preparation
        | (2-3 weeks later)          |
        v                            v
     Phase III                  Basic O.Q.I.
        |                        Training
        |                        (3 days)
        v                            |
     Phase IV                        v
        |                       Management
        |                         Review
        v                            |
     Phase V                         v
        |                       Advanced O.Q.I.
        |                       Training (2 days)
        v                            |
     Phase VI                        v
        |                         Approval
        | (After 3 months)           |
        v                            v
     Phase VII                    Update
        |                            |
        v                            v
     Phase VIII                   Yearly
        |                       Presentation
        v                            |
     Phase IX                        v
        |                       Recognition
        v                         Banquet
     Phase X                         |
                                     v
                                Ongoing O.Q.I.
```

FIGURE 3-2

Phase I: Introduction

Nowadays, companies are looking to improve the quality of their products and services. Many executives and managers have read about OQI in magazines, newspapers, or promotional advertisements. The concept must be introduced to top management, who must approve of it before it is implemented in the organization. If top management approves of OQI, then you can proceed to the next phase.

Phase II: Preparation

This is a very important phase. Management has many duties to carry out before it can introduce the OQI process. Some of the key duties in preparation for OQI are:

1. Formation of a quality council
2. Selection of a quality-council chairperson
3. Preparing quality policy
4. Selection of members for quality training
5. Obtaining training material
6. Selecting a trainer and location
7. Keeping the members informed of all the details

The author has already given more details about preparation in Chapter 2.

Phase III: Basic OQI Training

Basic OQI training lasts for three days; it is very intensive. Participants should work in small groups (usually three or four in each group). Each group preferably should be mixed (i.e., each group should have a cross section of people from various work areas, such as manufacturing, quality control, engineering, financial, and purchasing). The basic training outline is given on page 221.

Basic OQI Training for Management and OQI Teams (Duration—Three Days)

Topics
1. New quality era
2. Worldwide competition
3. Where are we?

4. Quality Wheel analysis
5. What is self-analysis? How to analyze your organization
6. Statistics for nonstatisticians
7. Industrial statistics
8. Looking at the process
9. Improving the processes
10. Charting the processes
11. Cost/benefit analysis
12. Quality Circles
13. Problem-solving system
14. Putting it all together
15. OQI implementation plans for our organization

(*Note:* One can add additional topics from Chapter 14, Training Programs for OQI, beginning on page 218.)

Phase IV: Management Review

This management review takes place at the end of the three-day training period. The objectives of the review are as follows:

1. To review the self-analysis process
2. To review the statistical understanding of the group
3. To review project presentation by teams
4. To review projects that are collected
5. To select certain projects for future analysis or implementation
6. To advise caution on certain projects
7. To form the quality-action committees

Once the teams have been given the green light, the work is cautioned by the teams for the next three to four weeks. After this, a second part of the training should be arranged which is basically a review of the self-analysis and statistical methods.

Phase V: Advanced OQI Training

Our experience in many organizations indicates that it is not easy to make management personnel understand and use statistical techniques. Hence, we recommend this training to make sure people use statistical methods at a later date.

Many exercises should be used that will give participants practical experience. Similarly, teams should be ready for a revised presentation on the projects that are selected and approved by the management. Projects should have appropriate cost-benefit analysis to convince the management of the feasibility of the project.

Phase VI: Approval

This phase generally follows the end of advanced training. Top management is present at this time to review the whole training and its benefits. Similarly, projects that have been implemented and then approved are presented to the management. Quality-improvement goals are generally established for the year. Quality-council meetings are scheduled and the OQI process really gains momentum at this stage.

Phase VII: Update

An update of OQI projects is generally done through quality-council meetings. It is highly recommended that the quality council hold quarterly meetings to review progress made. Projects can be divided into three areas:

1. Short-range projects (projects that will take less than six months to implement and ROI is acceptable)
2. Yearly projects (projects that will take one or two years to study and implement)
3. Long-range projects (projects that will take more than two to three years and ROI is unknown at this stage)

Phase VIII: Yearly Presentation

This activity should be planned generally at the end of the year or one year from the advanced OQI training. This will give sufficient time to get some projects under the belt, and the OQI process will establish some credibility in the organization. Completed projects should be presented to all management people; major Quality Circle projects should be included in this event.

Phase IX: Recognition Banquet

The organization should hold a recognition banquet to recognize good work done by the key management as well as by the people in Quality Circles. Most companies recognize sales achievements in the organization; it is about time for top management to realize and recognize the importance of good quality work. We would like to caution the readers that these banquets (recognition activities) should be arranged in such a way that everyone gets something, but at the same time giving more recognition to people who worked hardest.

Phase X: Ongoing OQI

Once the organization goes through the first year of hardship, the OQI process becomes simple to carry on. The quality council should watch progress via periodic meetings. Training should be expanded to include more management personnel. More OQI teams should be formed. OQI projects should be followed properly and more projects should be added for further improvement. If the quality council does its job properly, the OQI process not only gets a good start, but flourishes rapidly in the organization. However, many times our experience indicates that bottlenecks occur at the top; then the organization starts looking for new techniques for improving quality and productivity.

Factors for a Successful OQI

In order to make the OQI successful, there are many factors that are essential. Some of the key areas are listed here.

1. An active and enthusiastic quality council and chairperson
2. Good planning and follow-up
3. Realistic quality objectives
4. Top-management involvement
5. Accurate self-analysis
6. Good documentation
7. Widespread use of statistical methods
8. Ongoing training
9. Quality audits
10. Participation from all members
11. Quality cost analysis
12. Yearly quality goals and annual review
13. Recognition of good work
14. Customer-based quality goods
15. Continual quality improvements

Many organizations have realized the following benefits using the OQI process:

1. Improved quality
2. Cost reduction
3. Improved productivity
4. Fewer field complaints
5. Customer satisfaction
6. Better human relations and departmental relations
7. Better communication
8. Larger market share
9. Higher employment
10. Team spirit in the organization

OQI is not a fad or gimmick. It is a proven way to improve the quality and productivity of a organization. What we need is determination, training, and a desire to change. Organizations that realize the need are implementing the OQI process and reaping the above-mentioned benefits.

Case Study Number 1

An air compressor company involved 20 key management personnel in the training program. After three or four days of intensive training, the teams' formations were complete. Each team was first trained in statistical methods and then asked to analyze the organization, then Quality Wheel concepts. More than 200 questions were given for analysis.

The teams came up with more than 50 projects for the organization to implement to improve quality. Some of the key projects were as follows:

1. Standardization of parts
2. Better service to the customers (goal: parts should be delivered in less than 24 hours)
3. Statistical training to operators
4. Good gauging
5. Process-capability analysis

Case Study Number 2

This international company employs more than 20,000 employees. One of the divisions decided to implement the OQI process. Twenty-five management people were selected for the training. The members received statistical training and, using the Quality Wheel, analyzed the company. The total number of projects was more than 35 in this case. The key projects were as follows:

1. Quality audits by management and customer
2. Design reviews of the new product
3. Quality cost analysis
4. Visits to the major dealers and field cost analysis
5. Expansion of Quality Circles to the vendor's plants

Case Study Number 3

This company manufactures internal combustion engines. More than 35 management people were trained in the process. More than 20 projects were proposed for approval.

Key projects selected for quality improvement were as follows:

1. Reducing incoming inspection
2. Use of SPC on shop floor
3. Proper gauge control
4. Standardization of instructions and drawings through use of CAD
5. Customer-based quality improvement
6. Rigid design reviews

We would like to conclude this chapter with remarks from the famous quality consultant, Dr. Edward Deming:

Total quality assurance approach recognizes that good quality is not accidental and that it does not result from mere wishful thinking; that it rather results from the planned and interlocked activities of all the organizational levels of a company, that it enters into design engineers, technical and quality pre-planning, specifications, production control, production layout standards, and even into the training. It would put the man at the head of the quality program in the position to establish and make effective a company-wide policy with respect to quality, to direct that action to be taken where it is necessary and place responsibility where it belongs in each instance.

Today, more than ever before, the organizations that like to improve quality and productivity need to take this advice seriously and establish the OQI process so that organizations can survive for many years to come.

The total quality assurance concept puts its major emphasis on planning for quality by each activity, with the quality assurance activity serving as a service function to advise on past problems and recommend or suggest methods of avoiding such problems in new products. Quality assurance wants to spark quality approaches by each person to his job. Quality assurance objectives are not confined to one area of the company, but should be included in every activity's list of objectives.

Edward Stiles,
"Handbook for Total Quality Assurance"
National Foremen's Institute
Waterford, Connecticut

Chapter Four
STATISTICAL PROBLEM-SOLVING METHODS

There are a number of ways in which problems can be solved. Many times the solution depends on the complexity of the problem. Some problems are easy, whereas some are too complex. Some problems are solved immediately just by looking at the situation; some take months just to see the progress. Some you may never solve completely; some require patience and perseverance to see the solution.

In this chapter we will describe various statistical problem-solving methods. We recommend intensive use of statistical tools and a systematic approach to solve a problem. You should stop solving problems by using opinions and hit-or-miss methods. Preventive actions are essential to any solution; periodic follow-ups are necessary to make sure that problems are fixed and that corrective actions are followed religiously. Generally, people tend to forget the complete solution and will find that many problems recur due to negligence and incomplete implementation.

Many people fear the word *statistics*. But every one of us uses statistics daily, in our work as well as at home. When we listen to the news on radio or TV we hear a lot of statistical data—the average temperature for the month or the number of cars manufactured last month, for example. Computers also generate a volume of statistical data that is read every day. Statistics is a part of our life that can be applied in problem solving.

In simple language, statistics can be described as a systematic way of collecting and analyzing any given quantitative data. In order to use quantitative data effectively in making decisions, it is necessary to have a systematic method of organizing, summarizing, and analyzing individual facts. These methods of analysis can be called *statistical methods*.

The following five basic steps are generally used in applying statistical methods:

1. Defining the problem
2. Collecting relevant information
3. Investigation
4. Analyzing the data
5. Presenting the findings

There are many versions of this basic methodology in various applications.

Problem-Solving Methods

A number of different types of problems exist in our society today. No one method will solve them all, nor are there known "best" solutions to all our problems. We must keep trying and searching for better ways to do our jobs and to improve the world in which we live.

The following table shows briefly the various problem-solving methods that can be applied to problems in your organization.

PROBLEM-SOLVING METHODS (PARTIAL LIST)

TYPE	PEOPLE	SUGGESTED APPROACH
A. High level (design type; when cause is not obvious)	Engineering Manufacturing Engineering	Variation Research Creativity
B. Classical (when historical data available)	Engineering Quality Control	Cost-Avoidance Team Task Force
Scrap, rework, engineering specifications	Manufacturing	Value Analysis
C. Daily shop problems, rejects, maintenance, people-oriented problems	All	Quality Circles Foreman involvement

The following table shows some of the statistical methods that are common and useful in solving complicated problems:

STATISTICAL METHODS

BASIC	INTERMEDIATE	ADVANCED
Graph, check sheets	Multivary charts	"Red X" theory
Charts, sampling	Component search	Design of experiment
Pareto analysis	Stratification	Orthogonal arrays
Cause-and-effect analysis	Control charts	Reliability analysis
Histograms	Precontrol	Failure analysis
Activity analysis	Tolerance	Non-Paramametric
Process analysis	Process capability	Computer analysis

Statistical problem-solving methods generally use the following steps:

STATISTICAL

1. Problems are collected and selected.
2. One problem is defined clearly.
3. Data collection and analysis (experts from outside are also involved).
4. Solutions are generated.
5. Plan of action is drawn up.
6. Trial run.
7. Evaluation.
8. Implementation of improvement.
9. Follow-up.
10. Prevention checklist.
11. Periodic reviews.

You should keep in mind that this is a recommended procedure. Sometimes you may not need all the steps. If the machine is stopped or a person is injured, you don't have to go through each and every step. Immediate action is necessary. Sometimes it is possible to combine some steps or add some steps. However, the overall method should be productive and efficient. Let us go through each step and see what one does or is suppose to do in each case.

Statistical training is important at the beginning so that everyone understands the basic concepts and working of practical statistics. Once the

PROBLEM SOLVING PROCESS

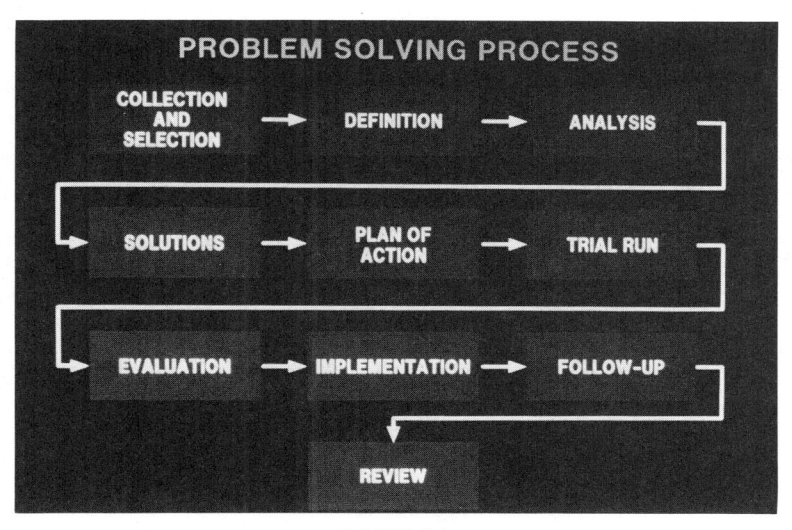

COLLECTION AND SELECTION → DEFINITION → ANALYSIS → SOLUTIONS → PLAN OF ACTION → TRIAL RUN → EVALUATION → IMPLEMENTATION → FOLLOW-UP → REVIEW

FIGURE 4-1

training is completed and the quality teams are formed, the groups can start collecting the problems. Brainstorming works very well in this case. Remember the old saying, "Two heads are better than one."

Once the problems are collected, the poor ones can be weeded out, and the productive projects can be presented to the quality council. The quality council in turn will approve the best one to work on. Once the project is selected and approved, it is important that the group define the problem clearly. A written definition is preferable to avoid confusion. This keeps the team on track. Also, objectives should be listed to achieve the final goal. Preliminary data can be collected or old data can be used to analyze the problem's intensity. Pareto analysis could be used here to separate the "vital few" from the "trivial many." It is a good tool to use in reviewing the problem and finding possible solutions. Next the team can try to find obvious clues as to what went wrong in the past contrasting data or recent changes. The analysis may include input from experts in other areas or even vendors or customers. A fishbone diagram can be used here to analyze cause and effects systematically. The group can generate solutions at this stage. Many solutions and alternatives are necessary, and you should take the precaution of not hanging on to preconceived ideas. Once the various solutions have been discussed and weighed, the group should decide which key area to work on.

The group then should prepare a plan of action to check the solution. Sometimes the solution may involve only verbal contact with other parties. Other ideas may require modification of equipment or other substantial

FIGURE 4-2

changes in process. The plan of action should be laid out in such a way that it will provide a run (or test) of the proposed solution. It is essential that data be collected efficiently and properly. Using one or more of the statistical tools available, the group may approach the trial run with a multivary chart, scatter diagram, component search pattern, histogram, or frequency distribution (Figure 4-2).

Control charts or precontrol can be also used to verify whether the process is in control or out of control.

FIGURE 4-3

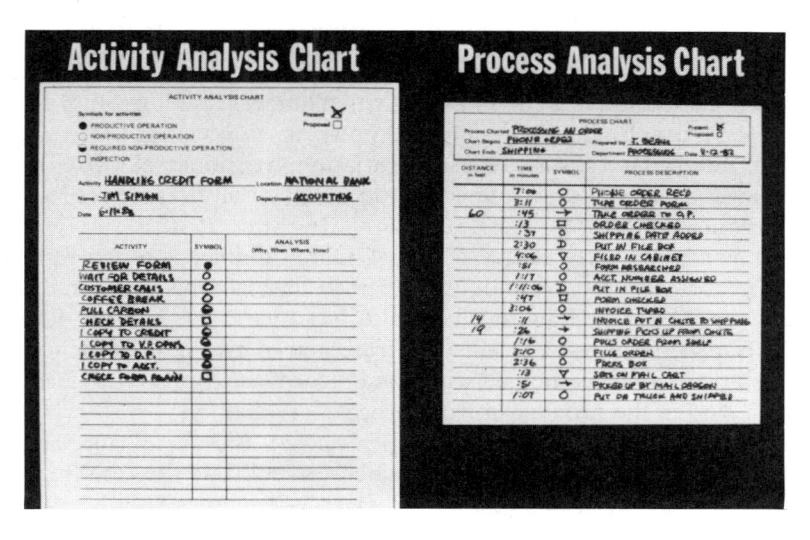

FIGURE 4-4

Activity and process charts are excellent charting procedures to measure how the trial run improves the efficiency of activities or processes.

Red X Theory

The statistical technique called the Red X theory has been well publicized by Dorian Shainin.[1] Through his hard work and many successful applications, this technique has been used by many companies to solve complicated problems.

Sometimes the Red X theory can isolate complicated problem variables more easily and show interaction between two or more variables. Every effect of importance, a Y (a product characteristic) is a result of a large number of causes—the variables in material ingredients, parts, machinery, operators, environment, and so on. The causes always include some that are easily recognized, some that are suspected, and some that are completely unsuspected. Caution should be taken to consider all the variables that control the causes, such as raw material, the human element, and so on. If enough time is allowed to analyze problems properly and let the parts do the talking to reveal the leading cause, one will find that Red X caused the largest variation in the process. Proper control of this variable

---

[1] Dorian Shainin, "How to Build Quality Products." Talk given at Mercury Marine, Fond du Lac, Wisconsin, February 1979.

can get rid of a major portion of the process variation and save wasted money.

Most times, one variable makes the largest contribution to the output variation, another makes the smallest, with all others ranging somewhere in between. X usually designates the unknown in an equation. Because we need to find the largest single cause of variation, we should let it continue to function and thereby draw our attention in a very noticeable red color—hence the Red X.

If you know the relative effect of each variable, you can rank the causes in sequence by the amount of their influence. One can then draw a Pareto curve to show how much of an effect each cause had on the final result. But the final result is not the direct sum of all the X influences.

All these tools, combined with good record keeping, pave the way for the next step in the problem-solving process—evaluation.

After the plan of action has been proposed and a trial run has been completed, the results should be evaluated carefully. Is the resulting data consistent with a workable solution? Here is a cost-benefit method of analysis that can point the way to the most beneficial course of action. If the solution is unworkable, the group can go back, review the data, and try another approach. By this time, the group has learned from previous experience in analyzing the problem more carefully, and a more workable solution is found in the second trial. Once the solution is agreed upon it can be presented and approved for implementation.

A follow-up procedure is essential to avoid future problems. A periodic check of the implemented solution is a good preventive action. The follow-up process can include problem prevention by listing first the causes of the problem, the lesson learned through the past mistakes, and preventive procedures for the future.

A preventive checklist can be for personnel who may be able to stop the problem from recurring. This kind of checklist guarantees the enduring values of the quality-improvement team and keeps the Quality Wheel rotating.

Periodic reviews are also essential in the future to see if the solution is complete and adequate over a long period of time. Sometimes further improvement is possible if the group is not satisfactory with the present situation. For example, if a solution cuts down the rejects from 14 percent to 7 percent, the group may wish to aim for a 4 percent reject rate. Later you may need to review your goals again. Figure 4-5 shows a case study of reduction in welding rejects in the automobile industry in Japan. The group achieved this goal in less than six months.

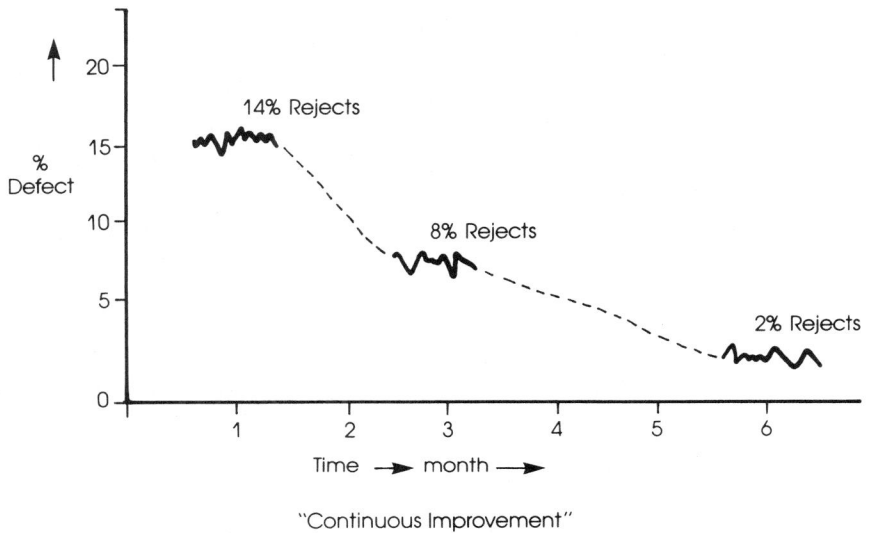

"Continuous Improvement"
FIGURE 4-5

EVALUATE YOUR ORGANIZATION

1. How do you solve problems in your organization?

| Don't know | Hit or miss | As a team, in a systematic way |

2. How much statistical knowledge do people have in your organization?

| Don't know | Statistical knowledge possible but most effective | Everyone knows and uses statistics |

3. What kind of statistical methods are used in solving problems in your organization that are described in the book?

| Don't know | Some of them | All |

4. Can you list the steps people use in solving problems in your organization?

| Don't know | Some | All |

5. Do people in your organization realize importance of statistical thinking?

| Don't know | Maybe | Definitely, yes |

Finally, one has to remember that in the problem-solving process patience is necessary, especially during the data-collection step of the cycle. This is often a slow procedure that threatens to stifle the enthusiasm of the team members. It is also necessary to remember the importance of teamwork. All members must participate and cooperate in each step of the process. Quality improvement should not be a method for laying blame; it is a procedure for solving problems systematically using statistical thinking.

When you can measure what you are speaking about, and express it in numbers, you know something about it; but when you cannot measure it, when you cannot express it in numbers, your knowledge is of a meagre and unsatisfactory kind.

Lord Kelvin, 1883

Chapter Five
QUALITY PLANNING

Managing for Quality

The importance of producing quality products or offering quality services has created completely different values in developing nations today. Nowadays, when you discuss the subject of quality with any top executive, you will hear nothing but 100 percent support for building quality products. Some of the remarks most commonly heard can be listed here:

"Quality is our number one priority."

"Quality is job number one."

"Nothing is more important to our organization than the quality of our products."

"We are all for quality."

"Quality is everyone's job in our company."

Even though a lot of these remarks are superficial, and not completely convincing, there is a change in understanding of the importance of quality. Any organization that needs to improve quality and productivity needs this support from the top; we can actually see an optimistic picture, since most top managers are thinking of quality and not quantity alone!

Most organizations are also aware of the realities of the next 20 years. Some of the facts are listed below:

1. In order to improve, organizations must have good cost control.
2. Organizations must build superior-quality products.

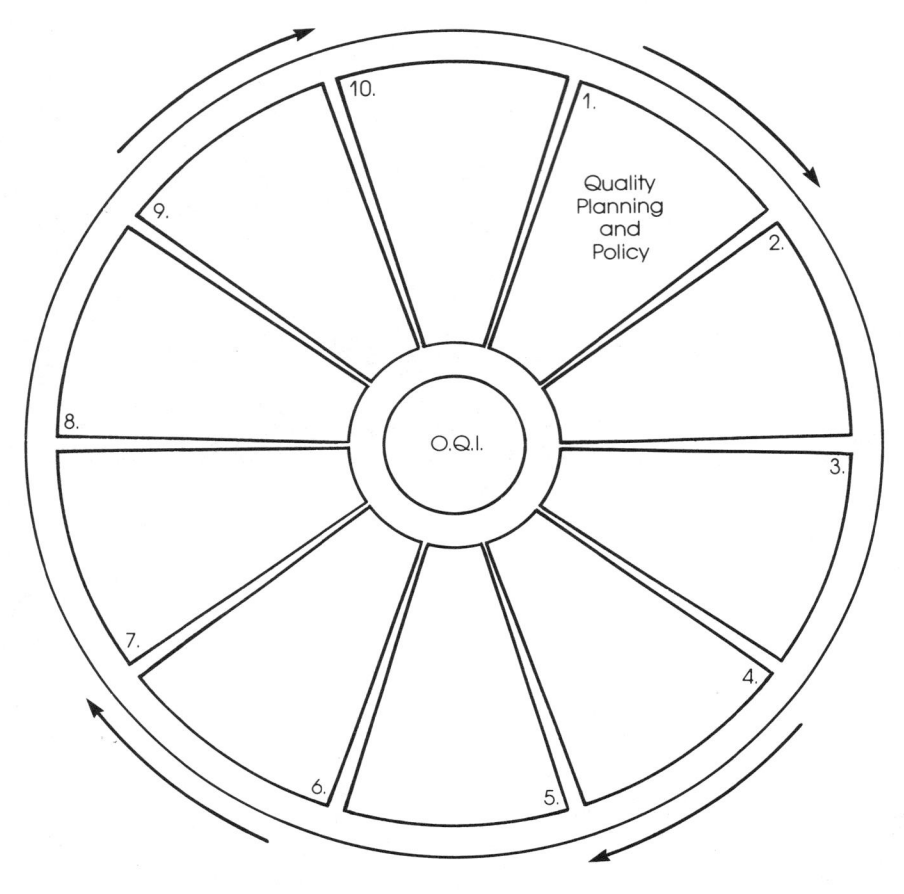

FIGURE 5-1

3. Teamwork is a must.
4. Organizations need ongoing improvements.
5. There is a need for a tremendous amount of ongoing education and training.
6. The world is getting smaller and competition is getting tougher.
7. It is not enough to do a good job. We must strive for ongoing improvements.
8. The customer is number one.
9. It is essential to understand customer needs and requirements.
10. Finally, we must remember that the customer is the next inspector.

Many organizations have already realized this need and have started many quality-improvement programs. However, many of them failed before they could make any substantial impact on the quality of products or services. We have already reviewed many general reasons, in Chapter 1, for the failure of these programs. Some of the major reasons for quality program failure in the organizations are listed here:

1. Many companies saw the quality program as another fad and did not take it seriously. Management looked at it as a suggestion system or MBO program (management by objective) and never sincerely believed in the need for ongoing quality improvement.
2. Many of the quality programs and training started by a quality department was offered at the worker or shop level. Top management never got completely involved. They were still watching the scene from outside the fence.
3. Often, quality training was made complicated and statistical training was too dry; people became confused and disenchanted.
4. Management looked for quick fixes and a magic wand. In reality, it takes years to change the management style and quality attitude in an organization. Patience is necessary to get things done. However, this is not easy for the management.

One can add many reasons to the list. The author would like to conclude, based on the above observations, that the quality movement is not a program; it is a process. It takes a long time and requires determination, training, and a willingness to change. Everyone needs to realize that the quality problem does exist and that we must change for survival or to improve the market share. Patience and systematic planning are required to make changes happen, changes that will add to the betterment of an organization for years to come.

Roadblocks to Quality Improvement in an Organization

We discussed, in general terms, the management's attitude toward quality and the reasons for failure of quality programs. You must realize that there are more than these general reasons already discussed. Each organization is different; it is necessary to understand the mix of people and the behavioral attitude of the departmental heads as well as interdepartmental relationships in the organization. Let us review roadblocks that one finds to improving quality in the organization.

1. Many organizations are not clear about their work standards. Specifications are not specific enough, and people are still expected to perform well.

2. Today more than ever, SQC (statistical quality control) is being promoted in organizations. However, the equipment and machinery that are used are old and need better attention. The lack of preventive maintenance also causes many quality problems.
3. Poor communication also causes problems in building quality products. Incomplete messages, unclear instructions, and incomplete drawings cause confusion; most of the time people carry on the work without waiting for an explanation. This often results in chaos.
4. When people do a good job, they expect recognition and also some remuneration. Many organizations do not implement adequate incentive systems, and when people become unhappy, poor-quality work results.
5. Many times people are accustomed to carrying on work in their own way. These past practices are hard to change. In fact, resistance to change is one of the deadly enemies in improving quality of products and services.

One can add many other roadblocks that may have been in existence for a long time in many organizations. Lack of pride, problems with vendors, lip service from the management, lack of documentation, and various other reasons contribute to the poor quality image in the customer's mind which, in the long run, could result in loss of market share.

Objectives of Quality Planning

There is an old saying, "An ounce of prevention is better than a pound of cure." Quality planning plays a very important role in improving the quality and productivity of an organization. Hence, quality planning must be done systematically, properly, and on an ongoing basis.

Quality planning must have two major objectives. They are planning for:

1. Quality management. Quality management involves quality organization, quality objectives, quality costs, and many other managerial aspects discussed in various parts of this book. (See Appendix B, Quality Costs.) Those organizations that are committed to quality are involved in quality costs and quality reporting.

2. Quality technology. Quality technology involves training, equipment, data collecting, data analysis, statistical methods, and computer-aided quality techniques. These topics are also discussed in detail in other chapters.

SUCCESSFUL QUALITY PLANNING
FIGURE 5-2

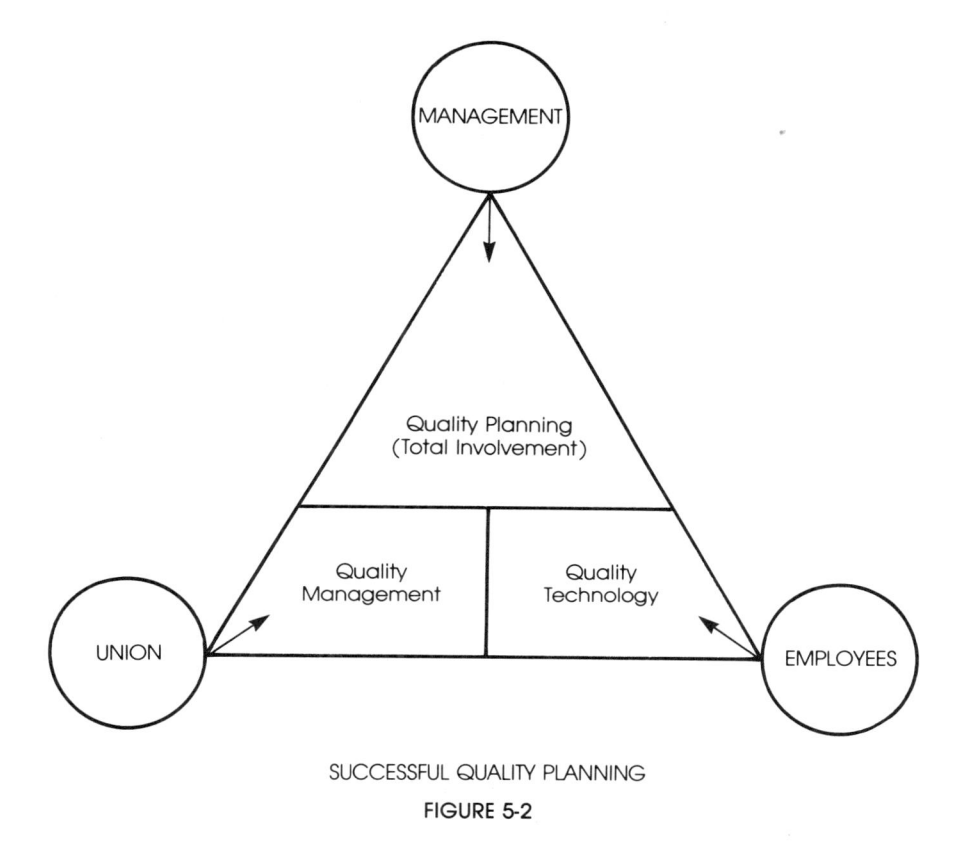

Figure 5-2 shows the key elements of successful quality planning. The triangle shows the three sides and the need to get management, employees, and union leaders involved in quality planning. The elements of a successful quality process are listed below. One needs to understand these elements and then plan quality objectives and quality plans for the organization.

Elements of a Successful Total Quality System

Quality planning and management are not easy in any organization. Quality products are built with the help of many people, many activities, many procedures and standards. One person as a quality-control manager, or one quality-control department, cannot achieve this. What an organization really needs is the commitment and involvement from top management to all the lower-level employees. However, this action has to start at the top through quality planning and establishing quality policy, because it is the top management who can change the culture of the organization and can guide the organization in the right direction.

The following list will give the reader an overall idea of the elements of the successful total quality system:

1. Management planning for quality:
    Quality policy
    Quality plans
    Quality assurance procedures/manual
2. New product planning for quality:
    Market evaluations
    Customers' needs
    Marketing specifications
    Competiton
3. Product design for quality:
    Design reviews
    Part/product specifications
4. Supplier/vendor quality:
    Incoming inspection
    Supplier certification
    Supplier studies/records
    Training
5. Manufacturing for quality:
    Preproduction review
    Manufacturing process information
    Manufacturing planning
    Inspection planning/instructions
    Process capability studies
    Precontrol/statistical techniques
    Quality standards/visual aids
    Control elements
        a. know what to do
        b. know what you are doing
        c. have the ability to regulate
    Nonconforming material controls
        a. material review board
        b. salvage procedures
        c. deviation system
    Traceability on key parts/operations
    Machine tool/gauge—qualification/certification
    Quality-improvement system
        a. prevention
        b. connections
        c. react to quality reports
        d. set goals and time tables

Calibration system
Warehousing/storage
Material-handling systems
  a. hardware
  b. software
6. Finished product quality:
   Customer service
   Packaging quality
   Field failure analysis
   Product manuals
   Field audits
   Product liability preventions
   Product recall methods
7. Information systems for quality:
   Quality loss reports
   Warranty reports
   Customer feedback
   Annual quality report
   Quality cost reports
8. Training for Quality:
   Job training
   Product training
   Quality Circles
   Use of statistics
   Suppliers

Quality Measurement

Quality planning should also include some kind of measurements to check the progress and measure the overall performance of the quality of the organization. However, it is not possible to measure the quality performance in one single index. The author's experience shows that it is valuable and very useful to devise different ways to check the performance. The following list will give the reader the methods to measure quality progress in the organization:

1. Production Performance in Quality

    a. Quality costs as a percentage of sales.

    b. Quality costs as a percentage of manufacturing costs.

    c. Quality costs as a percentage of production hours.

2. Customer Satisfaction
   a. Product audits
   b. Warranty
   c. Early-warning system
   d. Customer survey
   e. Customer, dealer vists
3. Quality Systems
   a. Quality audits
   b. Overall performance of the organization
   c. Overall quality training of the department
   d. Internal surveys on absenteeism, grievances, communications

Quality Policy

Need for a Policy

The quality of products and services directly affects a company's competitive position, profitability, and reputation for responsibly serving the interests of its customers and the public as a whole.

Evolving environmental trends have intensified the product-quality opportunities and challenges faced by all businesses. Among these trends are:

1. A continuing rise in expectations and sophistication of product users in all categories.
2. The enactment of legislation extending not only the range of products but also the civil and criminal penalties, and associated reputation loss, for noncompliance.
3. A general escalation of downtime costs, product liability costs, and repair costs relative to acquisition costs.

The challenge is further heightened by the extremely wide range of customer classes it serves; the interdependence of product-quality reputation among all company products sharing common use of the corporate name and trademark; and the broad range of technology, frequently at the leading edge of state of the art of its product offerings.

A product-quality policy is needed to give firm expression to the overall product-quality objective of the company and to set further procedures applicable to its fulfillment.

Company policies provide a guide to the proper courses of action, both present and future. They give a better understanding of the limits and regulations to which people should conform. Without a strong policy, the program can lack direction and continuity. Well-defined and properly constructed policies help managers delegate responsibilities to subordinates, as well as permit people at different levels of an organization to make appropriate decisions as long as those decisions fall within the limits of the published policy. Thus, the policy encourages uniformity of action and follow-up within the company.

However, it must be remembered that policies need to be reviewed periodically to maintain their effectiveness and must be updated constantly to reflect changes in the company. Even though it is recommended that companies have a policy for a quality system, it is not necessary to cover each and every detail. That will make the policy too tight and leave less chance of improving the program. Policies need to be flexible enough for the betterment of the program.

The well-defined policy eliminates a lot of confusion and misunderstanding. However, it is not easy to write such a policy within a short period of time. One of the first duties of a quality council is to write policies as soon as possible.

The American National Standard Institute (ANSI) describes quality policy in the following way:

A quality policy should be adopted to describe explicitly management's specific intentions with respect to quality. This document should specify an organized approach for carrying out those intentions and should address itself to all major quality parameters including user safety, product liability, adherence to legal requirements, and product fitness for use. It should be approved by the chief executive officer for company-wide policies or by subordinate officers for specialized policies, as applicable. Periodic organizational audits should be conducted to assure adherence to quality policy.

I have reviewed many quality policies of the major corporations. IBM has listed part of its policy in its annual report. It encompasses most of the items described earlier. Allis-Chalmers maintains that those who purchase Allis-Chalmers' products expect them to fulfill intended functions and operate satisfactorily for a reasonable period of time with proper use, care, and maintenance. Schlitz Brewing Company emphasizes that quality results from a total company effort and that quality must be built into the product.

In general, a quality policy should define the actual quality intent of the organization; it provides the foundation upon which the appropriate quality process is designed and built. Managers at all levels must be responsible for giving attention to product and service quality in business planning and in all opportunities for serving the customer.

We have described below a quality policy for the reader's use; however, one should modify and change it to suit his or her organization's total objectives.

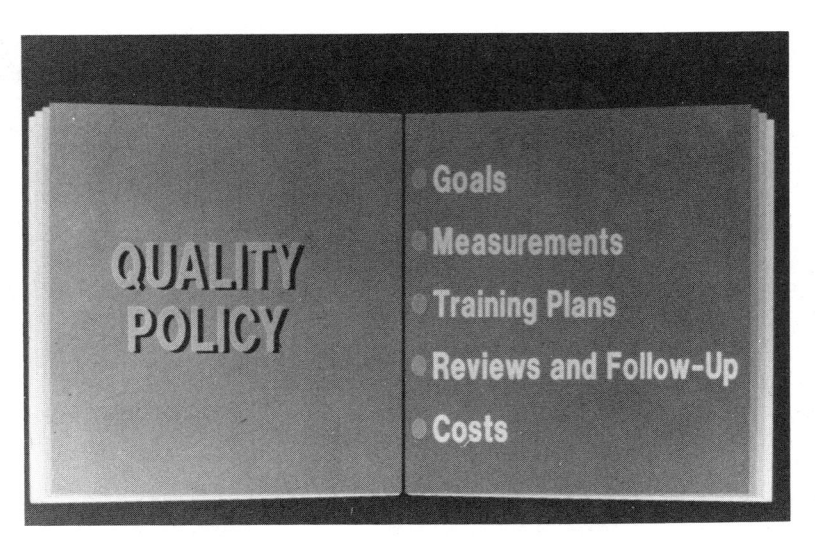

FIGURE 5-3

Quality Policy for ABC Company

It is the policy of ABC Company to design, manufacture, and market products that satisfy the customer's needs for quality, reliability, and performance. Safety is a property of our product, akin to quality and not separable, but it is dealt with in a separate policy.

Quality is defined as the sum of product characteristics and product support which ensures that the customer receives full value for his purchase price and that ABC Company obtains a fair return on its investment. ABC Company products are designed to the same exacting standards and manufactured to uniformly high levels of quality throughout the world. Maximum interchangeability of components and parts is maintained wherever they are manufactured.

Pursuit of quality also includes providing improved performance, safe operating characteristics, and timely after-sales parts and service availability. We continually monitor the impact of products on the environment, striving to minimize any potentially harmful aspects and maximize their substantial capability for the benefits of mankind.

This constant pursuit of quality must necessarily involve the dedication of all departments—particularly manufacturing, engineering, testing, and product assurance. Continual emphasis will be placed toward increased checking with gauging of components by production personnel and the "make it right the first time" philosophy throughout the company.

To ensure effectiveness, the quality-control function must be exercised in an objective and unbiased manner. As such, the independence of the quality-control function has been emphasized throughout the organization so that it has the power to prevent nonconforming products from entering the commercial stream.

Quality Plans

Quality plans are just like other plans in managing business. The plans help us see the goals and accomplish quality objectives based on the organization's quality policy. We should remember that quality plans should be established annually and that everyone should get involved in preparing the plan.

Some of the suggestions in preparing quality plans are listed below:

1. Items listed in the plan must be related to the quality of our products and services. Ideally, the plan would state known quality problems; proposed solutions; and procedures, with timetables, as to how the solutions will be accomplished.
2. The plans must be specific. Objectives in the plan must be stated as specifically as possible so as to be measurable. The audit system will review these plans and comment as to the degree of conformance a department has to its plan. For this reason, the more specific the plan is, the more objective the audit can be and the more positive the results.
3. The plan should provide for some form of training. This training might include people from outside your department that your department interacts with as well as the people within the department.
4. All plans should include a schedule for department review sessions to monitor the department's progress on the plan. Hence, quarterly plans are recommended.
5. The quality plan should encourage a systematic approach to improving quality.
6. The plan should reflect the effort and involvement of as many people as possible.
7. There should be a follow-up procedure to check the progress of the plans.
8. Once the plans have been accepted by the division quality council, they may not be changed without the approval of the division quality council.

A sample quality plan for one of the plants of a leading manufacturer is descibed below:

Quality Plans for a Manufacturing Division
(Sample)

I. General Manager's Plans:

Objective: It is the primary objective of the division to maintain and improve the quality of our products so that we can continue to supply a product of higher quality than any of our competition. Hence, it is essential that quality be considered as everyone's responsibility. Every part, every detail, and every function that you are a part of or associated with must be within the quality specifications required for a superior product. It is up to *you* to do it right the first time and not let the product out of your jurisdiction until it is *right*.

Procedure to develop a quality plan:

A. List of quality-related goals
  1. Goal
  2. Timing
  3. Measurements
B. Development procedure
  1. Foreman develops his or her own written quality goals, including timing and measurements.
  2. Plant superintendent collects, critiques, condenses, and summarizes to prepare departmental quality plans.
  3. All other departments follow similar procedures.
     a. Production control
     b. Quality control
     c. Manufacturing engineering
     d. Industrial engineering
     e. Inspection
     f. Accounting
     g. Shipping, receiving
  4. Quality council reviews the quality plan and incorporates the total organization quality plan.
C. Other items in quality plans:
  1. Quarterly review of quality plan by the quality council.
  2. Develop a more comprehensive divisional quality cases reporting system and analyze the quality cases every month.
  3. Establish a quarterly plan to reduce scrap and rework.
  4. Introduce operator control in the division.

5. Improve the content and availability of resource documents.
6. Maintain and improve products.
7. Constantly improve details in process sheets.
8. Improve methods of operation sheets.
9. Improve better setup instructions.
10. Confirm purge procedure.
11. Expand use of process capability and SPC in the division.
12. Develop a systematic procedure for sorting defective parts.
13. Constantly improve the quality manual for the division.
14. Improve communication by planning quarterly meetings with employees and monthly meeting with foremen and department heads.

II. Suggested Items for Other Departments
   A. Manufacturing engineer
      1. Meet drawing requirements and process development.
      2. Develop quality fixtures and gauges.
      3. Purchase and check all facilities, capital equipment, tooling, and gauging, using proper quality-control checks.
      4. New-product drawing review.
      5. Attend quality training.
      6. Use machine and process capability studies.
      7. Analyze tolerances and initial dimensions.
      8. Similar plans for plant engineering.
      9. Preventive maintenance system.
   B. Industrial engineering
      1. Training programs.
      2. Detail operator instructions.
      3. Better method for operation sheets.
      4. System to check bill of material.
      5. Operator control.
   C. Production control
      1. Purge system quality.
      2. Pick up list quality.
      3. Inventory and MRP quality.
   D. Divisional quality control
      1. Quality reporting.
      2. Written specifications.

64 QUALITY PLANNING

    3. Quality checks.
    4. Quality loss input data.
    5. Reject, scrap reporting.
    6. Quarterly quality planning.
    7. Vendor analysis.
    8. Technical information storage.
    9. Visual aids.
    10. Statistical analysis, including SPC.
    11. New product quality control.
    12. Product and service performance reporting.
    13. Key project analysis.
    14. Corrective and preventive actions.
    15. Quality training.
    16. Improvement reports.
    17. New and current product specification reviews.
    18. Customer complaints review.
    19. Warranty analysis and feedback.
    20. Yearly quality progress and review meeting.

III. Quality Plans for Machining
    A. First quarter
        1. Teach advanced inspection class.
        2. Implement gauge control and calibration system.
        3. Establish inspection procedures for new products.
        4. Continue process control program.
        5. Expand MERC (Mercury Employee Recognition Circles).
        6. Develop process for use of smart gauge.
        7. Develop computer-controlled SIR (Sample Inspection Reports) tracking system.
        8. Review capabilities and standards in automatic machining area with product and manufacturing engineering and production personnel.
    B. Second quarter
        1. Eliminate duplication layouts.
        2. Reduce deviations by 50 percent by having process or print changed.
        3. Follow-up on changes requested in MRP programs to permit collecting more pertinent data than system presently permits.

4. Complete SIRs on redesign projects.
5. Establish budget for following year.
6. Design and build in-process gauges for redesign projects.
7. Write inspection instructions for the many parts received from other plants.

C. Third quarter
1. Establish process control program for the new block line.
2. Perform capability studies in the automatic machining department.
3. Recommend changes in the quality loss reporting system that will provide management with meaningful data.
4. Complete training program for quality control supervisors.
5. Develop system for implementing a management-awareness program to educate management personnel in their role in quality.

D. Fourth quarter
1. Continue process control program on block line.
2. Review budget and establish goals for following year.
3. Prepare to receive machining of gear case and drive-shaft housing.
4. Continue to work with product and manufacturing engineering to upgrade print tolerances and standards.

IV. Quality Plans for Die Cast:
A. First quarter
1. Review redesign to make sure all prints meet die-cast standards.
2. Design and build gauging for gimbal housing, gimbal ring, and bell housing.
3. Modify current gauging to accommodate redesign products.
4. Assemble all information for the move to Mexico.
5. Establish MERC on second shift.

B. Second quarter
1. Write procedures for first piece inspection in the trim room.
2. Present all information on the image amplification system for following year's budget.
3. Establish budget for following year.
4. Conclude advanced inspection class.

C. Third quarter
1. Start end-of-run meetings with manufacturing, engineering, die repair, and production.

2. Teach supervisors a working knowledge of programming of cordax and portage.
3. Develop applications for the smart gauge.

D. Fourth quarter
1. Implement gauge-control system.
2. Update inspection instruction sheets to improve inspection of parts.
3. Expand Quality Circle program.
4. Review budget and establish goals for following year.

IV. Quality Plans for Assembly

Goals are not defined on a quarterly basis. The need for implementation is current. Progress will be reviewed on a quarterly basis.

A. Accomplish advanced inspection training.
B. Cross-train floor inspectors.
C. Develop inspection instruction sheets and pertinent visual aids for new product.
D. Weekly torque-wrench calibration on each assembly line, to be done by floor inspector and group leader.
E. Inventory all torque wrenches in assembly and catalog.
F. Refurbish existing gauging and backup equipment.
G. Standardize fasteners and torques on new engines.
H. Revamp process control meetings to be more goal-oriented.
I. Continue with visual aid format—one project per quarter.
J. Review all assembly method of operation sheets for correct call-out on adhesives, lubs, torques.

A Word on Quality Organization

During the last twenty years, I have studied many quality organizations in various companies. The historical development in quality organization has also followed closely for the last several years. One can find many versions of quality organizations, depending on the size of the organization, type of business, number of years the business has been established, and the type of product or services that are offered by the organization. Generally, one will find inspection-oriented quality organization for fifty years back. Later, the quality-control department was originated to monitor the quality of products and services. However, it created problems in the organization since production departments concentrated more on production (quantity) and neglected quality, assuming it to be a quality-control department's job!

Quality and productivity were thought to be two separate objectives, and management concentrated more on quantity and neglected quality. In the last several years, there have been many versions of the basic quality control department. In some organizations, departments such as quality assurance, quality improvement, product assurance, reliability, and quality engineering were added to improve quality.

However, I feel that most organizations forgot the basics and tried to shift responsibilities in higher production without much attention to quality. Based on experience and analysis, I believe it is about time quality responsibilities are put back where they belong: Quality is everyone's responsibility. In the manufacturing industry, it is the job of the manufacturing department to ensure and build quality products. Space does not permit a detailed discussion of the pros and cons of various organizations. However, a recommended overall organization is described in Figure 5-4.

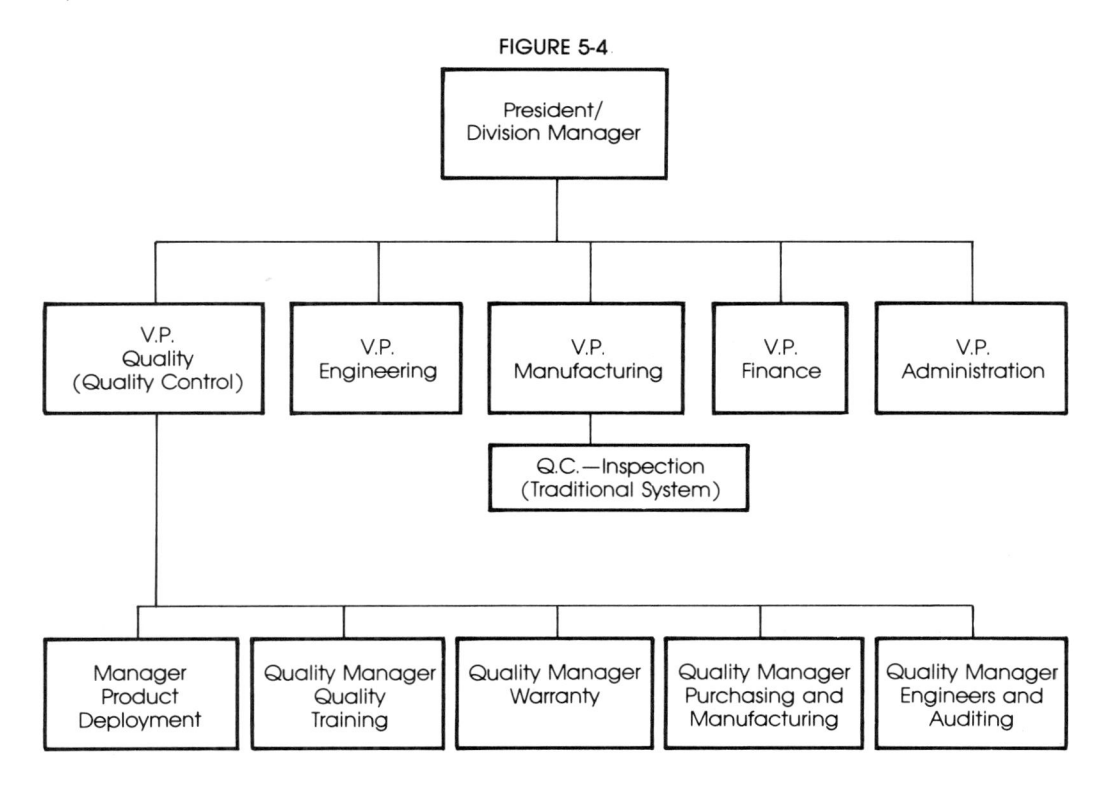

FIGURE 5-4

```
                    President/
                    Division Manager
                         |
    ┌────────────┬───────┴───────┬────────────┬────────────┐
   V.P.         V.P.           V.P.          V.P.         V.P.
  Quality    Engineering    Manufacturing   Finance   Administration
(Quality Control)                |
    |                     Q.C.—Inspection
    |                    (Traditional System)
    |
    ├──────────────┬──────────────┬──────────────┬──────────────┐
  Manager      Quality Manager  Quality Manager  Quality Manager  Quality Manager
  Product        Quality         Warranty       Purchasing and    Engineers and
 Deployment     Training                        Manufacturing      Auditing
```

This type of independent quality organization will achieve the following objectives through systematic quality audits:
1. Cost reduction
2. Customer satisfaction
3. Higher productivity
4. Improved quality
5. Improved relations between management and workers

QUALITY PLANNING

EVALUATE YOUR ORGANIZATION

(Self-analysis—Quality planning)

0 1 2 3 4 5 6 7 8 9 10

1. Our organization has established a quality policy that is known to all.
2. Our management spends time in quality planning; yearly quality plans are known to all.
3. New products and services in our organizations are evaluated very carefully and very few problems are encountered in product introduction.
4. Our organization works closely with vendors and very few problems exist due to poor vendor quality.
5. Our organization has established very good cost control and very good in-process quality checks in order to build quality products.
6. Our organization has very good quality training programs and everyone is involved in improving quality.
7. Our organization has well-established quality systems and quality cost reporting for all the employees.
8. Our organization promotes use of specialized thinking and SPC in the organization.
9. Our organization understands the new concept called product deployment and quality tables.
10. Our organization values customer satisfaction; customer complaints are handled immediately.

An ounce of prevention is better than a pound of cure.

Chapter Six
QUALITY DEPLOYMENT

During the next decade, customers are going to play an important role in building quality products and requiring quality services. Gone are the days when producers thought they could build and sell anything to the customer. The world is getting smaller, and more and more organizations are building quality products that are competing for the same market share. Hence, it is essential that manufacturers and service organizations pay better attention to customer demands and needs.

How Foreign Organizations Capture New Markets

The world is getting smaller and smaller due to improved communication systems, faster air travel, and ongoing improvements in various other aspects of daily life. All these aspects play an important role in expanding the market share for any product or service that organizations sell around the world. Generally, most foreign competition has used a systematic plan in entering into new world markets—whether it is the United States, Asia, South America, or Europe. In general, the new market is studied carefully from the customer's point of view. The currently available products and services are analyzed to find out whether they satisfy customers and what

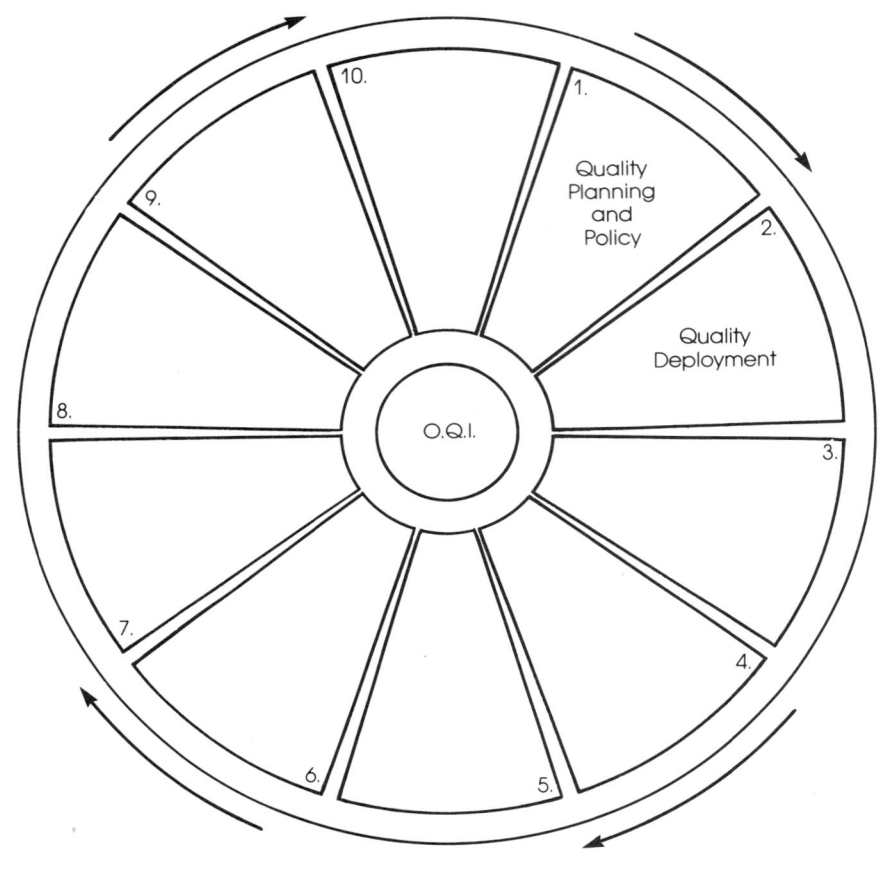

FIGURE 6-1

they might lack. The strategy for product introduction in the new market is carefully planned and then executed properly. Generally, today everyone is cost-conscious; hence, product cost is given high priority. For the last ten years, the trend has been for quality products to be introduced at a reasonably low price. Once the customer liked the product or service, prices were generally increased and kept just below the price of competitive products. I have studied various products available in the market, and most of the time the same marketing plan has been used to enter into new areas. Recently, industries making lawn mowers, machines, and air conditioners have become concerned with foreign competition. In some cases, it is a foregone conclusion that these businesses will be bankrupt unless the government interferes and helps the local industries.

What Can We Do to Beat the Competition?

1. Develop Closed-Loop Product Deployment Systems

Customers may think ill or well of an organization for reasons other than association with product quality alone. They may be entirely satisfied with the way the organization fulfills their needs such as delivery schedule, financial agreement, sales promises, and other details. We must realize that customer satisfaction depends only on product quality; organizational qual-

FIGURE 6-2

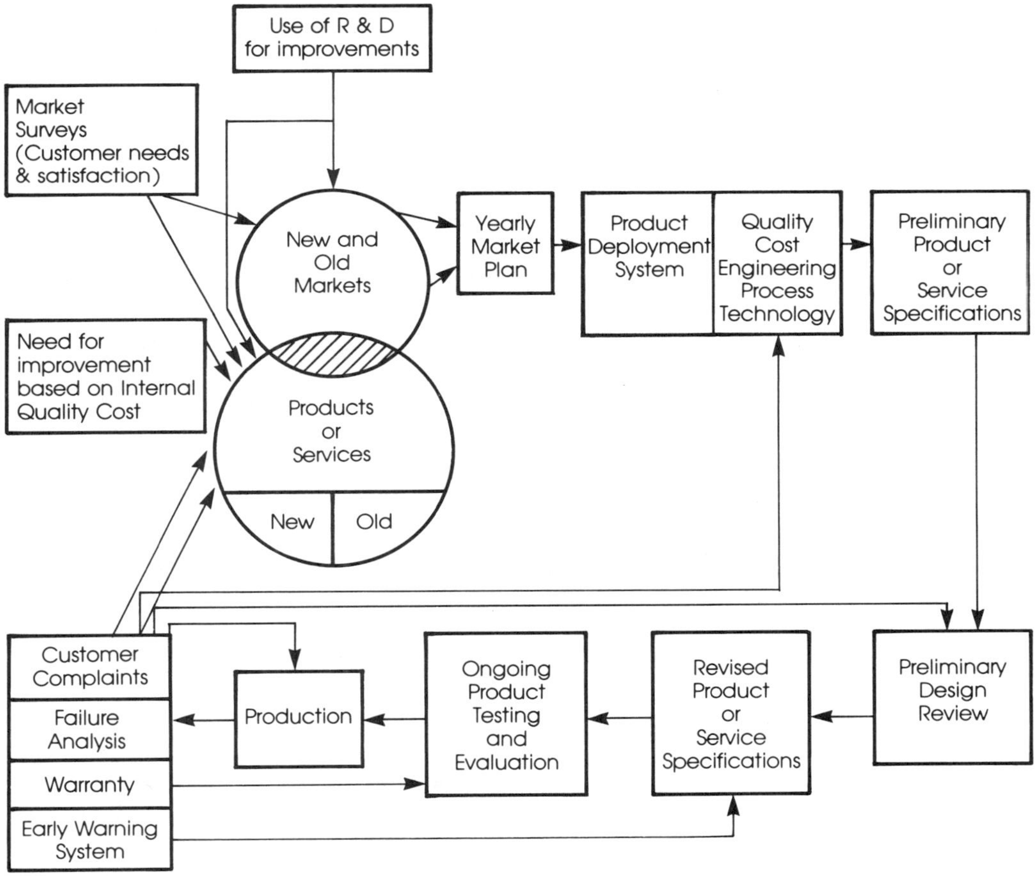

CLOSE-LOOP PRODUCT DEPLOYMENT SYSTEM

71

ity requirements are much broader than working only on product quality improvements.

Figure 6-1 shows a closed-loop product deployment system. The customer's needs and expectations are frequently difficult to determine. Determination of customer preferences starts with the broadest of product functions, such as food refrigeration or cooking, home heating, or clothes washing and drying. It becomes more specific as evaluations are made through the various market-sensing devices available, such as geographic or social group market surveys, competitive product analysis, evaluation of customer complaint data, and analysis by professional consultants such as market analysts, home economists, and product service specialists. There are several other key elements that one should consider in market analysis and new-product development. These elements can be classified in areas such as use of research and development for better products or creating new products; improving products to eliminate internal quality costs; and improving products to minimize customer complaints.

Once all the areas are analyzed and investigated, organizations should develop a yearly market plan which should be flexible, but must have a priority for product development. Many organizations prepare market plans, but generally they are completely different. The market plan for each product should be transferred into what is called a *product deployment system*. In the product deployment stage, various aspects of building the products are discussed, analyzed, specified, and reparaphrased. This gives birth to what is called a preliminary *product or service specification*. This specification, if accepted by quality council or top management, is used later for preliminary design review. The type of design review that is conducted by quality control engineering and manufacturing helps to revise product specifications. Using revised specifications we can build prototypes, test them thoroughly, and then either run mini-trial runs or preproduction lots, if possible. Production of the new products can be continued as long as revised products are not designed or needed by the market. The last key element of the closed-loop product deployment system is the active maintenance of customer complaints. Customer complaints can be collected and analyzed effectively through the use of a computer-aided quality system. Failure analysis, warranty analysis, and early warranty system play an important part in this regard. More details on each element can be found in other chapters.

The author believes the effective and honest use of this type of system will tremendously improve the market share of any product in the world market. However, one has to realize the importance of each element and follow it now, not wait until the competition takes over the business.

2. Emphasize Use of Quality Deployment System

Quality Deployment is the crucial part of the product deployment system described earlier. In order to satisfy customers' needs and requirements, it is necessary to understand them first and translate them effectively into characteristics in such a way that various departments in an organization can also understand them properly. In this case, one has to use common language that people know in these areas. Customer needs and expectations must be qualified in terms of overall product attributes such as weight, size, volume, and so on.

- Performance attributes such as output power and efficiency
- Aesthetic attributes such as appearance, style, texture, and so on
- Feature attributes such as remote control, automatic operation, and so on
- Integrating attributes such as safety, environmental compatibility, serviceability, reliability, maintainability, and so on

Determining customer needs and expectations is not an easy task. Both formal and informal customer specifications and requirements need to be addressed and discussed by various departments of the organizations. Reviews and discussions take place and the work responsibilities are divided among engineering, manufacturing, finance, and quality areas. The main objectives of these discussions are to assure that:

1. All significant product quality factors have been communicated to engineering, quality, manufacturing, and other appropriate people.
2. Interpretation of customer needs and requirements are understood by all concerned parties.

Figure 6-3 shows the short version of a quality deployment table being used in a large Japanese organization. This quality deployment is based on a free brochure received by the author from The Cambridge Corporation, Minato-ky, Tokyo, Japan.

In general, a quality deployment system uses the following procedures:

1. Various details on old and new market areas are collected and analyzed (information on market quality, claims, and information on competitive products).

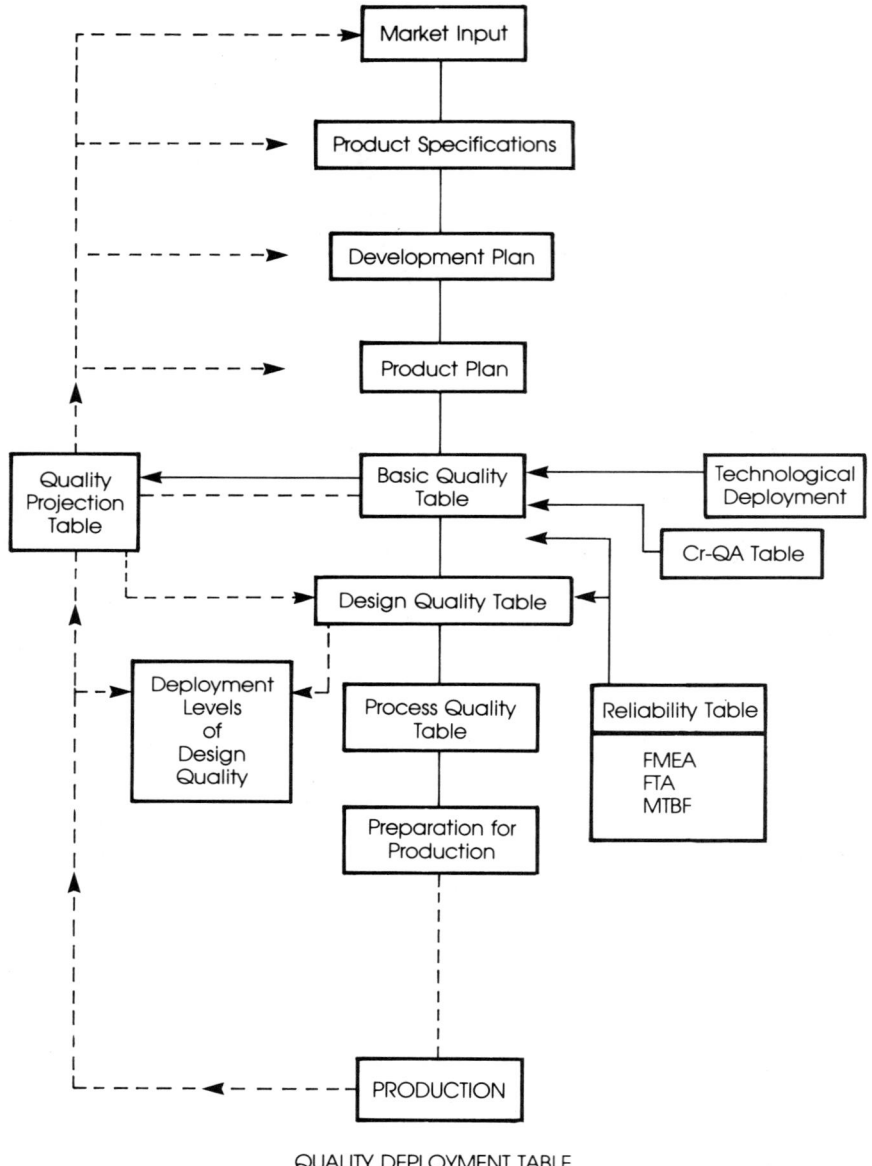

QUALITY DEPLOYMENT TABLE
FIGURE 6-3

2. Key areas for product improvement or new product developments are decided.
3. A development plan is prepared.
4. A product plan is organized showing the details regarding quality goals and quality objectives.

5. Basic quality tables are prepared.
6. Detailed quality tables are prepared for the following areas:
   a. design characteristics
   b. process characteristics
   c. assembly, subassembly, and part characteristics
7. In many cases, reliability analysis, cost analysis, and technological bottlenecks are also considered in developing quality tables.

A basic quality table is shown in Figure 6-4. In general, these tables are used to transfer customer requirements into quality characteristics. Later, quality characteristics can be subdivided according to their importance and also

FIGURE 6-4

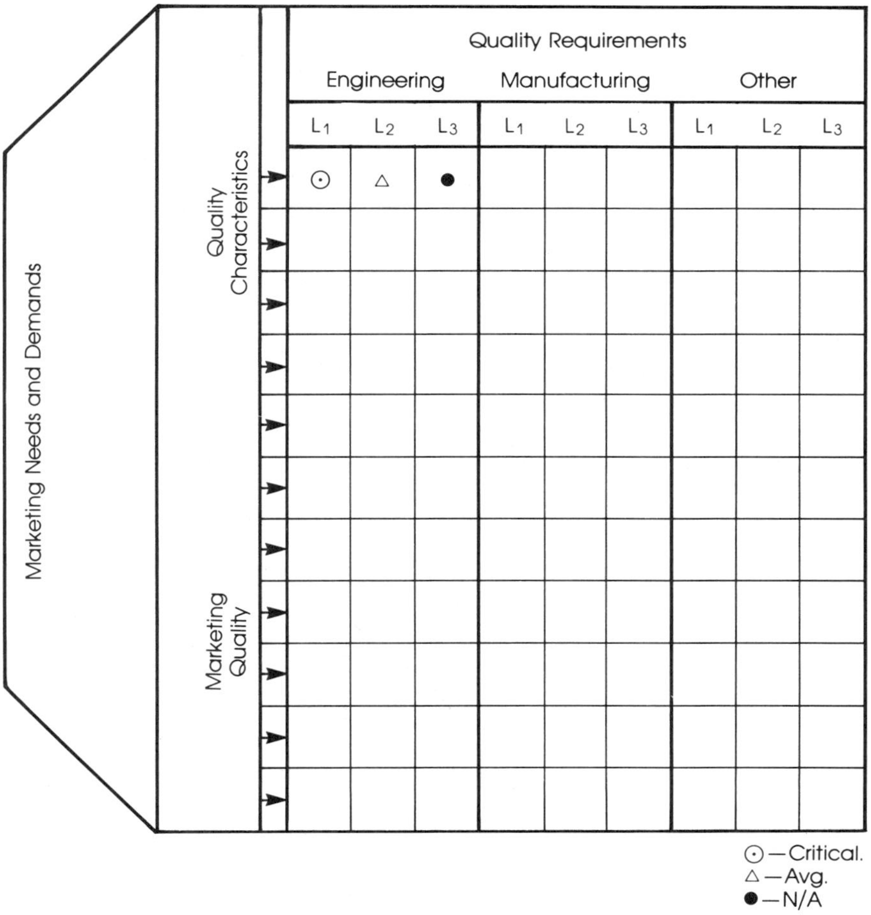

⊙ — Critical.
△ — Avg.
● — N/A

TYPICAL QUALITY TABLE

into subsystems such as components, processes, assemblies, testing, and so on. Effective use of quality tables plays an important role in the quality deployment system. Many organizations in Japan have expanded the basic concept of quality deployment into other areas, such as cost deployment or technological deployment.

In general, quality deployment helps the organization in the following ways:

1. Clear classification of the engineering issue
2. Clear clarification of customers' needs
3. Establishment of common language (quality table) for smoother communication
4. Clarification of companywide relations and responsibilities from planning to production
5. Establishment of priorities in various areas to meet quality objectives.

3. Establish Goals to Meet Specifications

The following information is based on the author's discussion with Yuin Wu, who studied and worked in Japan for several years.

If the customer requirements and specifications are analyzed with the help of the quality deployment system, once the quality tables are prepared, each area is given the responsibility for translating the requirements into specifications in a systematic way. Often products are also specified by JIS (Japan Industry Specification). However, companies generally try to aim at still lower specifications to make all products identical and well within specifications while manufacturing the products. Figure 6-5 will show the reader the relationship between these various specifications and the need for continual quality improvement.

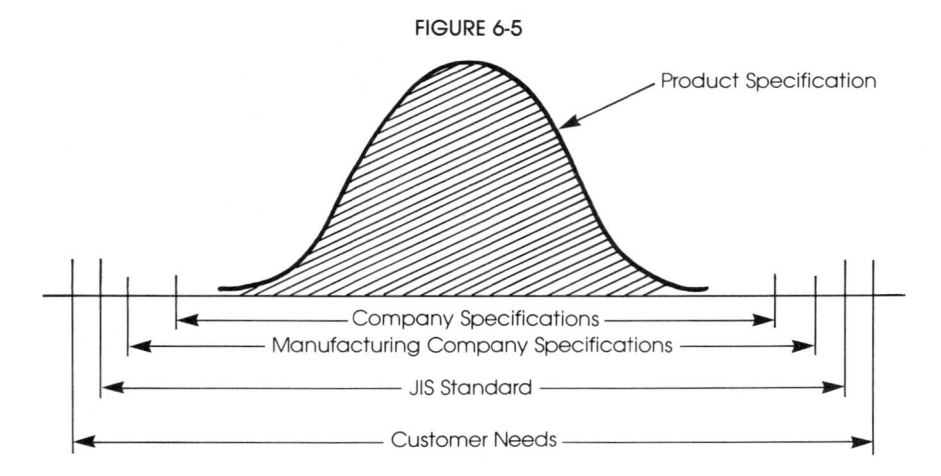

FIGURE 6-5

This type of work seems impossible and costly. However, we must remember that customer demands are increasing, and if one company satisfies these demands, people are going to buy that company's products. Hence, even though initially there is more long-range investment, it can pay off through a larger market share and repeated customer orders.

4. Use Customer-Based Measurements of Quality

Several methods are practical for obtaining customer-based measurements of the quality of products and services. Some are more appropriate than others. All involve a decision balancing the value and reliability of the information to be gained versus the cost of acquiring the information. The following methods are common in the customer-based measurement of quality:

a. Formal customer surveys. This type of survey is carefully planned to yield unbiased results. Questions are carefully worded or reworded; the method of asking them is also determined ahead of time. A sample of customers is statistically selected to represent the universe. Formal customer surveys are useful when the universe is large and one needs to get an idea of the acceptance of a new product or overall product quality.

b. In-depth customer interviews. When products are specialized and the market is limited, one can do in-depth customer surveys. However, it is not easy to interview a customer and get all necessary details, since customers may not be completely open and honest.

c. Informal visits to dealers or customers. A manufacturer can visit dealers and/or customers periodically and get an idea about product quality. Similarly, indirect questions can be asked about the quality of the competitor's product. This type of information can be very useful for improving product performance.

d. Published quality data. There are sources in the United States and other countries that independently test products available in the market and report periodically on their performance. *Consumer Reports,* published by the Consumers Union of United States, Inc., is a well-accepted publication. A manufacturer can use this information to compare his product's quality with the competition and learn its deficiencies. There are many other independent sources that publish similar reports on specialized industries.

e. In-house computerized reporting system. Every organization regularly gets in touch with customers when products are sold or services are offered. The service department, field people, marketing personnel, and sales force all have to work constantly with customers. All of these sources are

78 QUALITY DEPLOYMENT

valuable. However, one should watch for the biased opinion and try to siphon the information as much as possible. This type of information can be stored in the computer, and one can develop excellent files for future use. Many times customers' phone calls or letters can also be used to determine the acceptance or rejection of products in the market.

The following is one of the samples for dealer or customer interviews:

SAMPLE CASE STUDY

Name:_____
Address:_____
Telephone No.: _____

1. How would you rate the overall quality of the product you received from ABC Company during this year or the previous year?

   Excellent   Very Good   Good   Fair   Poor

   Explain: _____
   _____

2. What area of specific servicing have you run into most?

   Explain: _____
   _____

3. Please identify the biggest complaint out of the service shop.
   _____

4. What is the major size of the engines you sell and service? (percentages, please)_____
   _____

5. What are the primary applications of the product you handle and in what environment are they used?
   _____
   _____

Condition of the Product as Received

6. How do you rate the cosmetic appearance of ABC Company engines?

   Poor   Fair   Good   Excellent

7. What problems have you had with the following:

   Paint damage_____
   Decal problems _____
   Poor appearance _____

8. Have you received goods that incurred shipping damage?_____
   _____

   Who was the carrier? _____

9. Are you able to handle the product as received in the box? What improvements could be made to help you?

Condition of the Product Out of the Box

10. Have you found engines that appear incomplete; with loose fasteners, missing parts, or literature; not tested.
    Explain: _____

11. Are instructions adequate for installation? What problems have you had installing engines?

12. Do accessories install with ease? What can you suggest for improvements?

Initial Engine Performance

13. Are you confident the engine will start with ease out of the box?

14. Describe any particular problems you have had, such as starting performance. _____

15. Are engine-setup specifications proper?
    Timing _____
    Setting _____
    Speed _____
    Performance _____
    Setup Adjustments _____

16. What improvements could be made to improve the "out-of-the-box" performance?

17. Have you had specific electrical problems that could be improved on the product?

18. Are instructions and instruments adequate for diagnosing electrical problems?

19. Since you've been a dealer, has the finished product's quality improved or decreased from ABC Company's standards?
_____

20. How is the quality of service parts you receive?
_____
_____

21. General Comments:
_____
_____
_____

Note: This information is based on Ed Grimmer's dealer survey. Mr. Grimmer works as quality control manager at Mercury Marine, Fond du Lac, Wisconsin.

General Comments on Customer Surveys

The importance customers attach to various attributes is likely to vary over the life cycle of the product. When products are first received, customers may place the most value on appearance, completeness, and performance. Later the emphasis may shift to reliability and effectiveness of service. Once the warranty runs out, they may emphasize maintainability and the cost and quality of service. However, all these aspects should be included in measuring customer-based quality performance.

Similarly, we should realize the limitations of customer-based quality measurement due to the biased nature and use of information. Generally, we can learn from customers the key elements they deem most important for satisfaction and how much they are willing to pay for them. We can also learn the quality of performance of our products compared to those of the competition and deficiencies that customers see in the products or services that are offered by our organization.

EVALUATE YOUR ORGANIZATION

1. Our organization understands and uses the concept of quality deployment.		0	10
2. Our organization uses quality tables for new-product development		0	10
3. Our organization uses product deployment and product or service specifications for developing new products or services.		0	10

4. Our organization uses various types of surveys or interview methods to get customers' input in developing new products or services.   0 _____ 10

5. Our organization uses failure analysis, using FMEA (Failure Mode and Effect Analysis) and FTA (Failure Tree Analysis) as one of the key inputs in product deployment.   0 _____ 10

6. Our organization communicates to engineering and manufacturing what is important to the customer.   0 _____ 10

7. Our organization considers cost aspects, sales forecast, safety reliability, and other key features while developing new products for the customers, but customers' needs and requirements are considered first all the time.   0 _____ 10

8. Our organization considers marketing tests and evaluation for customer satisfaction on new products and services.   0 _____ 10

9. Our organization considers the need for spare parts and other components for customer satisfaction.   0 _____ 10

10. Our organization develops service instructions and service policies for new products and services as well as old products or services.   0 _____ 10

Note: The author has developed 300 similar questions to analyze the organization. This information is based on Ed Grimmer's dealer survey. Mr. Grimmer works as quality control manager at Mercury Marine, Fond du Lac, Wisconsin.

Quality must be standard equipment. We cannot view it as an operation for which the customer must pay extra. Rather, it must be the reason why customers buy from Brunswick.

Brunswick Corporation Annual Report, 1983

Chapter Seven
NEW PRODUCT INTRODUCTION: QUALITY OF DESIGN

Design engineering happens to be an area often overlooked in the industry's ongoing quest for quality. It should never be overlooked. Design is the starting point; some say it is the foundation of any effective quality process. Even though the United States is known for a number of inventions in worldwide use, even though the basic ideas are great, the finished product at times lacks high quality. It is known that many companies allow customers to test the quality of their product—testing which should have been done in the company before the first lot of production was released in the market. One of the major differences between the products built in the United States and Japan is the quality of design. In Japan, from the conception of the idea to the first production lot, the products are thoroughly tested at various stages, and the first production is not released to customers unless it is approved by the consensus of various departments. The product must pass many types of quality tests before it is released.

Problems in New-Product Introduction

We read in newspapers and hear on the radio and television about new products that do not work properly and companies that must recall some of

FIGURE 7-1

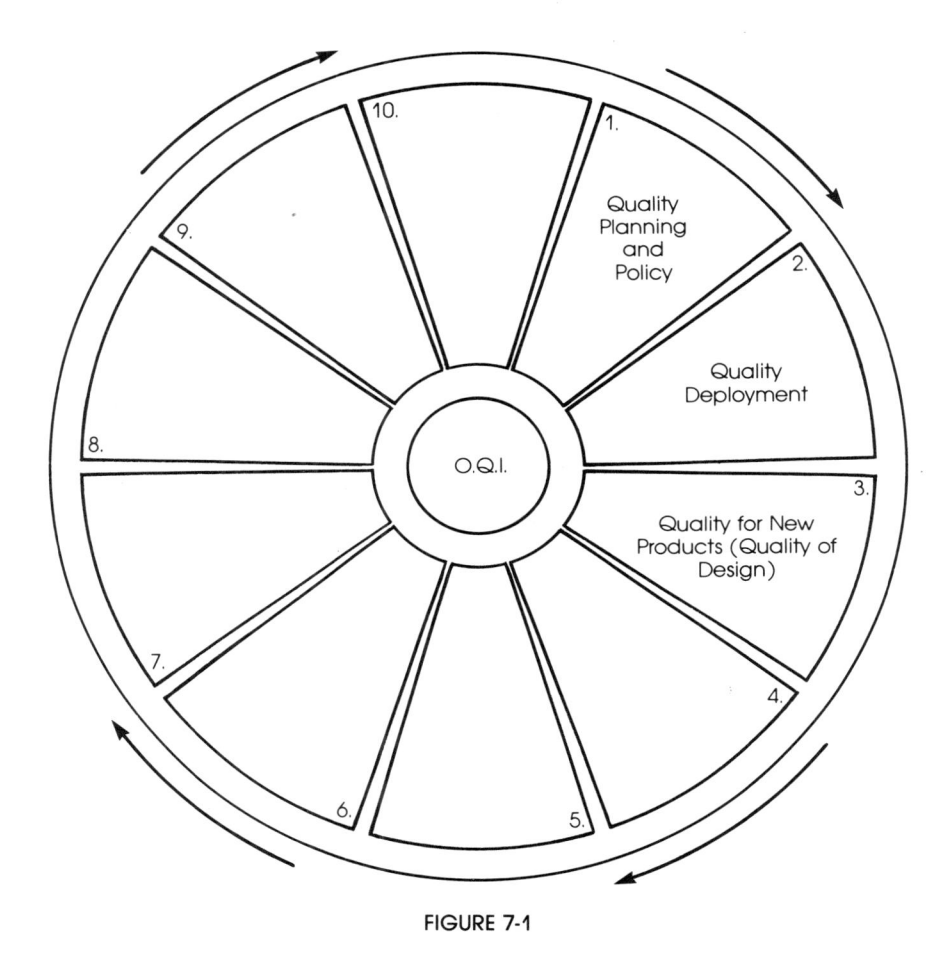

their products for rework. The automobile industry is an obvious example of this type of problem. Here are some of the reasons for this failure:

1. Too much rush to beat the competition. Many products require a number of years to develop an attractive, noteworthy design. However, in order to capture a larger market and beat the competition, the product is often introduced in a rush. With this ongoing, never-ending rush, products are introduced in the market without thorough testing, resulting in poor-quality products.

2. Financial pressure. Organizations invest millions of dollars in new products or services. Not all the new products and services work for a long time; many times organizations have to stop production or offer new services. Hence, management is always pressured to achieve quick financial returns.

"MARKET-IN" AND "PRODUCT-OUT" CONCEPTS

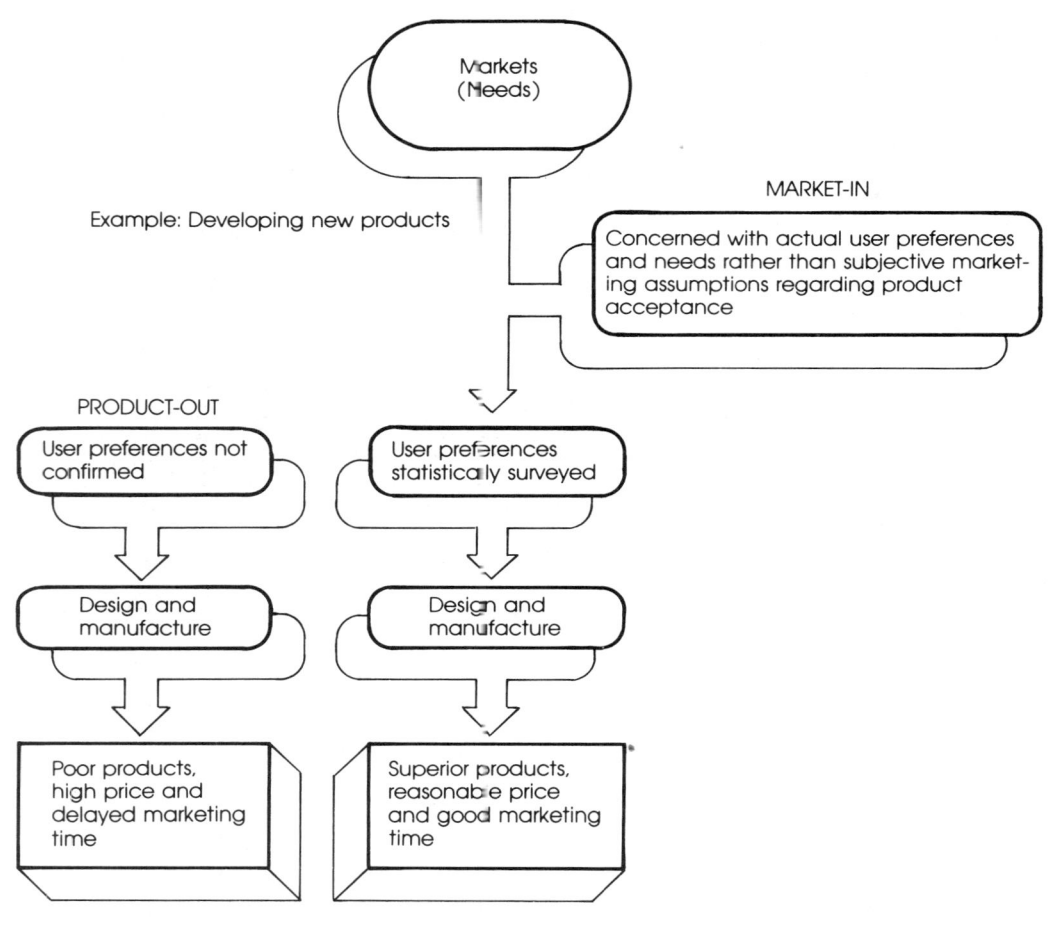

```
                    Markets
                    (Needs)

Example: Developing new products        MARKET-IN
                                        Concerned with actual user preferences
                                        and needs rather than subjective market-
                                        ing assumptions regarding product
                                        acceptance

PRODUCT-OUT
User preferences not          User preferences
confirmed                     statistically surveyed

Design and                    Design and
manufacture                   manufacture

Poor products,                Superior products,
high price and                reasonable price
delayed marketing             and good marketing
time                          time
```

A new marketing concept, called "Market-In" was developed by the Ricoh Company as part of the CWQC program. Rather than subjectively designing products and then looking for a way to market them, the so-called "Product-Out" marketing concept, Ricoh began by conducting statistical surveys of user preferences. This information was utilized in the design and manufacture of products, enabling the company to manufacture superior products for a reasonable price. Because the divisions concerned developed a better understanding of the market through these surveys, market timing was improved considerably (see graph).

The Ricoh Company's new corporate policy can be summarized in a few words:
"*To win customer trust and expand the company through quality.*"

FIGURE 7-2

Due to this pressure, many organizations rush to introduce products that are not up to par. I have experienced this type of pressure during the building of new products. Even though such organizations may make money when new products are introduced, in the long run the organization will lose money due to poor quality image of the product.

3. Poor communication in departments. Most organizations are broken down into various departments such as marketing, sales, finance, manufacturing, engineering, and so on. If communications between departments is poor and people interact by confrontation instead of with team spirit, with each department interested in pushing its own ideas, then poor design results. The outcome is poor customer satisfaction.

4. Late interface with the vendor. Any design of a product or service uses many purchased parts. However, vendors are generally kept in the dark regarding the new parts or new operations. This confidentiality is mainly to prevent information from getting into the hands of competitors. However, this late involvement causes more problems for the vendors. Since specifications or drawings are not available to vendors, their work has to be carried out blindly. It is not easy to control cost or check quality of the parts. Organizations need to review their policies and operation in dealing with vendors. We have discussed this aspect in detail in Chapter 8.

5. Poor understanding of manufacturing processes or services. Even when a new design is introduced that is supposed to be manufactured with existing equipment, I have observed that many problems occur in the manufacture of new products. Engineers generally work on the new product in their department, testing it in special laboratory conditions. These products are rarely field-tested. Many engineers do not get involved in manufacturing operations and rarely know the capabilities of the manufacturing equipment. Tolerances are given and drawings are based on old drawings or sometimes cut in half so that all parts will meet the specifications. In modern quality industries, use of process capability indices (Cp and Cpk) to communicate tolerances should be used between the engineering and manufacturing departments, rather than old documentation based on historical data.

6. Lack of statistical knowledge and use. One of the major reasons for the improved quality of Japanese products is the use of practical statistics. Statistics are applied in all phases of production. Workers use statistics in solving problems in Quality Circles; engineers use it in failure analysis; and so on. The use of experiment design and failure analysis play an important role in improving the quality of design of the product. Parameter design and allowance design are common. In the United States, the use of statistics is limited and many times ignored.

Design Phases

Any new product design or new service goes through various design phases. Let us review the process:

FIGURE 7-3

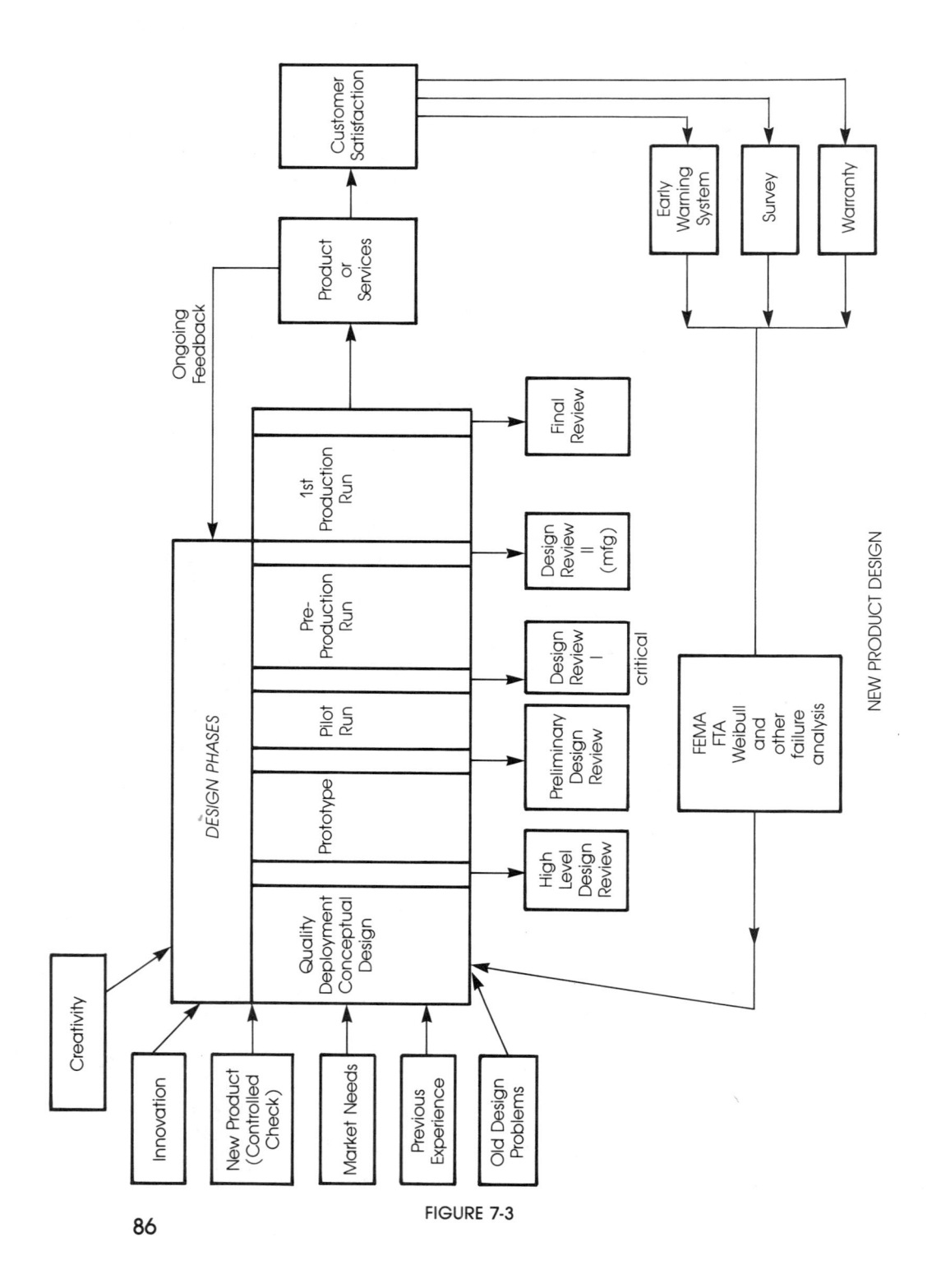

As shown in Figure 7-3, the design of a new product or service can be divided into the following four phases:

1. Conceptual design
2. Prototypes
3. Pilot or mini-pilot run
4. Preproduction

In conceptual design, engineers are generally assigned to find new products for the market and to invent new products and services for customers. This phase is nebulous and can take a long time. Sometimes one will find that time and money are wasted due to poor quality and unnecessary products or services. Designers must consider various aspects before putting together the product or service. Failure analysis should be made on warranty parts and other possible failures as shown in Figure 7-2. Similarly, present market conditions, previous experience, and old designs should be reviewed to avoid past errors. At the end of conceptual design, top management usually meets to decide whether or not to go ahead with the project. If approval is given, an informal specification is prepared and a high-level informal design review should be performed. In the prototype phase, samples are made to see the conceptual design carried out. Then, in the pilot phase, detailed drawings are done and decided upon, and design reviews are held so as to correct any mistakes. Drawings are released after the pilot run is completed.

Case Study

The following information describes, in detail, the various steps that one should follow in introducing a new product properly.

New-product introduction is to be effected in four phases, as follows:

Phase One—Advance planning

Phase Two—Pilot run

Phase Three—Preproduction run or mini-pilot run

Phase Four—Production run

Each phase will be initiated by a bill of material release from engineering. The following outlines the activity in each phase.

Phase One—Advance Planning

Bill of material format. The Phase One bill of material is to be a typed numerical listing of all parts released for advance planning activities; it should include all new purchased parts, castings (metal and plastic), forgings, and machined casting or forging part numbers. Both production numbers and experimental numbers may be employed.

Activities authorized. Activities authorized will be as specified by the bill of material cover letter. Typical activities authorized in Phase One are as follows:

- Die design and die steel procurement
- Die construction (only where considered necessary and requested by die design or product engineering to meet schedules)
- Maching tooling design
- Vendor quotes for costing

Drawing change control and distribution system. Drawings in Phase One will be under the control of product engineering. Drawings identified by experimental part numbers require no formal change control system. Drawings identified by production part numbers are to be released to manufacturing engineering using the confidential drawing release and change control procedure.

Distribution of drawings is as authorized by manufacturing engineering, and *all* print requests are to be processed through manufacturing engineering.

Parts procurement responsibility. The procurement of parts authorized by the bill of material cover letter shall be the responsibility of the manufacturing engineer assigned the project to initiate and product engineering to expedite. Materials management personnel will assist in this procurement by placing all orders as directed by manufacturing engineering and insuring that all purchased parts are delivered to product engineering on time.

Phase Two—Pilot Run

Bill of material format. The Phase Two bill of material shall be a typed, indented bill of material sequenced so as to facilitate the needs of product engineering. All known parts are to be listed in the Phase Two bill. The inclusion of a production number in the bill directs that a drawing is available. In many cases, a computer BOM may be created from the typed BOM for material control purposes; however, the authoritative Phase Two BOM will remain the typed engineering bill.

Activities authorized. Activities authorized will be as specified by the bill of material cover letter. Typical activities authorized in Phase Two are as follows:

>   Die construction and sample castings
>   Procurement of vendor tooling and samples
>   Procurement of in-house machine tooling and samples

Drawing change control and distribution system.

>   For in-house parts: same as Phase One control.
>
>   For purchased parts: drawings are released to Fond du Lac blueprint room control and the ECN (Engineering Change Notice) system and normal distribution are employed.

Parts procurement responsibility. Procurement of parts sufficient to build the quantity of pilot-run models directed by the bill of material cover letter shall be the responsibility of the applicable product engineering group. Materials management personnel will assist in this procurement by placing all orders as directed by product engineering and insuring that all purchased parts are delivered to product engineering on time.

Phase Three—Preproduction

Bill of material format. The Phase Three bill of material shall be an indented format, computer bill of material sequenced so as to meet the needs of manufacturing. All known parts are to be listed in the Phase Three bill, using production or temporary numbers. The inclusion of a production number in the bill directs that an ECN-released drawing is available in the Fond du Lac blueprint room.

Drawing change control and distribution system. Drawings are released to Fond du Lac blueprint room control and the ECN system and normal distribution are employed.

Parts procurement responsibility. Materials management shall be responsible for procurement of all parts under Phase Three as directed by the preproduction schedule and bill of material.

Phase Four—Production

The bill of material format, activities authorized, drawing change control and distribution system, and parts procurement responsibility for Phase Four are identical to those of Phase Three except that parts procurement is increased to the quantities dictated by the production schedule.

One of the key features of this four-phase system is to clearly define responsibilities of all the various departments in the new-product introduction phase. The key departments are listed here:

1. Marketing responsibilities
2. Engineering responsibilities
3. Product coordination responsibilities
4. Manufacturing engineering responsibilities
5. Production control responsibilities
6. Quality control responsibilities
7. Engineering services responsibilities
8. Manufacturing plant responsibilities
9. Purchasing department responsibilities
10. Financial department responsibilities

Importance of Design Review

In order to develop defect-free designs, it is necessary that teamwork be created in the organization. Manufacturing, purchasing, and engineering personnel, and others should talk with each other freely and openly. One of the best ways to achieve this goal is through design reviews. In order to establish proper sequence, the author recommends the following procedure:

Phase I—Product Specification

Once the conceptual design is approved by the management, it is necessary for a preliminary product specification to be written cooperatively by the manufacturing, marketing, engineering, quality control, and financial departments. This should be used as a guideline in the future.

Phase II—Preliminary Design Review

This should be conducted after the prototypes are made and tested.

Phase III—Detailed Design Review

This should start after the mini-pilot run and should be conducted on an ongoing basis until the first production is tested.

The following article, "Making the Most of Design Reviews"[1], will give the reader a good idea about the procedure and how to conduct good design reviews.

Making the Most of Design Reviews

A well-conducted design review offers several advantages:

- It shows how well a design will meet the customer's requirements.
- It provides information on product costs and profit potential.
- It gives data on product performance and reliability.

This article describes effective methods for conducting formal design reviews. It covers both the planning and doing stages, with emphasis on preparation. Although many of these techniques were drawn from military/space experience, most of them are applicable to commercial products—and for large or small companies.

Nearly all firms that manufacture new products face a similar problem. Engineering wants maximum time for development, Manufacturing wants to productionize the design before starting to make it, and Sales wants to introduce the product quickly. This causes internal conflicts between the various affected groups.

It's true that the market place applies competitive pressure to shorten the development cycle. However, the risk of a failure which could damage the firm's reputation must be weighed against the possibility that a late release could cause the firm to lose its share of the market.

Design review is a means of reducing the risks associated with the introduction of new or improved products. It brings together specialists from all affected groups with the prime purpose of optimizing the design from the standpoints of function, cost, reliability, and appearance. In government procurement situations, the contracting agency can evaluate, in advance of testing, whether the design will satisfy the program requirements.

To get the proper coverage, at least the following groups should attend formal or informal design reviews:

Design Engineering	Reliability
Manufacturing	Marketing
Quality Control	Field Service

Depending upon the product and the related market situation, it may be necessary to include other groups such as Purchasing, Stress Analysis, Value Analysis, and Technical Publications (manuals and handbooks). Attendance at a review should be

---

[1] John A. Burgess, Manager, Reactor Engineering Administration, Westinghouse Astronuclear Laboratory, Pittsburgh, Pa. "Making the Most of Design Reviews," Machine Design, July 1968.

limited to about a dozen persons. However, when customer representatives attend the review, it may be necessary to exceed this limit.

Design reviews provide an opportunity for bringing questions and viewpoints about a product out into the open. They also allow the firm to benefit from the experience of its senior personnel. This prevents one project from repeating the errors of earlier ones. A formal design review allows the specialists in the firm to make certain that the new product has been designed in accordance with the proper methods and standards.

Some firms select an ad hoc committee, consisting of knowledgeable personnel from many groups in the firm, to serve on a design review panel. Other firms simply invite all major departments to send one or two representatives to the review meetings. Still other firms use a full-time audit team which reviews the concepts, methods, and features of all new products. Each of these approaches will work if proper preparation is made for the design review.

Regardless of the method selected, the reviewers have an obligation to prepare for the design review. This means studying any previous design-review data on similar products, as well as reviewing available material on the new product. Also, the reviewers need to know "the rules of the game," such as funding limits, schedules, and the general competitive situation. Otherwise, their recommendations may not be reasonable for this particular product. There is a need for objectivity, but it must be tempered with practicality.

Without this preparation, the design-review meeting will degenerate into a low-level education session. Thus, it will fail to achieve its intended purpose of optimizing the design for function, cost, reliability, and appearance.

A question often asked and seldom answered is, "What does design review cost?" One NASA study showed that design review for several space programs amounted to one to two percent of the total engineering cost. Some firms may feel this is too high. Others ask, "Can you afford *not* to use design reviews?"

Design reviews are not the panacea for all problems. Improper planning, inadequate preparation, poor selection of participants, and a bad presentation can easily wipe out gains that a design review may offer.

Although many companies look to the Reliability Department to trigger design reviews, the basic responsibility for preparing and conducting design reviews lies with the Engineering Department. Normally, the chief engineer or project manager will appoint someone in the Engineering Department to be the chairman of the meeting. The person selected should have a broad understanding of the overall technical problem. He should be skilled in leading a technical meeting and have a high level of tact and discretion. He may be a product-line manager or a key engineer. However, he should not be in a direct line of authority to the designer, since they would be reviewing themselves. This person's job is to work out the details of the design review and make all the arrangements for the meeting.

Time and Place

When should design reviews be held? Firms sometimes schedule a design review at the end of development but before the design is released for production. The think-

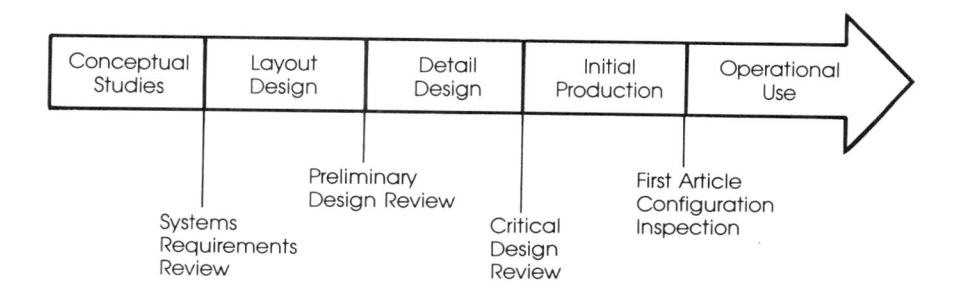

Design review cycle (Air Force Systems Command).

FIGURE 7-4

ing here is to let everyone know what Engineering has developed and is about to turn loose. However, this point in time may be too late to be helpful. Manufacturing may need changes in the design for ease of fabrication. Marketing may need time for planning the introduction of the new product. Quality Assurance may need special inspection equipment and procedures. To be effective, the design review must be held earlier in the development cycle.

For best results, a series of design reviews should be held at different stages in the design and development cycle. Several factors influence the frequency of reviews. These include product significance, degree of complexity, and the design timetable. Some firms hold a design review at the end of the conceptual stage, one after the layout stage, and one after prototypes have been built and tested. Several government agencies have established specific points in the cycle for reviewing the design of major equipment or systems. The Air Force Systems Command specifies three design reviews, Figure 7-4.

In addition to the formal reviews, informal reviews are periodically held at the working level. The design engineer meets with other engineers to discuss detail problems. Usually, the drawings are simply spread on a table, and the engineers review the design, raising questions as they go. Many of the preparation and follow-up techniques described in this article can be applied to both formal and informal reviews.

When a single component or a relatively simple product is being reviewed, about four hours should be allotted for the review meeting. But, if a system or a complex product is involved, it is advisable to review the major subsystems in separate meetings. This may take two or three days. For best results, design reviews should be scheduled in the middle of a week.

After the date is selected, the chairman must prepare an agenda for the meeting and specify which engineers should discuss the product design. The agenda should also indicate how much time each design engineer will be allowed. The chairman must also establish a planning schedule. Such a schedule, Table 7-1 (page 94), indicates when the formal meeting will be held, when the material must be available for review, and when rehearsals are scheduled.

TABLE 7-1. DESIGN REVIEW PLANNING SCHEDULE

ACTIVITY	WORK DAYS BEFORE DESIGN REVIEW
Schedule design review	D—30
Publish agenda. Assign personnel to topics. Invite review board members.	D—25
Initial illustrations available. Send out available review packages to review board members.	D—10
Dry runs	D—7 to D—3
Final illustrations available	D—2
Final dry run	D—1
Design review	D—Day
Critique	D+1
Issue design review summary report	D+10

The chairman is also responsible for inviting the proper persons to the review meeting. He should send out a written notice to each person invited. The notice should tell the topic of the meeting, when the meeting will be held, how long it is expected to last, who else has been invited, and where it will be held.

The chairman must select and reserve a meeting room for the review. The room must be large enough to seat everyone, yet small enough to encourage participation from the reviewers. This means everyone has to be able to see and hear everything that is going on in the meeting. The room must have adequate ventilation to permit smoking, and it must be private to prevent outside activities from interfering with the meeting. For military products security provisions should also be considered.

If a large meeting is planned, the chairman must see that a podium is available, along with screens, projectors, and trained operators. Lighting should be controlled, and a public address system should be available and operating. Although these items may seem incidental, they are often the cause of ineffective meetings.

Preparing for the Meeting

After the agenda is established the engineers must prepare for their participation. This is the point where many design reviews go astray. Inadequate and improper preparation are the most common faults. Significant points are often buried in trivia. And occasionally, the engineers do not cover all aspects of the product. For maximum effectiveness, the presention should:

1. Provide background information as an introduction.
2. Define the design requirements for the product.
3. Describe the design approach taken to satisfy the requirements.

4. Identify the problems encountered or expected.
5. Describe the approaches taken to solve the problems.
6. Present evidence that the design meets the requirements and solves the expected problems.

To assure that all persons are familiar with the product, its intended use, and any special information about it, each engineer should give an introduction to his portion of the design. Set the stage for the review by starting with the "big picture." Briefly tell what events or circumstances led to this design. How does it fit with other things the reviewers have heard? How will it fit in with the other items to be reviewed later? It is helpful to use comparisons or contrasts to illustrate how this is similar to or different from other products your firm produces. In this way, the reviewing panel can establish a baseline of understanding early in the meeting.

The degree of depth necessary in the introduction depends mainly on the specific product. The design engineer must gear the introduction to local circumstances. Approximately 10 percent of the total time can be spent on introduction.

The next step in preparing for the review is to define the requirements that the product must satisfy. This includes all technical performance requirements, safety, competitive factors, cost, styling, and reliability.

A factor of growing concern is the liability aspect of the product. How serious are the effects of failure or malfunction? What legal significance would failures have? Where lives or public property could be affected, the review must evaluate the product with particular scrutiny.

TABLE 7-2. DESIGN CHECKLIST

1. Design Requirements
   Documentation
   Specifications
   Standards
2. Functional Requirements
   Strength
   Motion, travel, operating time
   Cost
   Size, weight
   Appearance, simplicity
   Useful life
   Interfaces with mating parts or systems
   Use of proven components
3. Environment
   Loads (mechanical, electrical, thermal, etc.)
   Temperature (operating, transportation, storage)
   Humidity (operating, transportation, storage)
   Vibration (operating, transportation)

TABLE 7-2. DESIGN CHECKLIST (continued)

      Shock (operating, transportation)
      Corrosive ambients (salt air, sea water, acids, etc.)
      Foreign materials (dirt, oil, grit, moisture, etc.)
      Immersion (water, oil, inerting agents, etc.)
      Pressure and/or vacuum
      Magnetic field
      Sound ambient
      Weather
      Radio interference
      Nuclear/solar radiation
      Galvanic corrosion
      Friction

4. Production
   - Reasonable tolerances
   - Materials and processes definition
   - Value engineering considerations
   - Identification and marking
   - Inspection/nondestructive testing requirements
   - Workmanship requirements
   - Finishes (surface and protective)
   - Assembly requirements (torque, fits, sequencing, etc.)
   - Component interchangeability

5. Operational Use
   - Field installation
   - Instruction sheets/service manuals
   - User maintenance requirements
   - Field service/replacement
   - Special tool requirements
   - Operating experience data (test reports, field service reports, customer complaints)

6. Special Consideration
   - Hazardous materials/environment
   - Hazardous operation
   - Failure mode analysis
   - Product liability

A tabulation of requirements is helpful as a summary for this portion of the review. This same listing can be used later as a checklist to show how the new design satisfies the requirements.

Next comes the technical portion of the design review. This is where you describe the design in depth. Tell what its features are, how it works, how it satisfies the requirements, and why it was designed as it was.

Trade-off studies are an effective means of showing how one design was selected from a series of alternates. The various concepts are evaluated against the requirements for the design and the pros and cons for each concept are listed in a matrix format. From this data, one design is selected.

Failure mode analyses are often included in such trade studies. The potential failures and the effects of these failures for the various concepts are compared on the basis of safety and reliability. In a failure-mode analysis, list the modes of failure considered, the consequences of such a failure, and the possibility of this actually happening.

Another tool for supporting a design selection is the design checklist. Although much of the literature recommends the use of checklists in design activities, not many firms actually use written checklists. Many persons claim to use mental checklists, but this practice is not reliable. Others say that the checklists are stereotyped and attempt to make all products fit the same set of parameters. This is true if an engineering department simply applies someone else's checklist without tailoring it to the particular application. A list used in a manufacturing industry would not suit a process industry. Nevertheless, a checklist designed for your own products and markets can prevent accidental oversight of significant features or characteristics.

Table 7-2 is a typical listing of functions which should be considered for a new product. This can be used as a starting point for constructing a checklist for particular products. To be effective, two or three specific questions should be listed under each functional heading. For example, under the topic "Operational Use" you could ask questions such as: 1. Can this product be serviced by the owner? 2. Are service manuals needed? Available? 3. Are any special tools needed for normal servicing? In addition, many generalized questions can be asked of any design.

Earlier in the review, it was recommended that a list of design requirements be prepared to show what the product must satisfy. At this point in the review meeting, the design group must show how the design satisfies each of the requirements.

After the basic design is described, any problem areas associated with the product should be discussed. This includes both actual and expected problems and the steps taken to solve the problems.

As a final part of the design review, it is necessary to show evidence that the design will, in fact, satisfy the requirements and will successfully overcome the expected problems. This evidence may take several forms: analysis, testing, or pilot-line results.

Depending upon the type of product, different forms of analysis may be appropriate; such as, performance analysis for operations and stress analysis for structural adequacy.

In a formal design review, the results of analyses are usually shown in tables or curves. The data presented should include basic assumptions, the method used to make the analysis, a summary of the results, and conclusions. The conclusions are as important as the results. If sound conclusions cannot be drawn from the data, the analysis does not support the presentation and should not be included.

Test data from prototypes or pilot line operation also give evidence of performance. Information briefly describing the test setup, a summary of the test results, and conclusions from the data should be presented to verify that the design is acceptable.

Purchased parts or vendor-designed components present a special problem, since many vendors consider their designs proprietary. In this event, the design review must question the validity of the vendor design and its compatibility with the rest of the system. Also, the design review should produce evidence that the purchased parts of vendor-designed components will meet the requirements. Thus, the inputs and outputs are examined, but the design process itself may not be. Wherever possible, the vendor should be required to conduct his own design review.

Thus, a design review must cover all facets of the product. It must not be limited to a single discipline, or specialty, such as mechanical design, producibility, or reliability.

Review Package

It is a good practice to provide the review team with detailed information about a product prior to the review meeting. Examples of such material are product drawings, schematics, design criteria information, specifications, performance and reliability analysis data, and cost figures. Review material must be sent out early enough to allow the people time to review it. Minimum time is approximately two weeks.

In a formal design review, charts, graphs, and sketches are frequently used as supporting data in the technical discussion. Table 7-3 summarizes a number of helpful hints for preparing effective illustrations.

TABLE 7-3. TIPS FOR EFFECTIVE ILLUSTRATIONS

The biggest fault with illustrations is that they are not prepared from the audience's point of view. Over and over, it is discovered too late that the audience cannot read the charts or slides. Whether the illustrations are viewgraphs, lantern slides, or flip charts, the size of the meeting room dictates the size of the printing used. The following table provides guidelines for print sizes:

LETTER SIZE (IN.)	DISTANCE TO AUDIENCE (FT.)
½	15-20
1	30-35
2	40-50

When determining what type of visual aid to use, consider both the size and shape of the meeting room, the expected number of people, and whether or not you can dim the lighting in the room. If the room is small and the audience will be within 20-25 ft. of the speaker, flip charts (30 × 40-in. posters) may be used. If the people will be farther away, plan to use projected slides. Viewgraphs (overhead projectors) are versatile and do not require total darkness to be visible. Lantern slides (35 mm., 2¼ × 2¼ in. or 3 × 4¼ in.) are useful with large groups, because the image can be projected with good resolution. But in both cases, you will need a large projection screen.

Another common problem stems from trying to put too much information in the illustration. If it is a table or an outline chart, the maximum number of words or numbers that can be seen and understood is 20 to 25.

NEW PRODUCT INTRODUCTION: QUALITY OF DESIGN

TABLE 7-3. TIPS FOR EFFECTIVE ILLUSTRATIONS (continued)

This means a chart of about four lines of five or six words each. Let the chart be an outline. Tell only the high points. Limit each chart to a single theme, and use a brief caption or heading on each one.

If the illustration is a curve, make the curve stand out heavier than the grid lines. Use only faint grid lines, broadly spaced. Check to see that the markings on the axis can be read, and limit the number of curves to three on any one illustration. Using colored backgrounds for slides reduces glare, but too many different colors can be distracting.

One other type of visual aid may also be helpful in the design review. This is a full size or scale model of the actual product or facility. The third dimension of the model adds to understanding and is especially helpful to persons who are not familiar with the new product or concept. Models constructed of wood, plastic, and soft metals, such as aluminum, are easy to build and low in cost. If the product or concept is complicated, a model may be well worth the investment if it helps the reviewing personnel grasp the idea quickly.

Dry Run

Before a formal design review, a practice session is in order. A dry run is especially important if customer personnel will be attending the actual review. The dry run should be conducted in the scheduled conference room, and the actual illustrations should be used. If it is held two or three days before the actual design review, there will be time for corrective action, if necessary.

A few senior members from the engineering or project department can serve as the review panel. Their job is to ask questions they would expect to be raised and look for weaknesses during the discussion of the design.

Conducting the Meeting

The success or failure of the design-review meeting depends mainly on the chairman. He is responsible for the preparation for the meeting, and he is also charged with conducting it. Tables 7-4 and 7-5 contain suggestions of interest to the chairman. Failure to keep the meeting on course (and reasonably on schedule) will ruin even a well-prepared presentation. The chairman must keep the meeting under control—firmly but not dictatorially. He must see that the meeting gets started on time, that introductions are made as needed, and that time is allowed for questions and discussion. The chairman must maintain a climate of free interchange in which all participants question and comment openly. Above all, the chairman must not let the meeting seem like a board of inquiry, where the designer is on trial.

To assist the chairman in documenting the meeting, a member of the Reliability Department could serve as the secretary for the design review. He records comments, questions, agreements, and action items. This record is the basis for the summary report.

TABLE 7-4. CHAIRMAN'S LAST-MINUTE CHECKLIST

- ☐ Sufficient chairs available and seating arrangement checked
- ☐ Room ventilation and air conditioning settings checked
- ☐ Display material available
- ☐ Security measures checked
- ☐ Chalk and eraser available for chalkboard
- ☐ Projection equipment and screen available (including spare projection bulbs)
- ☐ Trained projectionist available
- ☐ Receptionist alerted if persons from outside the company are invited
- ☐ Arrangements made for coffee breaks
- ☐ Pencils and paper available for note taking
- ☐ Person assigned to take minutes (record action items, questions and significant comments)
- ☐ Ash trays available
- ☐ Podium, pointers, public-address system available if needed
- ☐ Person available to operate lights (or window shades) if room is to be darkened

TABLE 7-5. DESIGN REVIEW LEADERSHIP TECHNIQUES

- Start on time, break on time, stop on time.
- Introduce outsiders and newcomers.
- Make sure everyone can see and hear what is going on.
- Start the meeting by stating the objectives of the meeting. (Stress the fact that Design Review purpose is to help the designer, not criticize.)
- Make sure that minutes are taken.
- Keep the discussion on the track.
- Encourage participation by everyone but discourage debates.
- Ask searching questions to assure the group has considered all aspects of the subject.
- Maintain impartiality. Avoid giving your own personal opinion.
- Sum up periodically to keep the review moving forward.
- Keep firm control, but do not be a dictator.
- At the end of the meeting, summarize the conclusions. Identify what action must be taken, when, and by whom.

Since the reviewing personnel usually includes experts from many disciplines, it is not uncommon for them to raise questions that the design group had not expected. These questions should be recorded and investigated after the review.

Comments or recommendations by customer representatives frequently introduce a legal problem. Often, the question is whether or not the resulting action is within the scope of the existing contract. If the point should arise, it should be noted in the minutes and resolved outside of the design review.

Followup

After the design review, the chairman must see that the minutes of the meeting are published and that action items or questions from the meeting are assigned to the appropriate engineer for resolution.

Documentation from design review meetings has significance, both for direction and for historical purposes. Without documentation, the various participants in the meeting go their separate ways with uncertain, or differing, viewpoints. A final report of the design review should be published to state decisions reached on questions referred to the designer for investigation, and to note significant comments and agreements. If the engineering department decided not to incorporate recommendations made during the meeting, the original recommendation should be stated in the summary report along with the logic for rejecting the idea. Later, the questions and the replies provide insight into the review process. This is helpful in providing continuity for future reviews.

The design-review method is an important tool for decision making, and it also offers a learning experience. To capitalize on this training opportunity, the chairman should hold a critique on the day after the design review. He should tell the engineers who led the review what he thought went well and what went wrong. This provides immediate feedback to enhance the learning process. The good points should be singled out for incorporation in future design reviews, and the problem areas should be corrected or avoided in the future.

Different types of design review methods used by General Dynamics, in Dallas, Texas, were reviewed in the August 1983 issue of *Iron Age Magazine*. Edward McClure, vice-president, Quality Assurance, explained the design of the F-16 fighter plane. During the design phase, divisional QA proposed a design to support a function. The support function was conceived with three primary phases. They were:

- To provide quality requirements to design engineering during the initial design phase
- To review the drawings and specifications prior to release to assure the adequate inclusion of quality requirements
- To achieve early familiarization of the design in order to focus the implementation of the QA program

The initial implementation of the design-support function was accomplished in mid-1975.

Mr. McClure reported at the end of the article that this provided a net cost avoidance for the F-16 program of $3,423,951 for the first year. This example shows what can be accomplished through the proper use of quality design reviews.

What Can We Do to Improve Quality of Design?

It is not easy to answer this question with a simple recipe. I cannot offer any gimmick or panacea to cure all the problems. We must realize that in order to build good-quality products or offer quality services, a design must be thoroughly tested and retested for reliability and whatever it proposes to do for the customer. I have already given some ideas in this chapter. Some of the modern techniques on the horizon are described here:

1. Use of computers
2. Involvement of all departments and other employees
3. Use of CAD/CAM (computer-aided design and computer-aided manufacturing)
4. Failure analysis
5. Product deployment
6. Standardization and specification
7. Off-line quality control

1. Use of computers. Computers play an important role in data collecting, data analysis, and finite element analysis. Many new designs can be tested or simulated without really spending money on actual tests. A lot of statistical analysis as well as manufacturing problems can be solved with the help of computers, robotics and automation.

2. Involvement of other departments and employees. Employee participation programs are growing rapidly, and companies are trying to create teamwork within the organization instead of the traditional compartmentalized atmosphere. More and more people are able to talk freely and openly with other department personnel. It was reported recently that the Ford Motor Company involved production employees in the design of the Ranger truck. The employees came up with more than 15 changes which improved the quality of the truck design tremendously. Ford gained better acceptance of the truck and also gained a larger market share. Organizations willing to do this will improve the quality of their design. The process does take longer than the usual method of designing and manufacturing the product, but a heavier price is paid when the design is of poor quality and not tested thoroughly.

3. Use of CAD/CAM. This is a specialized version of computer use. Computer-aided design and computer-aided manufacturing are highly publicized. However, it seems these methods are still in the infant stage; more time is needed to make them practical, cost-effective, and a reality. Thousands of articles have been published on this subject, and I recommend for those who see the need for future improvement to read these.

4. Failure analysis. In order to design products or services effectively and successfully, it is necessary to find and keep track of the problems and complaints on present products and service. The organization must use warranty data effectively and analyze it thoroughly. The following four techniques are common in analyzing warranty failures:

1. FEMA
2. FTA
3. Weibull distribution
4. On-line computer analysis

5. Product deployment. This system for understanding customers' needs is gaining in popularity in both Japan and the United States. We have described the methodology and ways to obtain details in Chapter 6.

6. Standardization and adherence to specification. Engineers like to imagine and design products that are unique, and the aspects of commonality of parts and cost-effective design are generally neglected. This creates problems later on in manufacturing and service-parts areas because companies need to carry more parts and products to satisfy the customers. However, I feel that in the future, this trend will change; more and more designs will use standard parts, and commonality of the parts will be instituted for cost effectiveness.

Another important change that will occur is adherence to specifications. Organizations will insist that the designs, as well as the manufactured products, conform to specifications. This will force discipline on the system, and everyone will know what to expect of each department and each area of the organization.

7. Off-line quality[2] (Dr. Genichi Taguchi Method). Dr. Taguchi describes the quality of design by calling it *off-line quality control*. It includes activities in product planning, research and development, design research, and quality countermeasures in production engineering.

---

[2]This information is prepared from discussion with and valuable input from Professor Yuin Wu, based on his work and book, *Off-Line Quality Control.*

TABLE 7–6. TRADITIONAL QC VS. OFF-LINE QC APPROACHES

Stage of the study	After drawings and specifications are made.	Before drawings and specifications are made.
Content	To meet specifications. To adjust average values.	To dampen environmental effects. To reduce variations.
Method	Allowance design.	Parameter design
Cost	Could result in a higher cost.	Starts from the lowest cost materials and parts.
Continuation	Stops when the problem is solved.	Can be continued.
Attitude	Problem solving, failure analysis. Studying existing problems.	Optimization. Trying to avoid future problems.
Philosophy	Mathematical models and statistical methods are important.	Discovery of controlling factors whose effects are consistent. Such factors may also be effective for unknown factors. It is a substitution. It can not be proven on paper, but is based on our experiences.

Dr. Taguchi divides the quality design into three different parts:

1. System design (or primary design)
2. Parameter design (or secondary design)
3. Allowance design (or tertiary design)

1. System design (primary design). In this step, knowledge from a specialized field is applied—from electronics, research into the kind of circuit used to convert alternating current into direct current; from the chemical industry, studies concerning the specific chemical reaction needed to obtain the best process, given the available technology.

3. Parameter design (secondary design). Once system design is finished, the next step is to determine the optimum level of individual parameters of the system. Such research has been neglected, especially in developing countries. In these countries, researchers look for information from literature, designing power circuits that "seem to be best." Secondary design is the most important step in developing stable and reliable products or manufacturing processes. In this step we find a combination of parameter levels that are capable of damping the influences not only of inner noise but of all noise sources, while keeping the output voltage constant. This is the most important quality-control countermeasure in developing countries where variations in raw materials or component parts are frequent, making secondary design techniques more important there than in developed countries.

3. Allowance design (tertiary design). Once the system design is completed, we have the mid-values of the factors comprising the system elements. The next step is to determine the tolerances of these factors. To make this determination, we must consider environmental conditions as well as the system elements. The mid-values and varying ranges of these factors and conditions are considered noise factors and are arranged in orthogonal tables so that the magnitude of their influence to the final output characteristics can be determined. A narrower allowance will be given to those noise factors imparting a large influence to the output. Cost considerations determine the allowance.

Dr. Yuin Wu and Dr. Taguchi compare standard quality control versus off-line quality control in Table 7-6.

General System for New-Product Introduction

In order to introduce new defect-free products, an organization needs to institute good control in its various areas. Everyone has to do their best and carry on their function properly. The key areas for initial control are listed here:

1. Schedule control
2. Product control
3. Cost control
4. Process control

A systematic procedure in each area is essential. Let us review briefly the salient points. One can expand these and prepare detailed procedures if necessary. These four areas are just like the four wheels of an automobile; the organization needs all four of them working properly for effective performance.

1. Schedule Control

The following steps can be used for effective schedule control.

Step 1—Prepare a preliminary schedule. The planning department or product coordination department generally discusses with marketing and other concerned departments preliminary planning for new products or services. Once the basic concept is accepted, the planning department prepares one assignment and schedule to be approved by top management. Quality tables, performance requirements, and reliability analysis are considered to be vital parts of the analysis. Cost targets are also determined. Once the preliminary schedule is approved, the function can be transferred to production or the material-control area.

Step 2—Preproduction control. Once the preliminary schedule is approved, the product coordination department then works with other areas to determine how to handle bottlenecks. Policies are made regarding preproduction work and areas of responsibility, critical parts, and control procedures on critical parts.

Step 3—Preproduction schedule. Once the initial areas are identified, production control prepares a detailed scheduling chart and distributes it to concerned parties for their information and for more input.

Step 4—Scheduling by respective department. Similar activities take place in each department; once again, the information is distributed to other concerned parties.

Step 5—Preparation of master schedule for pilot and preproduction. Based on the input from other departments and discussion with key personnel, production control prepares the master schedule and the program is checked periodically.

Step 6—Follow-up. The production control department or product coordination department collects the details of preproduction results on the following subjects:

1. Quality evaluation
2. Case evaluation
3. Critical parts and equipment evaluation
4. Overall progress and scheduling problems

Preproduction evaluation and control are essential for long-range effective schedule control.

2. Product Control

Step 1—Market input and product specifications. Preliminary product specification is established based on market input, quality needs, customer needs, customer complaints, and research and development input.

Step 2—Design reviews. This step is discussed in other parts of this chapter.

Step 3—Test prototype. Prototype products are built and tested. The engineering department confirms the final quality of the prototype and collects the following information for final approval:

1. Conformance to specifications
2. Quality and reliability performance
3. Process precaution
4. Warranty precaution

Step 4—Preproduction run evaluation. In many cases, prototype testing reveals a need for major redesign or changes. In this case, it is customary to do preproduction runs to evaluate the results more closely. All the results should be carefully put together and submitted to the quality council through the vice-president of quality for final approval of the product for production.

Step 5—Release for production. Production should be resumed only after final approval is given by the quality council, which generally represents top management.

3. Cost Control

Step 1—Establish target cost. Product coordination departments generally set up the target costs based on marketing, purchasing, engineering, and manufacturing input.

Step 2—Make-or-buy decision. Organizations need to make this type of decision on various parts based on cost-benefit analysis.

Step 3—Ongoing evaluation and follow-up. Internal as well as vendor production cases should be evaluated constantly through the financial or cost control department. Any variation should be reported periodically, and the decision should be made as to whether to make or buy parts or change part design if the cost is getting out of control.

Step 4—Preliminary cost target evaluation. When the total costs are collected and the project looks feasible according to well-established Return-On-Investment procedures, top management should approve the project for production.

Step 5—Final release—a final cost evaluation. The final release should be given after rechecking the costs, obtaining agreements with the vendors, and making sure the cost targets are met.

4. Process and Manufacturing Control

Step 1—Establish process sheets. Processes are established on new products based on close discussion with manufacturing, engineering, quality control, and material control departments. Men, machinery, and manufacturing techniques are evaluated to get the product cost down and within target limits. In some cases, new equipment or processes are proposed and approved for new products.

Step 2—Establish standards. Once the process sheets are established in prototype, the final standards are established for the preproduction run, which includes equipment to be used, jigs, fixtures, process details, machining specifications, and other details such as inspection sheets and gauging. The details should be such that new job instructions can be written for operators or foremen so that there is less confusion or less chance of making mistakes.

Step 3—Investigate process capabilities. The manufacturing department checks the various processes and reviews the process capabilities through statistical methods or via past experience. In places where processes cannot meet standards, precaution should be taken and countermeasures should be planned for. Design specifications can be reviewed and perhaps relaxed if they do not affect the final quality of the product; use of the new processes can be revised if necessary.

Step 4—Release for production. Production should be only resumed once Step 3 has been followed and clearly documented by manufacturing.

In general, process and manufacturing control plays an important role in producing a quality product in the long run; preproduction and prototype production control are crucial so that final production does not suffer too many interruptions, which can result in poor-quality products.

EVALUATE YOUR ORGANIZATION (SELF-ANALYSIS QUALITY QUIZ)

The following questions will help you to analyze your organization with respect to new-product introduction. Again, self-analysis can be used to find where your organization stands.

1. Our organization understands the four phases of new-product introduction.	0 Not at all	5 Somewhat	10 Yes, definitely

2. Our organization uses customer-based analysis in new-product introduction.	Not at all	Somewhat	Yes, definitely
3. Our organization uses failure analysis and other statistical tools discussed in this chapter.	Not at all	Somewhat	Yes, definitely
4. Our organization uses the design review method in product development phases.	Not at all	Somewhat	Yes, definitely
5. Our organization employs designers with good ability and recommends ongoing training programs to update the new knowledge.	Not at all	Somewhat	Yes, definitely
6. Our organization keeps good records of old products and uses them to improve future products and services.	Not at all	Somewhat	Yes, definitely
7. Our organization encourages use of standardization and always tries to minimize new-part design unless it is necessary.	Not at all	Somewhat	Yes, definitely
8. Our organization encourages good cooperation between engineering, manufacturing, and quality control; new drawings are always reviewed and analyzed for quality improvements.	Not at all	Somewhat	Yes, definitely
9. Our organization keeps good design records, and standards and specifications are developed and used religiously.	Not at all	Somewhat	Yes, definitely
10. Our organization does not release products or offer services knowing that problems or deficiencies are unresolved.	Not at all	Somewhat	Yes, definitely

Note: The author has developed more than 300 similar questions to analyze organizational performance.

Quality is a commitment, a philosophy. It is not a manufacturing science. The product has to be designed right at the beginning.
—Derian Apelian, Drexel University,
Philadelphia, Pennsylvania

Chapter Eight
VENDOR QUALITY CONTROL

The Traditional System

David Schwinn's statement quoted on page 124 shows the importance of getting good-quality parts from vendors. When the organization is constantly engaged in buying parts from vendors, it is necessary that the parts be of high quality. Low-quality parts can cause problems such as production delays and scrapping or rejection of parts. It is true that the quality of in-house parts is important. However, if the quality of the parts supplied by vendors is very low, the organization can experience many problems due to the difference in quality standards. Based on my experience in 15 years in the industry and my knowledge of various other organizations, the traditional system of vendor purchasing that exists in many organizations is as shown in Figure 8-2.

An organization usually orders purchased parts through the purchasing department. Most of the time purchase orders are used to indicate quality, cost, and delivery. Quality requirements are very seldom spelled out on the purchase order. It is generally assumed that the vendor will deliver quality parts on time. This assumption creates many problems between the vendor and the buyer. Several other departments may also get involved dealing with vendors at times. Engineering people may follow newly designed parts; material control may follow missing parts or rush the orders. One way to control the quality of parts is through incoming inspection and

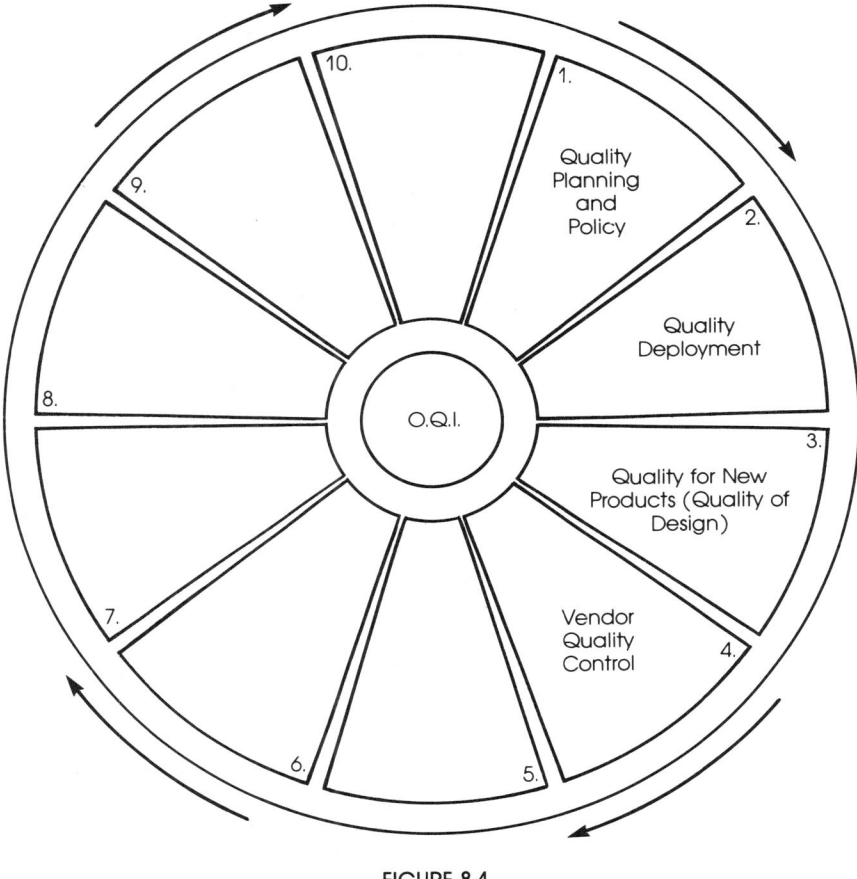

FIGURE 8-1

Wheel segments labeled:
1. Quality Planning and Policy
2. Quality Deployment
3. Quality for New Products (Quality of Design)
4. Vendor Quality Control

Center: O.Q.I.

other techniques such as vendor evaluation and vendor certification. These parts are generally checked by acceptable quality level (AQL) and most of the time are accepted with the designation "Engineering deviation." This means the parts do not meet the drawing specifications, but still can be used. Once the vendor and the buyer know these deviations, many parts are purchased with deviations for several years and drawing specifications are neglected. Later, when the conditions get worse due to too many final rejects or an excess of scrap, rework, or customer complaints, the company establishes a material review board (MRB) system to evaluate rejected parts. The basic idea behind MRB is good. However, in practice, some companies use MRB the wrong way; if the buyer can influence the MRB, it becomes ineffective and problems worsen.

Most of the time rejected parts stay in the guaranteed area for one or two months and either get shipped back, are used in the production, or get

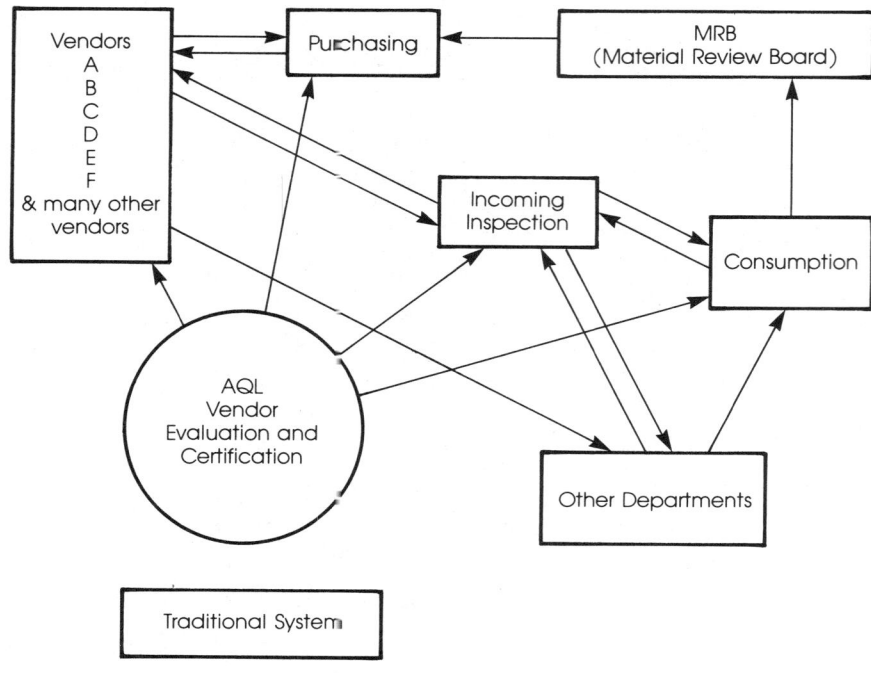

FIGURE 8-2

scrapped because of delays in action. Vendor certification and vendor evaluation procedures are also generally loose; my experience indicates that most evaluation procedures concentrate on system evaluation or a cursory evaluation of the company. This type of evaluation never results in much corrective action.

Problems We Face Today

The current vendor quality-control system and the relationship between vendor and buyer have caused many types of problems, resulting in different quality expectations and poor harmony between the two parties. There are numerous causes for quality problems; these have been described in many articles and books. Basically, the causes for quality problems can be categorized as:

1. 30–40 percent due to poor vendor parts quality
2. 30–40 percent due to management or system problems
3. 15–20 percent due to workers' unclear standards and poor communication

Let us review some of the major problems experienced today:

1. Cost first, delivery second, and quality sometimes. When the purchasing department is asked to purchase the material or equipment that are cheap and can be delivered quickly, buyers are generally interested in seeking a market for their products; hence, they buy the final product regardless of its quality. The next consideration, generally, is delivery. Most purchasing agents are used to judging a product based on cost and delivery. Quality requirements given in the specification or drawings are generally assumed. Naturally, most vendors also concentrate on cost and delivery aspects, using cost-cutting techniques to get a larger number of customers. Until recently it was not realized that productivity, quality, and cost go hand in hand. Products built in Japan have proven that one should not be concerned with cost alone, but rather in buying a high-quality product at a cheaper price!

2. Low quality, too many rejects, loose MRB. When more attention was paid only to cost, many times organizations suffered in quality. Vendors will shop for products below the agreed-upon quality level, or sometimes buyers will request even a rejected shipment to be delivered to avoid production delays or line shutdown. Organizations believed that the customer would not know the difference in final consumption. However, this myth didn't last long after 1970. Customers found that products from Japan and other countries offered better quality and were still cheaper than competitive products built in America. Many times, even though the organization rejected the products or parts, the MRB would allow rejected products to get into the system due to high-level pressure. This all resulted in poor-quality products.

3. Too many vendors. While searching for cheaper parts or products, organizations also get into the habit of having multiple vendors. Many argue that this practice is necessary to have a smooth supply of parts. Some vendors thought it was just a way to threaten the original vendor. Even smaller companies started similar games. It is said that many automobile industries in the United States have between 2,000 and 3,000 vendors, while in Japan similar industries deal with only 200 to 300 vendors. Multiple vendors create more paperwork, poor communication, and a lack of clear understanding.

4. Mistrust. Another problem predominant in western industries is a lack of trust between the vendor and the buyer. It is not easy to create harmony when each sees the other as an enemy. Incoming inspection, even though it occurs too late, is used to get vendors in trouble or for checking parts. If parts are rejected, it takes next to forever either to accept them or to correct the problems between the vendor and buyer, although most times the vendor-vendee relationship is not that exciting.

5. Large orders. To avoid loss of production dollars due to poor quality, many buyers realize that companies make mistakes; they usually allow an extra 10–20 percent for poor quality. This "padding" helps vendors to hide mistakes and doesn't cost too much money. However, because of hidden defects, organizations often suffer production delays, scrap, or rework. The organization ends up paying for this, since parts are required on the assembly lines or have been used and cannot be returned to the vendors. Once vendors get used to this practice, they will request an allowance for scrap and rework; most of them expect the organization to pay for additional work!

6. Too many people involved. As you can see in Figure 8-1, in the traditional vendor quality-control system, even though the purchasing department generally orders the parts, many times other departments get involved due to miscommunication or urgent needs. Material control sometimes tries to choose the purchased parts and ends up working with vendors. Engineering gets involved when drawings are not clear and parts are needed badly in the production phase. Data processing or accounting personnel get involved when problems arise in payments. In this way, when many people try to handle the work, communication becomes confusing unless the system is clearly defined and responsibilities are clearly delineated. In reality, many times boundaries are overstepped and quality is neglected in handling purchased parts.

7. Engineering involvement too late. Nowadays it is necessary for organizations to bring out their products and services before the competition to acquire a larger market share. However, this puts more pressure on the engineering department or departments that are involved in generating new services. The engineers try to buy parts in the assembly that are not completely tested or parts that are based on a drawing or specification that is not done completely. Vendors don't have the time to become familiar with the requirements, although they try their best to meet these requirements. This late involvement of the engineering department does tremendous damage to the quality of the final product. It is essential that vendors know early in the game what is expected of them and what are the specs and requirements of the purchased parts.

8. Drawings and specifications not clear. This problem was mentioned earlier. However, I would like to emphasize once again the importance of clear specs and drawings. Many quality problems are created because of misunderstanding and misinterpretation of drawings and specifications. The purchasing department may not be familiar with the details, and in search of a better cost offer, certain aspects may be neglected. I have seen many times incomplete drawings that were sent to vendors just to meet a deadline. Organizations will take a chance in this case and hope for the best results. In some cases, vendors are given responsibility to develop the process and are asked to do the best they can. Most results do not lead to quality in the long run. I have listed only a few problems here. You can expand the list based on your own organizational situation and quality priority.

What Can We Do Today?

1. Establish "quality and reliability agreement" with vendors. We have discussed earlier the traditional vendor quality-control systems. The current system has caused many problems such as higher rejects, higher costs, mistrust, and delays, among others. One way to improve this situation is to establish a quality and reliability agreement with the vendor, which should make clear the quality requirements. This agreement should be specifically written with each vendor, depending on the type of parts the vendor supplies and their criticality.

The agreement should list some of the followings:

Quality and Reliability Agreement

Vendor _____

Date of Agreement _____

Parts Purchased _____

Major Requirements
1. Objectives, quality needs
2. Specifications and quality measurement system (use of PPM (parts per million), if useful)
3. Engineering information and other information
4. Vendor's manufacturing plans
5. Statistical process control and use of process capability indices (Cp and CpK) on critical dimension
6. Quality audit methods
7. Process, design change feedback
8. Data collection systems and data feedback
9. Reliability analysis
10. Customer's claim analysis
11. Cost analysis and cost control
12. Rejected parts analysis
13. Monthly meetings with engineering and vendors
14. New-parts control and analysis
15. Settlement regarding disputed items

Many items can be added to make the responsibility clear and agreeable to vendors. This type of agreement is common in Japan. Many Fortune 500 companies also utilize similar agreements with their vendors.

Companies using this approach have accomplished the following advantages:

1. Better understanding of quality
2. Improved communication
3. Improved quality
4. Less scrap
5. Less rework
6. Better cost control
7. Fewer rejected parts
8. Less incoming inspection

2. Get engineers involved early. One of the critical needs that I have found in improving vendor quality is the involvement of the engineering department early in the system. Once a product or service is accepted by the manufacturing department, it is most desirable for a vendor to get to know the requirements of the parts and its design. The drawings and specifications should be spelled out accurately and in detail. The discussion with a vendor should concentrate on the aspects of quality and processing, not on the cost and delivery of products and services. The vendors should be comfortable with the engineers and should know in detail what is expected of the parts they will manufacture. The requirements should be negotiated, not forced. The measurement system should be clear and mutually agreed upon.

Precision Metal magazine, in its July 1981 issue, published an article called "How Xerox Is Beating Japan at Their Own Game." The details given in Figure 8-3 will be helpful in seeing the change that is taking place in vendor-vendee relationships.

3. Cut down number of vendors. I have described why and how organizations work with multiple vendors, who are kept for safety's sake. When you have to deal with many vendors, the paperwork and communication become more complicated and often unclear. The buyer has to spend hours of time working with many rather than with a few. The same details have to be conveyed so many times, sometimes part of the information is left out. Hence, it is desirable that the organization take a close look at its current system, review the number of vendors, and try to cut it down to a minimum. Working closely with vendors and treating them like a part of the family would benefit the vendor-vendee relationship.

QUALITY SENSITIVE PARTS SUPPLIER INVOLVEMENT CHECKPOINTS

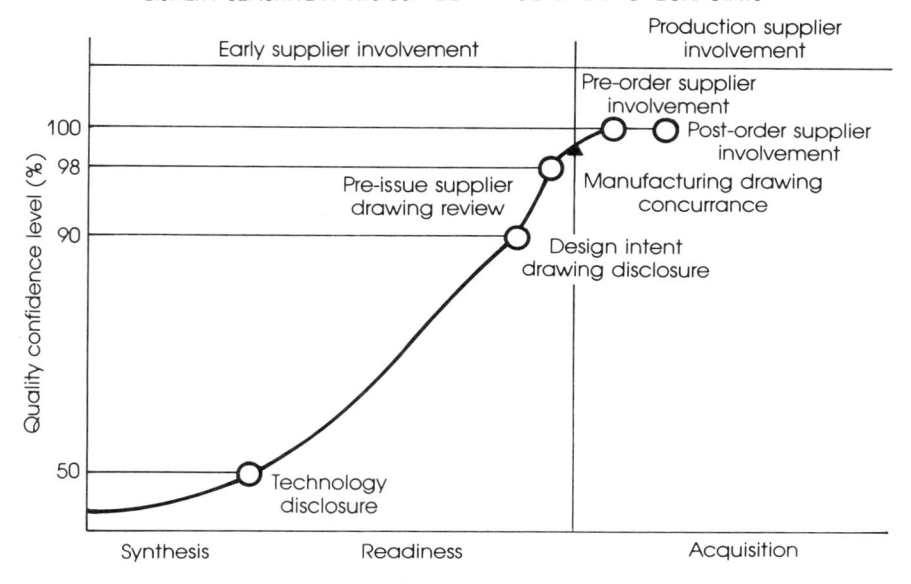

Xerox's plan for assuring a 100% quality level on quality-sensitive parts. These parts have been identified as being critical to machine performance and life. Technology disclosure is the first step and occurs at the first customer/supplier meeting. Note that the quality confidence level is at 90% before anything is even committed to paper. The "Early Supplier Involvement" phase finalizes the design, while "Production Supplier Involvement" is geared toward assuring a 100% confidence level in production. Xerox acknowledges suppliers that have done an outstanding job in design, production and delivery performance with an annual excellence award, typically given to less than 1% of its suppliers.

FIGURE 8-3

4. Revise vendor certification program. Many companies have developed what is called a "vendor evaluation and vendor certification" program. However, most of these certification programs are superfluous and do not carry any substance. Most of them are copied from other organizations; the typical certification process will last one or two days, during which auditors look at the plant briefly and spend most of their time ordering activities. Very rarely will auditors work on the shop floor to check processes or demand statistical evidence to show quality requirement.

I would like to recommend that organizations revise the certification program and add some of the following key items.

1. Demand proof of use of SPC (statistical process control).
2. Demand that sample data on process control be shipped with the parts.

3. Review closely, during incoming inspection, gauging and operator-control procedures.
4. Assist vendor in statistical training.
5. Review ongoing training programs in vendor's plants.
6. Review usage of drawings and data collection system.
7. Review vendor's plan in getting operator involvement.

In the long run the organization should pursue the goal of changing a vendor's quality system as given below:

Phase I	Vendor control
Phase II	Vendor certification
Phase III	Vendor surveillance
Phase IV	Vendor assistance

With the vendor, you should insist on the old saying, "Do it right the first time!"

5. Quality first, cost and delivery second. It is essential for organizations to understand the need of quality priority; they should emphasize the same in their training and communicate to all buyers the importance of quality parts. Cost should be reviewed and negotiated, but cannot necessarily be the primary goal in purchasing parts. If quality parts are purchased, many times rework or scrap is avoided later in production. Similarly, a lot of hassle in communication and correspondence can be avoided. The same time can be spent more efficiently in getting new parts or services. One should remember that time is money; use time effectively.

6. Promote SPC training. For a long time quality systems have depended on defect detection. Parts were manufactured and inspection introduced at various stages to weed out the rejects. These defect-detection systems caused more rework and scrap, and never gave operators the responsibility of making quality parts from the beginning. Recently the emphasis has shifted to prevention, where operators are made responsible and emphasis is also placed on statistical process control. Organizations should emphasize statistical process control training to the vendors, helping the vendors train the operators in SPC. The SPC process is described in detail in Appendix C.

7. Family parts buying. Many companies manufacture products or offer services that are similar in nature; many times these purchased parts are interchangeable. The buyer often ends up buying similar parts from different vendors, creating more paperwork and communications. Purchasing policies and the purchasing system should be revised. The company should try to concentrate on *family parts purchasing,* buying similar parts from one or two vendors. This will help to cut down the number of vendors and will help the few vendors to expand their base. This mutual exchange should help, in the long run, both build quality products and create more harmony between vendor and buyer.

8. JIT purchasing. We discussed earlier the typical purchasing system in which buyers purchase a reserve to cover up scrap and rework or defects. However, many good companies are changing the system and using what is called JIT (just in time) purchasing, in which purchased parts are bought in small lots—enough for one or two days' production. Vendors must adhere to the quantity and a schedule; a close watch is kept on these requirements. Vendors are also expected to supply good-quality parts; rejected parts are scrutinized carefully. Warnings are issued to the vendors; vendors are often notified that business is given to someone else. JIT purchasing does help to improve quality, but it is not easy to maintain in critical times.

9. Look for better suppliers. Buyers are used to looking around for new vendors who supply parts at a low cost. It is now necessary to look around and try to find vendors who will supply better-quality parts. Buyers should require vendors to supply statistical data and evidence that they will supply better-quality parts.

This Serves the Following Purposes:
1. Better-quality parts are acquired at no extra cost.
2. Cost is less in the long run since less rework or scrap will take place.
3. There is no need for a large stock since all parts received are of good quality and usable.

10. Annual convention. Organizations should arrange an annual convention with vendors. The vendors should be invited for one or two days; the organization should arrange the following:

1. Awards to vendors for the best-quality goods
2. Familiarizing the vendors with the product
3. Present the quality level of the organization or future goals
4. Worldwide competition to sell products that are quality built at reasonable price
5. Statistical training and other topics (automation, robotics, just-in-time systems)

120 VENDOR QUALITY CONTROL

This type of convention achieves the following objectives:

1. Vendors get to know the products and services.
2. Vendors realize quality needs.
3. Communication is improved.
4. Teamwork is created between vendor or vendee.

11. Gradual use of PPM (parts per million). Recently there is a lot of interest regarding the use of PPM (parts per million). Many companies are trying to specify in purchasing orders that they require their vendors to accept PPM requirements instead of traditionally used AQL (average quality level) system. What is PPM? Why is there so much interest in PPM? Let us look at the origin of PPM and its feasibility in vendor's purchase orders in order to acquire higher-quality parts.

PPM terminology is another import from Japan to this country. Most electronic components purchased in Japan generally require PPM defects. This means when an organization buys parts like electronic chips or resistors, defective parts are generally in parts per million (e.g., a 10 PPM defect is acceptable per lot). This means the company will accept only ten defective parts out of one million pieces delivered to the user. Organizations used to specify this requirement using AQL terms (acceptable quality level). The AQL rule is generally between 0.1 percent and 1 percent in electronics components. These numbers showed high rejects, implying that these types of defects were acceptable. A PPM specification shows the vendor has to improve quality; the PPM number is so small it seems impossible in some cases. However, the required quality level indicates that this PPM specification is a reality in many cases in the electronics industry. At least one American company has shown the same improvement in recent years.

Meaning of PPM

One should understand the meaning of PPM before applying it blindly. As most of us know, Japan is constantly busy improving quality levels, with the ultimate goal being to reach the zero defect level. Defects used to be reported in percentages. The use of PPM shows that there have been strides made toward improvement. This has been achieved in the electronics industry, but in many other industries it is not possible to use the PPM concept. PPM terminology is not common yet, and I recommend that an organization should research the subject carefully before trying to enforce PPM specifications on vendors.

Let us see how to interpret PPM and traditional AQL systems.

    1 percent AQL = 10,000 PPM
    0.1 percent AQL = 1,000 PPM

VENDOR QUALITY CONTROL **121**

What does this mean? It shows the results of constant improvement. Figure 8-4 shows what has been accomplished and the relationship between AQL and PPM.

One of the meaningful messages in the PPM concept is that continual improvement is essential and that an organization should not stand still and assume that 1 percent or 0.1 percent defects are good enough. The following are different ways to establish PPM specifications:

1. PPM can be established using in-house production capability.
2. Number of parts returned versus number of parts produced by a company.
3. Number of parts received divided by number of parts rejected.
4. AQL specification converted to PPM using a reduced number.

Introducing PPM concept. (Parts per million language)

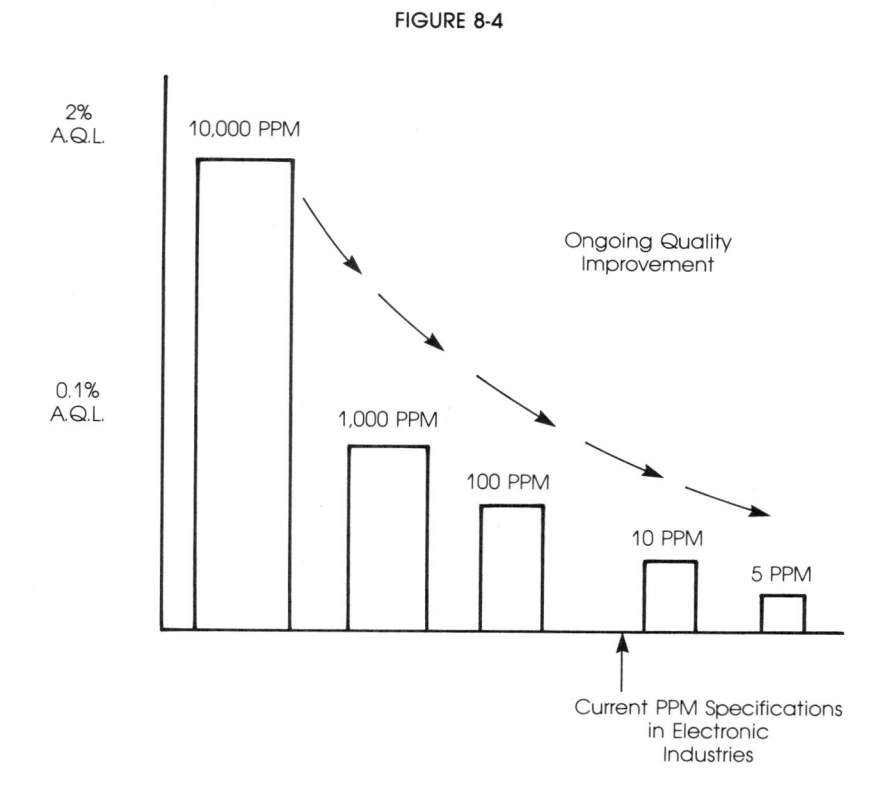

FIGURE 8-4

INTRODUCING "PPM" CONCEPT

Steps:

1. Work with vendor.
2. Review present quality level with incoming inspection.
3. Discuss the need for improvement.
4. Establish goals and plans.
5. Check processes and capabilities.
6. Collect information.
7. Establish targets for defective products and agree to reduce level of defective parts.
8. Establish feedback and corrective-action system.
9. Write procedures for follow-up.
10. Follow-up and review.

References on Additional Information on PPM

The following three articles contain more detailed information on PPM (all are from *Reports of Statistical Application Research,* Union of Japanese Scientists and Engineers, 20, no. 3, September 1981):

Article 1. "The concept procedures for PPM control" by the quality assurance department (Matsushita Ede. Component Company). A very good article on the PPM concept and PPM maintenance in the organization.

Article 2. "PPM control in the manufacturing of photo-sensitive materials," by Akira Kuma. This is a general article on PPM control.

Article 3. "PPM control for ceramic capacitors" by Mamory Koizumi and Eij Saka.

Quality requirements in electronics industry are becoming tighter and brighter. We feel that our capability in the area of quality has a fatal effect on the progress of electronic industry. Rather, we deem it to be our responsibility to take a positive stance to supply electronic parts of the ultimate high reliability with the ultimate low price. By this concept, we are making our best effort to achieve PPB (defective parts per billion) to say nothing of one PPM (parts per million).

Hence, PPM control is strictly a combined activity of systems, engineering, manufacturing, equipment, and material control.

Future Needs

It is essential that organizations work closely with vendors to improve the quality of purchased parts. One should keep the following objectives in mind in this respect.

1. Incoming inspection is too late to detect poor-quality materials. All it does is cause delays and unnecessary additional work. Hence, it should be eliminated as soon as possible or should be kept minimum.
2. Vendors must be treated as an extension of an organization. Instead of vendor certification, vendor support is essential to build team spirit.
3. A minimum number of reliable, quality-minded vendors is the way of the future.

Figure 8-5 shows one of the ways an organization can work closely with vendors in order to achieve optimum use of various available resources.

Fewer vendors should mean improved communication in the vendor-vendee area. The purchasing department should act as a liaison or clearinghouse for paper flow. Communications should be effective, and the loop should be short but workable; unnecessary work must be eliminated to improve the quality and productivity of the organization.

FIGURE 8-5

VENDOR SURVEILLANCE
AND
SUPPORT (Q.C.)

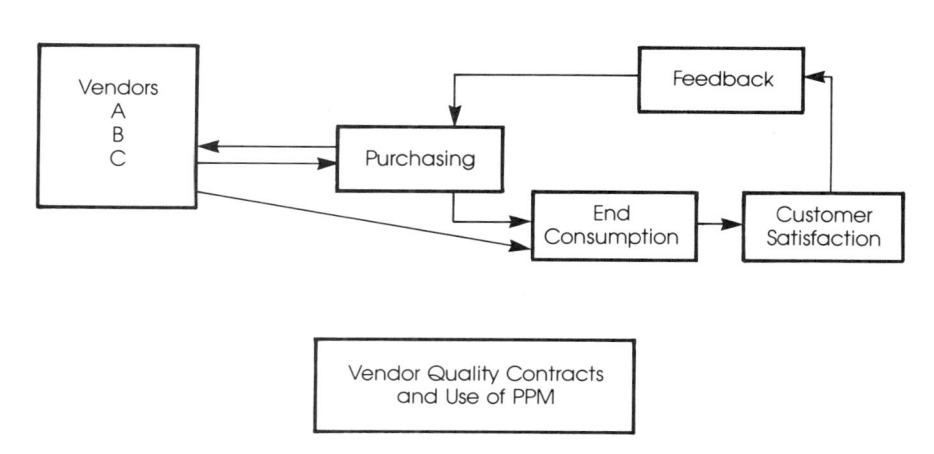

Key Features:
1. No large-scale incoming inspection
2. Quality auditing
3. Vendor surveillance and support
4. Fewer vendors
5. Family parts purchasing

"Future Needs for Effective Vendor Quality Control"

124 VENDOR QUALITY CONTROL

TABLE 8–1. EVALUATE YOUR ORGANIZATION (VENDORS; PURCHASED PARTS)

ASPECTS	EVALUATION			
	Poor	OK	Above Average	Excellent
1. How adequate is the vendor selection?				
2. How is the vendor rating system for the current vendors?				
3. How is our defect control on purchased parts?				
4. How well do we certify vendors?				
5. How well do we survey vendors? (What do we check?)				
6. How do we deal with rejected parts? Do we review our requirements with vendors?				
7. How would you rate our incoming inspections?				
8. How do we check mechanical parts? How do we analyze critical specifications?				
9. How do we check electrical and electronic parts? How do we analyze critical specifications?				
10. How much statistical quality control and statistical knowledge do we expect from vendors?				

Note: The author has developed more than 300 questions to evaluate organizational performance.

Outside supplier quality contributes heavily towards a vehicle's quality performance. At General Motors, 53% of each sales dollar goes to suppliers, at Ford, it is 62% and at Chrysler, 73%.

—David R. Schwinn, 1981
Ford Motor Company

Chapter Nine
MANUFACTURING QUALITY

Today, a number of manufacturing processes exists to satisfy customers' needs and requirements. Various products and services are offered by a number of industries; organizations are always looking to improve the quality and productivity of their products and services. In general, production processes can be divided into the following major areas:

1. Continuous processes—processes such as beer industries, chemical industries, and the like.
2. Batch processes—batch operations like equipment building, construction projects, and so on.
3. Physical processes—drilling, grinding, welding, or other machining processes.
4. Assembly processes—electronic assemblies, equipment assemblies, and many other assemblies.
5. Service and administrative processes—office operations; procedures and services in various service industries.

Conventional In-Process Quality System

In most organizations, one will find a system as shown in Figure 9-1.

This is generally known as the defect-detection system. In this type of system, some sort of inspection is used after the products or parts are

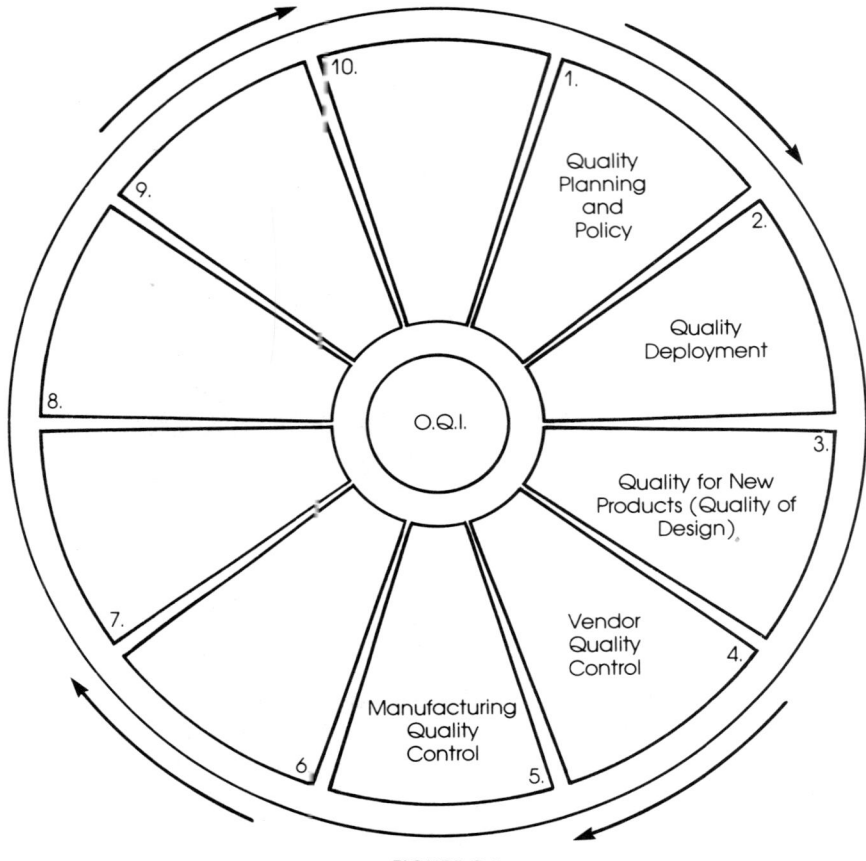

FIGURE 9-1

manufactured to sort out the good ones from the defective ones. Based on this information, the processes are adjusted to minimize or eliminate scrap. The inspection department or quality-control department is generally responsible for carrying out this work.

The following problems can occur with this system:

1. The responsibility for producing good-quality parts or products is divided between operations and inspection.
2. The corrective measures are too late to fix the system. Poor quality has already been produced.
3. There is too much unnecessary scrap and rework.
4. Product costs are high.
5. Organizations get used to accepting rejects.
6. Quality improvement is slow and sometimes hard to achieve due to divided responsibilities.

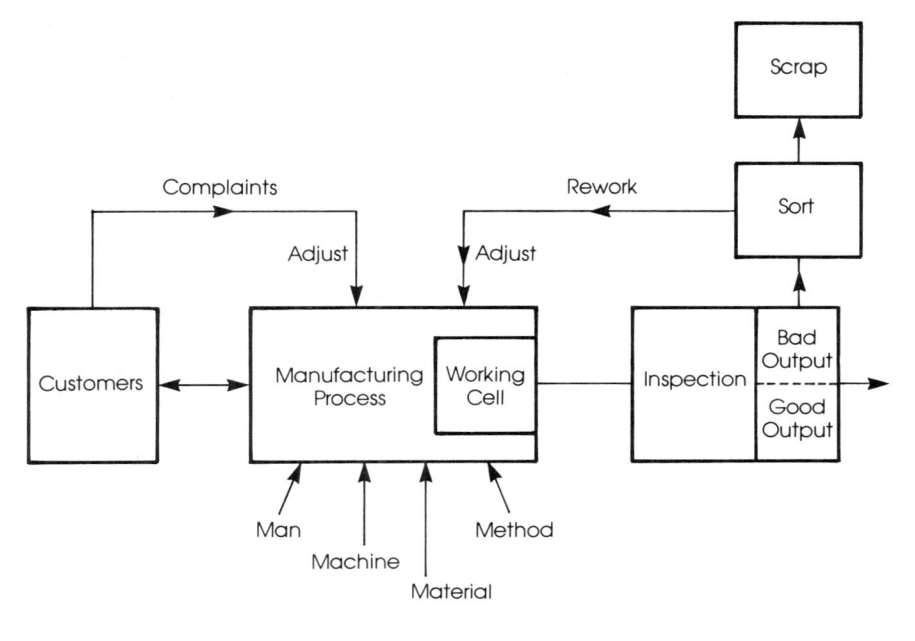

DEFECT DETECTION SYSTEM

FIGURE 9-2

Statistical Approach—Defect Prevention

The statistical approach, as advocated by statistician Edward Deming, fits well in the new quality era that we are entering in the 1980s. He has added the approach called *defect prevention* to that of *defect detection*. (See Figure 9-2.)

In defect prevention, processes are monitored continually on a periodic basis; corrective actions are taken immediately, as required. Variations take place due to various elements such as man, machine, material, equipment, and other unexpected changes in the processes. Based on the real-time measurement, processes can be monitored and adjusted as necessary. Statistical techniques are among the best tools for evaluating these selective measurements, as they provide a method for logical and systematic evaluation of information. Specifically, these methods help to determine process capabilities: the ability to meet consumers' expectations and to detect the causes of problems, and many times how to correct the problems without incurring too much quality loss. We need to remember that defect prevention will require inspection. However, it plays a different role than detect detection and does not require sorting good from defective parts.

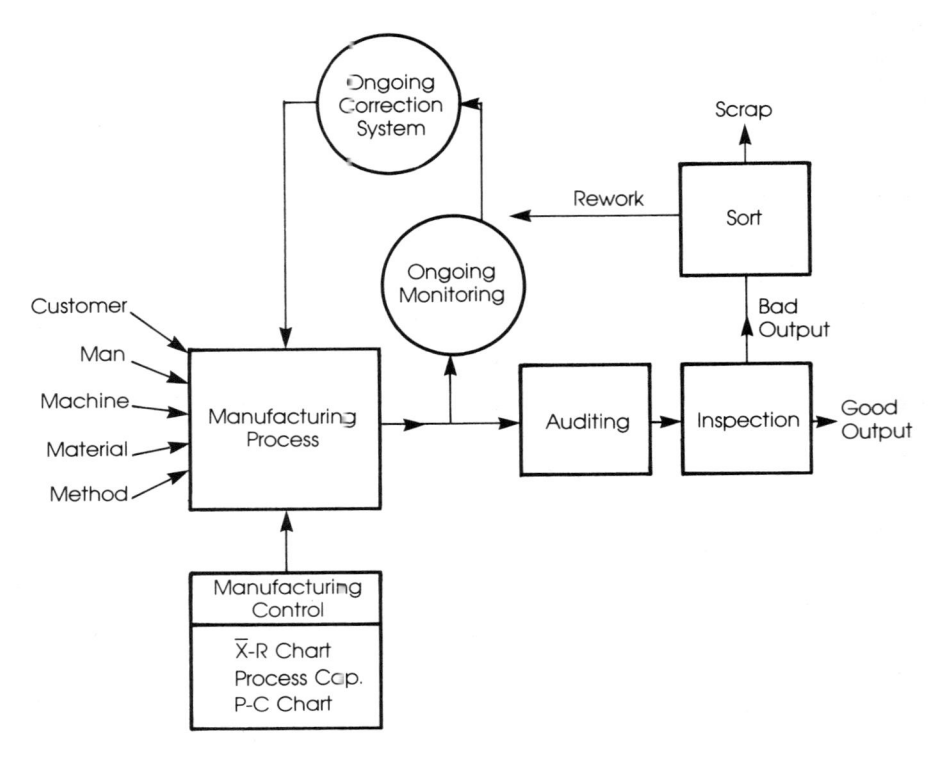

DEFECT PREVENTION SYSTEM

FIGURE 9-3

Maintenance of In-Process Quality

Organizations have to promote quality-control activities throughout the organization using in-process quality checks and in-process quality audit systems. In order to establish controlled processes, we have to pay attention to the four famous M's—namely, man, machine, material, and methods. Let us review each of them separately.

1. Training Programs for Improving Skills of the Operators

Various ongoing training programs for operators and management are essential to improve skills, teach the importance of quality, and create interest in doing quality work.

Basic training for supervisors and operators can be outlined here:

1. Basics of quality control
2. Importance of quality

MANUFACTURING QUALITY

3. Statistical process control
4. Charting process and activities
5. Improving processes
6. Cost-benefit analysis
7. Problem-solving process
8. Product familiarization
9. Special techniques
10. Teamwork and good job skills

(The details of other training programs are discussed in Chapter 14.)

2. Quality Control of Machinery and Equipment

It is necessary that organizations establish good quality-control systems for machinery and equipment in order to build quality products and other quality services. Well-maintained equipment helps to maintain the good spirit of the operators and supervisors. One of the key elements in successful quality systems is preventive maintenance of the equipment and processes. This follows the well-known philosophy that "an ounce of prevention is better than a pound of cure." Poorly maintained equipment and fixtures not only create poor quality, but they also discourage the operators from thinking about good-quality work.

Some of the elements in maintaining equipment are as follows:

a. Machinery and equipment
Daily inspection—check operations, movements, abnormal noise, leakage, and so on
Periodic inspection—as specified by equipment builders

b. Jigs and tools
Periodic inspection—for looseness, precision checks, and replacement of parts

c. Gauge Control
Daily and periodical. More details are discussed in Chapter 10.

Note: One can develop many types of checklists to collect information for corrective actions.

3. Raw and Component Material Control

The quality of material purchased and the dimensional accuracy of the parts are two critical factors that will determine the quality of products. Once such materials are found to be defective and of low quality, there is no effective way to use them other than remanufacturing them to meet specifications. Hence, the quality of the material plays an important role in building quality products. The following three areas need careful attention in this regard:

a. Procedure for selection of materials. It is necessary that an organization spend enough time in evaluating vendors properly. Preliminary tests and checks should be performed to determine whether the parts meet specifications for material quality, dimensions, finishing, heat treatment, and so on. Specifications should be clear and agreeable to both parties.

b. Purchasing of specialized items (steel, rubber, chemical products, etc.). We can ask the suppliers of such specialized items to perform inspection of each lot to be delivered. The organization must insist that each lot be delivered along with inspection data. It is necessary for vendors to take the responsibility for delivering quality products, not just meeting the shipping deadlines.

c. Confirmation of properties. It is often difficult to detect the mixing of different materials. Use of the wrong material can cause serious problems and costly liability suits. Hence, one needs to check properties of materials very carefully. Organizations should write clear documents, standards, and procedures, and must follow them in accepting critical items.

4. Accepted and Approved Standards

In order to create stable quality, it is necessary to standardize procedures to handle machines, material, and so on, and clarify the standards that must be observed by the operators. The instructions should be clear for all the areas listed below:

a. In-house standards. The following control methods are applied to maintain quality levels which are approved at the preproduction stage.

Area	Controlling Method
Continuous Process	Design of experiment, control charts, (cumulative summation chart)
Batch Process	Statistical process chart, histograms, Red X theory
Physical Process	$\bar{x}$-R chart, task analysis, scattered diagram
Assembly Process	P-chart, C-chart, Kanban system, component search pattern
Services and Administrative	Flow chart, process chart, function analysis, activity analysis, principles of motion economy, paperwork simplification methods

b. Purchased parts quality control. Organizations should work with vendors and instead of using the vendor certification system that is prevalent today, they should move toward vendor surveillance. Organizations should consider vendors a part of the organization and try to help them as much as possible in supplying quality parts or equipment. More details regarding this topic were discussed in Chapter 8.

What Can We Do to Beat the Competition?

1. Charting and Analyzing Processes

There are a number of processes that take place in the organization while building products. Generally, the processes are defined and evaluated at the start. However, as time goes on, people add unnecessary operations and sometimes try to bandage the process to eliminate problems.

I believe that the processes can be improved through systematic charting and involving people in analyzing the work. The following techniques are useful in this regard:

1. Activity analysis
2. Process analysis
3. Man-machine charts
4. Left-hand and right-hand charts
5. Use of principles of motion economy

2. Use of Process Capability Studies

Once the processes have been reviewed, it is necessary to collect the information and analyze the processes to understand their capability.

3. Use of Cp and Cpk indices

In order to promote the use of statistics all over the organization, various simple, new terms are being used in Japan. Many of these are also used today around the world. *Cp* and *Cpk indices* are two common terms used by the manufacturing engineering, quality-control engineering, and engineering departments to convey the capability of the processes. The *Cp* index is defined as follows:

$$Cp = \frac{\text{Upper specification} - \text{lower specification limit}}{\text{Process capability}}$$

The Cp index helps to make clear the process capability to the tolerance limits.

Cpk index:

$$Cpk = \frac{Z \text{ min.}}{3} \text{ where } Z \text{ min.} = \min. \left\{ \frac{USL - \bar{x}}{\sigma} ; \frac{\bar{x} - LSL}{\sigma} \right\}$$

The Cpk index helps to explain the process average shift from the nominal dimensions that one likes to achieve.

4. Use of Statistical Process Control (SPC)

Statistical process control is one of the major factors contributing to the high quality standards of Japan and other countries. Many industries and nonmanufacturing organizations today in the United States and other countries are rediscovering this cost effective, productivity-oriented tool. The author has described this in more detail in Appendix C.

Remember, implementing SPC takes a long time (six months to two years) and the financial investment is high. However, the returns are much greater if one sticks to principles and follows the well-defined discipline. Some of the known advantages are listed here:

1. Higher up-time
2. Reduced scrap
3. Reduced inspection
4. Higher quality
5. Reduced rework

One can add many other benefits to this list of key items.

5. Statistical Evaluation of New Equipment

Capital expenditure is one of the highest dollar investments in any organization; organizations spend thousands of dollars on new equipment purchases. As time goes on, we will find more and more need for better equipment to compete with other countries, as well as getting rid of the old equipment, which may be less productive. Hence, we need to be careful in spending the money—it takes very little effort to systematically evaluate new equipment. It is my experience that a lot of equipment is purchased because of contracts; in general, quality control plays a very minor role in accepting the equipment based on sound statistical evaluation.

The following sample proposal will give the reader an idea of how to write specifications for new equipment and how to evaluate new equipment based on statistical methods:

ABC COMPANY, MANUFACTURING ENGINEERING DEPARTMENT

EQUIPMENT SPECIFICATION

Specification No. _____

Specification for
suppliers offering
quotations on machine tools
and industrial equipment

PREFACE

This specification has been written to present ABC Company requirements for industrial equipment in an orderly manner. It is not intended to limit or inhibit development in industrial equipment design.

All specifications will be adhered to on each project and are to be considered an integral part of purchase orders.

Any exceptions must be authorized by ABC Company's Manufacturing and Quality Control Departments.

TABLE OF CONTENTS

ABC Company—Fond du Lac, Wisconsin

Machine Tools and Industrial Equipment Specifications

Section 1	General
Section 2	Machine Tool and Auxiliary Equipment
Section 3	Tool Design Standards
Section 4	Hydraulics
Section 5	Electrical Specifications
Section 6	Pneumatic Standards
Section 7	Equipment Lubrication
Section 8	Quality Standards
Section 9	Coolant Standards
Section 10	Safety and Health Standards
Section 11	Machine Drawing and Layout
Section 12	Material Handling Equipment
Section 13	Progress Report and Payment
Section 14	Other—Miscellaneous

Note: This specification is an integral part of the ABC Company's purchase order.

SECTION 8: QUALITY STANDARDS

1. *General Acceptance of the Equipment:*

    A. Equipment will be checked for compliance to specifications by a capability study at the vendor's plant. Permission to ship to ABC may be withheld by ABC Manufacturing or Quality Control until compliance has been demonstrated at the vendor's plant. Any deviations to this policy must be clearly stated in the quotation.

The equipment will also be checked for compliance to specifications by a capability study on ABC Company's floor. In the case where a system comprising a number of machines has been provided, the complete system must be checked. When this test has been satisfactorily completed, the vendor's responsibility with respect to compliance in specifications will be deemed satisfactorily discharged.

- B. The standard alignment performance of the machine will be verified by a certificate outlining the alignment tests and checks made by the supplier and the results at supplier's plant. Duplication of these tests in ABC Company's plant, for verification, will be done at the time of installation.
- C. Metal-cutting performance will be evaluated by the supplier utilizing the machine and its control to produce an agreed-upon test part.
- D. Positioning accuracy and repeatability is to be checked for all machines.
    1. NC machines are to be checked according to the procedure published by NMTBA.
    2. All other machines are to be checked by a procedure agreed to by both ABC Company and the supplier.

2. *Capability Study: General*
    - A. It is the policy of ABC Company to give each new machine tool the proper quality evaluation at the plant of the supplier to whom the contract has been awarded. This is done to insure that a machine is capable of producing parts to the specifications required by ABC Company. In order to explain what ABC Company considers a capable process, and how this determination is made, the following is provided. If tryout of the quoted equipment is to be done in any other location than the vendor's home plant, this fact should be clearly stated in the quotation.
    - B. Analysis of Data:
        1. Two-sided tolerance where the machine tool can be retargeted, such as diameters, lengths, etc. After taking data, the standard deviation is calculated using the following formula:

$$s = \sqrt{\frac{(\Sigma X_i - \overline{X})^2}{n-1}}$$

and C = Machine capability = $6S$ where X_i is the measurement of the i th part, n is the total number of parts measured, and $\overline{x}$ is the mean. For acceptance,

$$C = \text{Machine capability} \leqslant .6\,T$$
$$\bar{x} + .5C \leqslant X_n + .43\,T$$

and

$$\bar{x} - .5C \geqslant X_n - .43\,T$$

where

$T = $ print tolerance, and
$x_n = $ nominal dimension

2. One-sided tolerance where the machine tool cannot be retargeted, such as roundness, concentricity, runout, etc.

After taking data, rms deviation is calculated using the following formula:

$$S = \sqrt{\frac{\Sigma X_i^2}{N}}$$

$C = \text{Machine capability} = 2.5\,S$

For acceptance,

$$C \leqslant .6\,T$$

3. *Conditions for Capability Study*

In order to achieve the greatest possible validity from the capability study, the following conditions must be met:

1. The machine must be properly tooled and adjusted.
   a. The machine must be cycled at specified operating speeds and feeds.
   b. Tool grind must occur as it would during normal operation.
   c. The tests must be made on all the materials which the machine will run.
2. No machine or tool adjustments will be made during run of test.
3. Measurements will be made with the most accurate and economical production gauging available for checking the characteristics being studied.
4. All fixtures (pallets) must be used at least twice while machining qualification lot.

4. *System Acceptance:*

   Phase I: Each machine will be checked independently and will be qualified as described above.

   Phase II: A check of the complete system supplied by the vendor will be performed to qualify specified production capacity within specified tolerance.

6. Promoting Statistical Thinking

Edward Deming once remarked, "In Japan, statistics is a second language." In other countries, people are even afraid of the word *statistics*. We must find simple and commonly used methods to promote the use of statistics. One of the best ways to do this is through daily conversation meetings or informal communications. Various in-house newspapers or bulletin boards can also be used in this respect.

One can start by first using basic statistical techniques, such as

1. Graphs, charts, check sheets, checklists
2. Sampling methods
3. Cause and effect analysis
4. Pareto diagrams
5. Problem-solving process

As time goes on, one can start introducing more advanced techniques, which are listed below:

1. Histograms
2. Process capability studies
3. Component search pattern
4. $\bar{x}$-R chart
5. P-chart
6. Np chart
7. Cum-sum chart
8. Scatter diagram
9. Multivary chart
10. Stratification
11. Planned experiments
12. Red X theory

It is the function and responsibility of quality-control personnel to promote the effective use of statistics. There is no limit to how much you can teach to others.

7. Using Quality Costs Effectively

Quality costs speak another language that management likes to hear and most of them are familiar with—that is, dollars and cents. One should also promote the use of quality costs in various manufacturing operations. It is important to reduce internal quality costs which, in the long run, will also cut down external quality costs. It has been proven that there is always a high correlation between internal quality costs and external quality costs.

More discussion about quality costs and their use is offered in Appendix B.

8. Integrated Gauging

This new terminology is discussed in detail by Vearl A. Williams, editor of *Production Magazine* in detail in the March 1982 issue (page 79). An integrated gauge is defined as an automatic gauging system, fully integrated with a production machine's controls, which provides automatic size control cutting tool compensation, whether the actual gauging sequence is performed simultaneously with or at a statistic following the "machining operation."

Integrated gauging was normally thought to provide benefits only for medium- to high-volume production operations. However, that is not the case. Parts complexity and cost also play important roles. There are thousands of new pieces of gauging equipment available in the market; organizations should look for new features and try to implement a new gauging system effectively. Use of digital gauges, lasers, noncontact gauges, and NDT (nondistinctive testing) gauging is becoming more common along with integral gauging systems.

9. Self-Inspection

Equipment and gauges play a vital role in building quality products or offering quality services. However, there is another key aspect that should not be neglected in improving the quality of an organization: people. They need to be motivated constantly to build quality products. Many times, people are neglected and the organization faces problems in producing quality goods. People need to be properly instructed. Inspection and instruction have to be cleared and thoroughly tested. To achieve the desired goal, people need to observe self-control in the long run; this can be done by motivating them in the right direction. The management should also provide the necessary written specifications and inspection instructions to the operators.

10. Training, Training, and Retraining

Based on my last several years of experience in industrial organizations and visits to various operators, I find this area needs strong continual commitment from the management. Many organizations provide training in various areas, but at times this happens in bits and pieces; most of the time it is a one-time deal where the employee must depend on his or her personal resources for further advancement. Organizations need to establish training departments and construct new training courses on topics such as robotics, computers, management participation, statistics, and so on.

Recently, *Iron Age* magazine (September 1982 issue) published a description of the training program that is being used by the Nissan Company in Smyrna, Tennessee. It seems the well-planned quality of the products depends on who builds them—well-trained, well-educated employees or less-trained, less-educated ones.

11. New Role of Quality Control or Quality Assurance Department

Most organizations today have well-established quality control or quality assurance departments. However, most of the time these people are engaged in "fire fighting" (working on day-to-day problems without planning and without objectives). I believe that the roles of quality-control managers, quality control engineers, and quality control technicians are changing. Most of them need to get involved in training, evaluating results, helping people to understand the use of statistics, and learning new inspection methods for improving quality. Involvement in fire fighting should be avoided as much as possible.

12. Changing Role of the Inspection Department

Inspection systems are going to shrink in the future. Incoming inspections are going to play a less important role. Vendor parts will in many cases, be accepted, using quality audits, where once again statistical methods and analysis will be used heavily. Vendors will be required to show proof of the use of control charts and process capability studies. In the process, inspections will again be changed to auditing functions, and operators will be doing more and more self-inspection. Final inspections will be reduced to a minimum also, and quality audits will play an increasingly important role. Inspections will be needed to evaluate, update, and improve inspection procedures on a periodic basis.

13. Make It Right the First Time

I believe in this philosophy to improve the quality and productivity of an organization. However, it is not easy to achieve this goal anywhere. One of the quality control managers at Mercury Marine, Brunswick Corporation, at one time discussed this subject at great length with the author. You will realize the magnitude of the total involvement of various functions and the complexity of the responsibilities of various departments by reading the following summary.

Make It Right the First Time

During every step of this planning, consideration must be given to answer one specific question: What can go wrong? The obvious answer is, A hundred things.

At this stage of part development, every major department will be required to look at these possibilities and collectively agree on the best methods to use to produce that specific part.

The engineer must keep in mind his or her design specifications as to weight, shape, durability, and cost.

The raw-material producers' tool designers must keep in mind material, die designs, draft angles, strength, parting lines, machine availability, volumes, and so on.

The machining manufacturing engineers must determine tooling needs, fixtures, gauges, capacities, tool wear, volume, and so on. The secondary operations of welding, bending, heat treating, chemical treatment, and the like usually require heavy emphasis on operator skill and judgment. Consideration must be given to design of nondestructive-type tests to assure that the operations are completed successfully.

Industrial engineers must precisely measure the time required to do the operations, which ultimately determines cost and volume.

Process engineers determine proper sequences, routings, measurement intervals, and instructions for the operator.

Other departments such as purchasing, material control, production control, and so on also enter into this planning.

Consideration of all the above plant functions need to supply input so that when drawings are made, the best materials, processes, and procedures are used to make the part right and at the least cost.

Like the others, the quality and inspection departments have their job to do: to assure that specifications exist in every phase of production to allow a judgment of conformance to be made. If the plant will produce the raw part, these departments should answer questions of conformance to material and how best to determine it, how to maintain that conformance (holding frequent checks of nondestructive tests), and systems to handle nonconforming materials.

The same requirements exist in the machine shop. What instructions exist to permit the operator to make the part, insure that he has done the operation correctly, and recognize and report when the operation has produced a bad part? What audit checks will be necessary; which characteristics should be measured and at what frequency? Are destructive and nondestructive tests necessary? Has the inspection department provided the proper instructions to permit the audit check to be done correctly and with the right gauges and equipment? What will be the final inspection requirements, if any, to insure that the various lots meet all requirements before shipment is allowed?

The assembly quality department will need to insure that the complement of parts will fit together properly and function as the design engineer intended. What standards are required for the assembly operator to determine if the parts he or she works with are producing the correct function of that assembly? Are tests required before the engine is run? Are sufficient operator instructions available to assure that each unit the operator works on will be like the previous one?

There are questions of audit checks on items such as torques, function tolerances (shimming), leakage checks, correct lubricants and seals, paint thickness, and cleanliness of assemblies.

Finally, the culmination of all these operations should be a product that will start and perform to all the specifications the product engineers have designed.

In the final test, attention is given to proper specification of the individual characteristics of the running engine. Are they defined properly, with the correct tolerance to allow the tester's judgment as to whether the engine is performing correctly? Individual judgments of senses such as sound, feel, and smell should be minimized.

Over and above all of these considerations are the correct systems requirements. The systems that affect some control of parts and assemblies being made are as follows (just to name a few):

Material review boards

Sample inspection report procedures

Forms and tickets

Traceability

Inspection records

Reports and report procedures

Inspection instructions

Test instruction

Purge procedures

Control of defective lots

Receiving inspection procedures

Reports for purchasing
Reports for production and their foremen
What reports are not useful
Acceptable salvage procedures
Lot control
Shipment control
Proper quality-loss reporting
Quality-cost reporting
Analysis of these reports
Proper staff
Training needs
Process-capability needs
Supplier qualification
Supplier audits
Vendor gauges
Gauge-calibration system
Sampling procedures
Problem-solving tools
Special study capabilities
Quality information feedback
Drawing sign-off
Corrective action procedures
Deviation procedures
X-ray procedures
Material analysis
Problem cost recording
Audit procedures
Audit reports
Warranty reports and evaluation
Contribution margin
Data storage and retrieval
Application of simple statistics
Minimum-part sample techniques
Operator control

Precontrol
Reduction in inspection costs
Control chart applications
Plant certification requirement
Vendor training

The interaction of these systems, when performed properly, results in a quality product made with the least amount of quality loss. Together, they make up a total quality program.

14. Gradual Introduction of PPM Concept

Most organizations today use some kind of inspection system. The use of MIL-STD-105 D in many organizations is common in accepting loss on maintaining batches. The use of AQL (acceptable quality level) is based on the MIL-STD-105 D table. However, today this concept is not good enough. Dr. Edward Deming and others are already promoting the need for continual quality improvement instead of accepting a certain level of defective products. Use of PPM (parts per million) is becoming quite common in electronics industries. Organizations should look into studying the PPM concept and try to introduce its use gradually. I have already discussed this topic in detail in Chapter 8.

Continual Improvement (Case Study)

I recently viewed a videotape made by one of the automobile industries. The top management at this company is convinced that organizations need to work on continual improvement of quality. The videotape compares the automobile transmissions built in the United States with those built by a foreign country. Ten sets were examined for quality and performance. All ten made by the foreign country performed well, and service records indicated fewer warranty problems. When the parts were checked dimensionally, the statistical record showed that while the parts made in the United States used 70 percent of the tolerance, the parts made by the foreign country used only 27 percent of the total tolerance. When we use tolerances, naturally the variation is less, which ultimately helps to improve the performance of the products.

The message is clear: Quality improvement is a never-ending job. We need to strive for ongoing, continual improvement.

(I) C_p INDEX :

$$C_p = \frac{\text{Upper Spec.} - \text{Lower Spec.}}{6\sigma'} = \frac{\text{Spec. Width}}{\text{Process Width}}$$

LS | ▨▨▨ | Us
   $\underbrace{}_{6\sigma'}$

Suppose: Upper Spec. − Lower Spec. = 12
$6\sigma' = 6$

THEN, $\boxed{C_p = \dfrac{12}{6} = 2}$

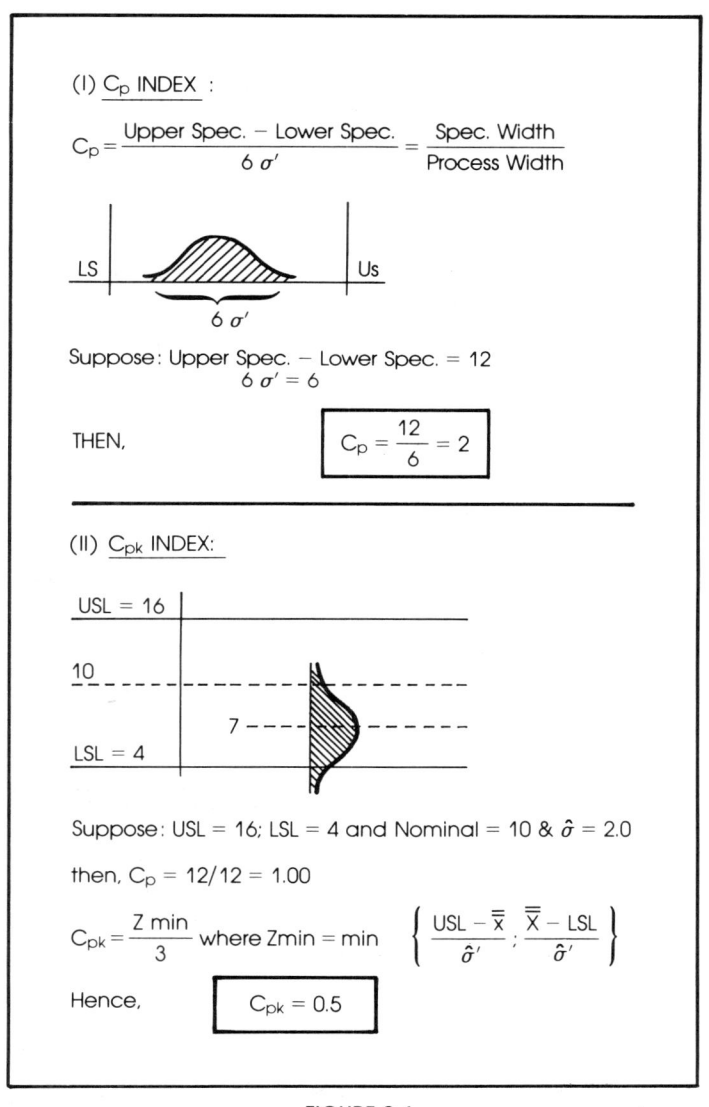

(II) C_{pk} INDEX:

USL = 16
10 - - - - - - - -
7 - - - - -
LSL = 4

Suppose: USL = 16; LSL = 4 and Nominal = 10 & $\hat{\sigma} = 2.0$

then, $C_p = 12/12 = 1.00$

$$C_{pk} = \frac{Z_{min}}{3} \text{ where } Z_{min} = \min \left\{ \frac{\text{USL} - \bar{\bar{x}}}{\hat{\sigma}'} \, ; \, \frac{\bar{\bar{X}} - \text{LSL}}{\hat{\sigma}'} \right\}$$

Hence, $\boxed{C_{pk} = 0.5}$

FIGURE 9-4

PROCESSES IN MANUFACTURING

1. Check variations in processes—

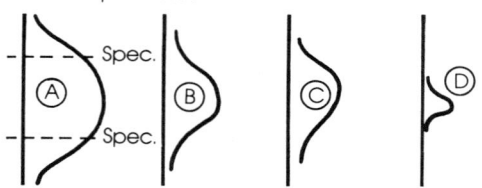

   (A) (B) (C) (D)

2. Select process A ⟶ For improvement—

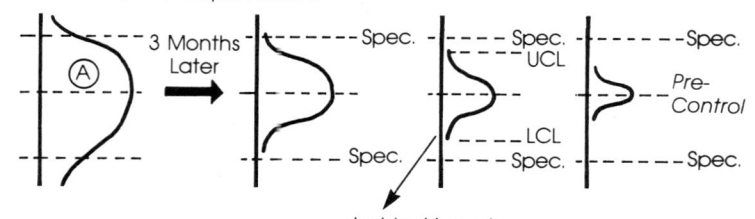

   3 Months Later

   start looking at other processes at this stage for overall improvement

3. Process B

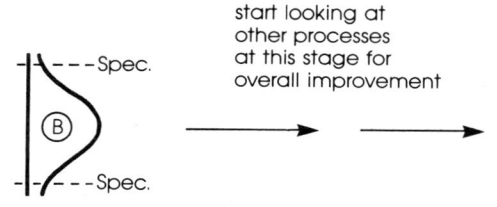

   "Continuous Improvement"

   FIGURE 9-5

EVALUATING YOUR ORGANIZATION

1. Our organization has very good job-instruction systems, and many instructions are visible.

0	5	10
No	Average	Yes

2. Our organization has good systems to analyze reject products or services.

0	5	10
No	Average	Yes

3. Our organization uses statistical training in various stages of process.

0	5	10
No	Average	Yes

4. Our organization conducts process capabilities as part of running business.

```
0          5          10
```
No   Average   Yes

5. Our organization has good new-equipment accepting procedures based on statistical studies.

```
0          5          10
```
No   Average   Yes

6. Our organization promotes the importance of quality through various quality programs.

```
0          5          10
```
No   Average   Yes

7. Our organization involves top management in promoting quality programs.

```
0          5          10
```
No   Average   Yes

8. Our organization believes in ongoing training programs; employees are trained constantly for new techniques.

```
0          5          10
```
No   Average   Yes

9. Our organization works closely with vendors, and vendors are invited periodically to visit our operations.

```
0          5          10
```
No   Average   Yes

10. Products and services are tested constantly in-house and, if necessary, corrective actions are taken immediately.

```
0          5          10
```
No   Average   Yes

Every process and every system is beset with variation. We live in a sea of variation. It blankets our operations like a fog, interfering with our ability to see the truth of our actions. It causes our processes to produce something other than what was intended.

Lloyd Nelson, Nashua Corporation

Chapter Ten
COMPUTER-AIDED QUALITY INFORMATION SYSTEMS

Nowadays we often hear the slogan, "Get it right the first time." However, very few organizations have implemented the quality information systems that are needed to achieve this goal. We must realize that things don't happen by themselves. It is necessary to plan, identify, and then implement the various quality systems. One of the best ways to start organizing this work is by using the MIL-Q-9858A standard. The MIL-Q-9858A need not be expensive to administer. It is merely a commonsense document that helps to start a method of examining quality in your business. Even though MIL-Q-9858A is used by the U.S. Government and its suppliers, I feel it is a very important document to help many other organizations initiate basic quality information systems.

Elements of Effective Quality Information Systems

The following elements are necessary in implementing successful quality information systems.

1. Goals
2. Communication
3. Implementation

4. Review
5. Feedback

1. Goals. Goals should be established to achieve desired objectives. They must be expressed in definitive and quantifiable terms with a timetable. Goals should be established for current as well as new products, engineering areas, manufacturing areas, service areas, and other areas of the business that affect quality.

2. Communication. Quality information systems goals should be communicated to all personnel in the organization. Each area should communicate its specific goal to salaried as well as hourly people. Getting people involved in initiating quality systems helps tremendously to make these systems successful. Training programs can be used to make outsiders such as vendors familiar with quality systems.

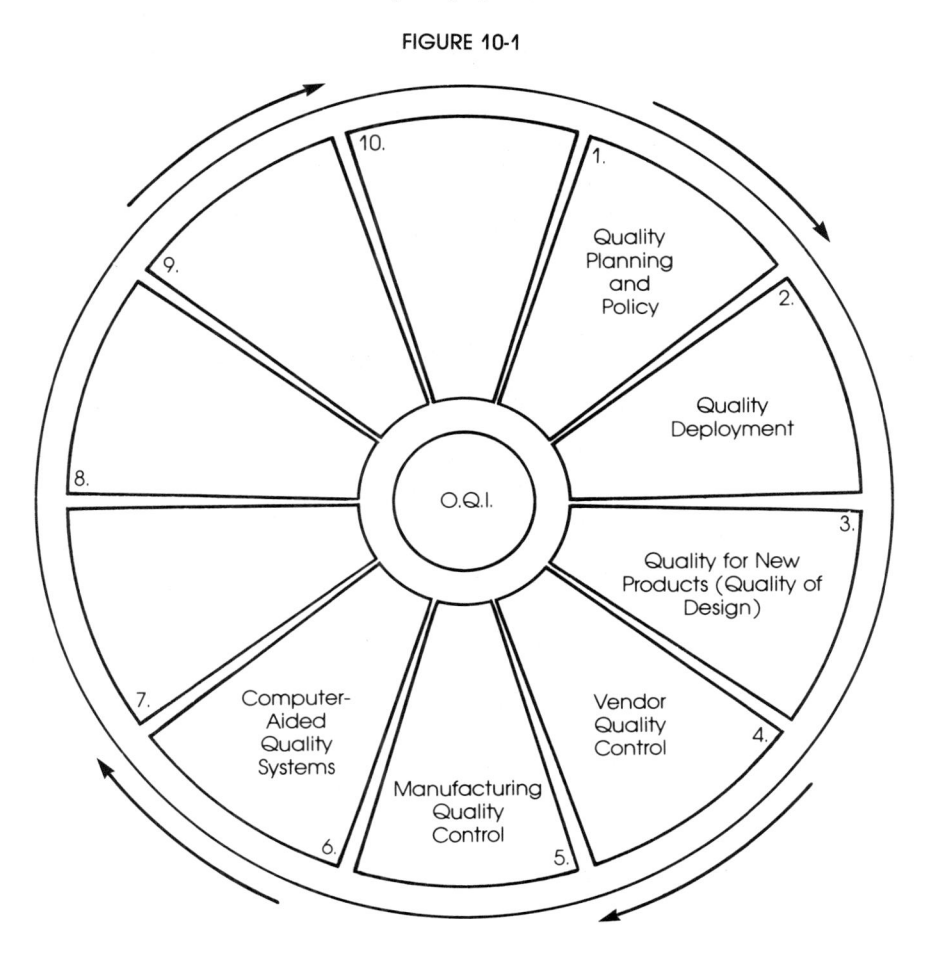

FIGURE 10-1

3. Implementation. Implementation of a new quality system will depend on the area it is to work in. You can prepare or computerize reports; however, you must make sure that the report is necessary and useful. Do not keep people busy reading reports that are not useful in quality improvement. Quality information systems should help to analyze problems, report other progress, or communicate a necessary message to other parties.

4. Review. It is necessary for periodic reviews to be made of the system by product engineering, manufacturing, suppliers, and warranty departments. Engineering must analyze the feasibility and capability of manufacturing systems and identify historic concerns associated with other reports. Manufacturing checks the feasibility of adapting the systems from a usefulness and cost point of view. Periodic checks of reviews will help determine the validity of the quality system and get rid of unnecessary work.

5. Feedback. This helps to close the loop and confirm the success of the quality information system. Sources of feedback information include customers' reports, quality analysis, costs, field returns, supplier surveys, and many other related reports. Feedback should be used, just like reviews, to check the progress and usefulness of the quality information system.

The Role of Computers in Quality Information Systems[1]

The computer is fast becoming the telephone of the modern beginner. When the telephone was first introduced, people were often afraid to use it; so now we find a phobia within the top management of companies about using computers.

However, it must be realized that the state of quality is evolving rapidly and at the least, a working knowledge of the computer is essential, just as a working knowledge of the telephone is required in everyday life.

The speed of the computer makes it an ideal tool for the rapid analysis of the large amounts of data collected in quality-control work. In typical quality-control work, a lot of the data collected is done because somebody, some time ago, set up the collection process that way. This data, though necessary for process projection, may not be immediately useful; hence it is often filed away and forgotten. If analyzed, (e.g., failure rates, scrap, etc.) this data could be used to enhance quality. The timeliness of data analysis can be achieved by utilizing the speed and storage capabilities of *Time* magazine's 1982 Man of the Year: the computer.

---

[1]This information is compiled by Anil Ingle, Master of Science Student at Marquette University, Milwaukee, Wisconsin.

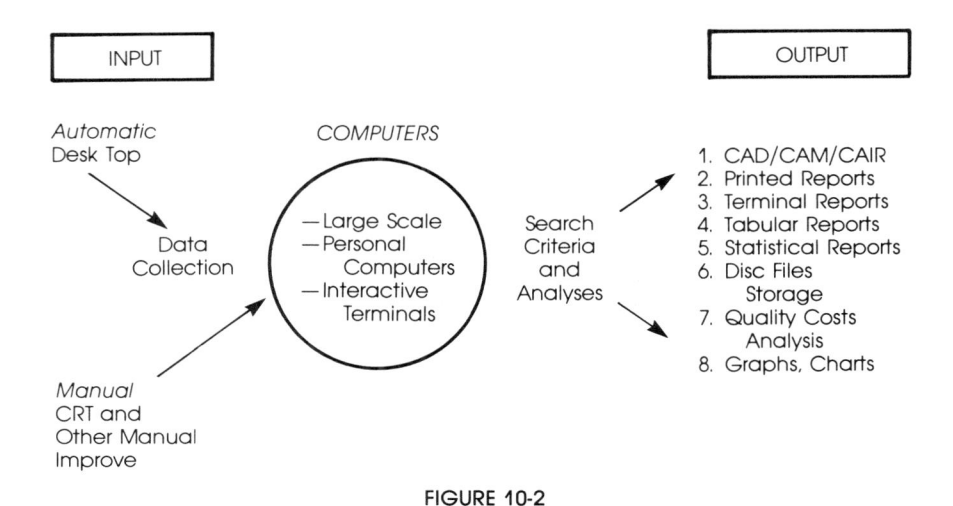

```
     INPUT                                              OUTPUT

Automatic            COMPUTERS              1. CAD/CAM/CAIR
Desk Top                                    2. Printed Reports
                                            3. Terminal Reports
          ↘    — Large Scale    Search      4. Tabular Reports
       Data    — Personal       Criteria    5. Statistical Reports
       Collection  Computers    and         6. Disc Files
          ↗    — Interactive    Analyses       Storage
                  Terminals                 7. Quality Costs
                                               Analysis
Manual                                      8. Graphs, Charts
CRT and
Other Manual
Improve
```

FIGURE 10-2

A logarithmic increase in their processing power and a logarithmic decrease in their cost and size have brought computers to the middle-management desktop. Tedious data manipulation, as found in a typical quality-control application, can now be easily programmed into a computer instead of the executive burning up his sleeves to do it, thus freeing middle management for the more productive job of looking at the results and deciding what to do with them. It is important to realize that the computer will not solve all quality problems. It is not an end in itself, but the means to an end. It can manipulate the input and present it to the user in whatever way the user wants it to, but the action to be taken is still the responsibility of the user.

Why Use Computers?

Let us now look at some of the reasons why quality assurance is so well adapted to computer applications.

1. Quality assurance generates a lot of data. Keeping track of all this data requires a lot of paperwork. This can be easily reduced by punching all this data into a computer and storing it on magnetic disks or tapes.

2. Most quality-assurance processes are computational and tedious. Processing the data collected for quality assurance usually consists of statistical calculations, which can be tedious. All this time-consuming, repetitive work can be avoided by programming, after which all that remains is keying in the relevant data and asking for the output in the format desired—for example, graphs, tables, and so on. All these can be repetitively reproduced at almost no extra cost or time.

3. Improved measuring systems now allow for automated data gathering, which allows data to be fed directly into the computer and analyzed without the possibility of human error.

4. The speed with which all of the above can be done can allow for 100 percent inspection, which in itself raises interesting possibilities. The production manager, for example, can know almost immediately if his or her process is going out of control instead of having to wait for a batch of rejects. If, say, one of the machines in a process is messing up that process, the manager can look up the history of that particular machine almost immediately, instead of having to wait and see what happens.

These and other common advantages, like having word-processing capability (because it makes no sense for the boss to write up a memo and then have the secretary type it up, bring it back for approval, and then send it out, when he could have done the whole thing himself on the computer far more quickly) make the mainframes and reword computers an essential part of the modern quality-assurance system.

1. Fast (for "small" data sets)
2. Accurate
3. Convenient (no phone-line or mainframe bottlenecks)
4. Inexpensive, compared to time sharing
5. No cost for data storage other than diskettes
6. Ability to tie in with mainframe if needed
7. You can take your time, since no time charges
8. Easy to include statistical output in reports with word processing

Disadvantages compared to mainframe are:

1. Slower for some very heavy computational procedures
2. Current micropackages not quite as extensive as mainframe ones
3. Usually can't handle very large data sets easily

These disadvantages can be easily ignored if one buys a MODEM and has access to a mainframe. A MODEM is a modulator-demodulator that allows one computer to "talk" to another. Using this feature, you can perform the few analyses that your micro-computer cannot handle by dumping the data to the mainframe package when needed. Another benefit of this feature is that data entry can be done off-line. Why tie up a multimillion-dollar computer for something as simple as data entry?

Use of Personal Computers

Using a personal computer will probably mean that the user has to develop his or her own quality-assurance system. As this would not involve the company's data processing department as completely as developing a quality-assurance system for a mainframe would, it can probably be done faster and be more personalized than it otherwise would be. Some important points to be kept in mind when developing your own quality-assurance system are:

1. Do it yourself whenever possible. This will serve as a learning experience so that you get to know your machine well, and will also be a great boon when you try to change the program. Trying to understand somebody else's code is not fun.

2. Buy off-the-shelf quality-control software if it meets your needs. This will not only save you time, but also hours of frustration trying to bebug a program and get it working.

3. Get a good data-base management system (e.g., dBase II) to maintain, enter, and retrieve data selectively. A good data-base system can be extremely helpful in fault analyses, especially when you have to selectively look up data collected over a period of time.

4. A statistical package is a must to create control charts and analyze data. Until recently, serious statistical analysis was confined to mainframes. However, good statistical software is now available for microcomputers as well. Out of the more popular mainframe statistical packages like SPSS, SAS, BMDP, MINITAB, and P-STAT, both SPSS and BMDP have packages designed to run on microcomputers in the $10,000-and-under range. SPSS runs on the Digital-PC and IBM PC with hard disk. BMDP sells a software/hardware package called STATCAT. SAS has recently released a version of their package for the IBM XT/370. MINITAB is also working on a release for Digital and IBM PCs.

Which package is right for you? If you are relatively sophisticated in your statistical capabilities and are used to using a mainframe package, you may want to consider one of the following.

1. STATPRO
2. STATGRAPHICS, PC
3. SYSTAT
4. SPSS
5. BMDP STATCAT

6. SAS
7. MINITAB

Most of the above packages contain much more than the normal quality professionals would ever use—and they are expensive, between $500 and $2,000. Less expensive packages are available that perform the majority of analyses a quality professional would need for everyday use. These packages are generally less expensive ($125-$500) and may prove to be better values. Some of these are:

1. MICROSTAT
2. ABSTAT
3. STATPAC
4. The Explorer

5. A good word processor can be a boon to the quality professional. Electronic spread-sheet packages like LOTUS 1-2-3 and word-processing packages like WordStar can be used effectively in quality control. Uses and advantages of word processing in quality control are:

1. Correspondence and memos. They usually improve secretarial productivity and reduce frustration. Why handwrite it on paper, have someone else type it, proofread it, retype it, reproof it, when it can be done by yourself on a computer? Though this assumes a certain amount of basic typing ability—which most professionals have—mistakes can be corrected easily before they are printed.
2. Report writing. Why retype from scratch a monthly report that is essentially unchanged? It can be stored easily in the computer, recalled when needed, and modified.
3. Directly combining output from quality control and statistical packages into reports eliminates the need for cutting or pasting of computer printouts. This can be done with a few keystrokes instead of being laborious.
4. They improve document control and reduce the time necessary to change documentation. For similar documents, a set of template specs can be created and customized when needed. The basic capabilities to look for in a good word processing system are:
    a. Automatic word wrap at end of line
    b. Deleting and inserting words
    c. Moving and copying blocks of text
    d. Searching documents for a particular string of words
    e. Searching for a string of words and replacing it with another

f. Underlining and boldfacing
   g. Changing a document's format easily
   h. Spelling check
   i. Producing page numbers automatically
   j. Headings and footnotes
   k. Merging material from two or more documents

There are many very good products available for word processing. Below is a list of popular word-processing software in the $100–$500 range that have most of the features necessary for effective word processing. This list is certainly not inclusive. There are many good products available, with more being introduced every day:

   a. Microsoft word (word-key or word-mouse)
   b. WordStar
   c. Multimate
   d. Volkswriter
   e. Wordperfect

6. Get a good communications package if your work involves "talking" to another computer (e.g., your company's mainframe). The primary method used involves using a MODEM (a modulator-demodulator) to send data over telephone lines between computers. The equipment you would probably need would be:

   a. An RS232 output part on the PC
   b. MODEM (Hayes, Racal-Vadic, Bell, etc.)
   c. Communications software (PC-intercom, Crosstalk, etc.)
   d. Telephone line

Some mainframes, notably the IBM, may require a board that allows terminal emulation. This is because the IBM mainframes use bisynchronous communication and an EBCDIC character set instead of the asynchronous communication and ASC11 character set used by most other computers, including the IBM PCs.

7. Try to modularize your system so that parts of it can be reused for other applications. This helps a lot, as you do not have to spend time redoing what has been done before. You just reuse it.

8. Develop separate systems for different applications, as this insures portability, and an error in one application will not affect the others.

9. Last but not least: In choosing any software package, it is usually a good idea to keep certain points in mind.

  a. The package with the most capabilities or the highest price is not necessarily the best for you. Find out what you need before you buy it.
  b. Select a package most suited to your computing abilities. Some packages require programming knowledge.
  c. View a demonstration of the package if possible and try it out yourself. In general, a good package should be usable after a few minutes of coaching by the vendor or instruction manual. Trade shows, seminars, and sales representatives offer excellent opportunities for instruction.
  d. Find out if the package will handle problems like missing data effectively.
  e. Check out the limits of the package.
  f. Check if the package will create files that can be used by other systems if your work requires it.
  g. Talk to associates already using the package. In lieu of this, try to obtain a review of the package in magazines such as *BYTE* or *Quality Progress,* or by a review team such as SIGSTAT.

Be open-minded to change. Probably the fastest-changing area today is software. Take time to find out what is available before settling on something.

Implementing Computer-Aided Quality Information Systems

A wealth of information exists about the capability to produce goods in an organization. A tremendous amount of data has been collected about scrap, rework, machine down-time, and many other characteristics of the products. Unfortunately, most of the data is filed away with a little or no analysis. The original purpose of the collection data may be known or unknown, but it is definitely clear that better utilization of existing information can be made with the help of computers today. Some major corporations have recognized the need for a computerized quality information system and have written customized software to collect and analyze manufacturing data. General Electric, IBM, Hewlett Packard, and other major companies have already implemented this type of computerized quality system in many of their operations. In the automated factories of tomorrow, computer-aided design systems will communicate directly with the computer-aided manufacturing system. It is necessary to add computer-aided quality-assurance systems to close the loop and augment the CAD/CAM system. Another important factor in using computer-aided quality systems is the competition with Japan. We must substitute the effective use of computers to counteract the effective and sophisticated paperwork for statistical quality control, which leaves quality control engineers and technicians plenty of time.

There are a number of areas in organizations where one can implement computer-aided quality systems effectively. Some of them are listed here:

1. Gauge control
2. Supplier quality performance
3. Parts and product performance
4. Statistical analysis
5. Quality-improvement inspection plans
6. Data collection systems
7. Quality costs
8. Quality management
9. Reliability analyses
10. Special applications

1. Gauge Control

Every organization uses a number of gauges to manufacture products. A great deal of scrap and rework may result if gauges are not calibrated periodically. Gauge control must serve two purposes: recalibration and usage file.

Recalibration systems should help to generate the data on previous gauge calibration, and future calibration needs the usage system, which should maintain the complete history of all gauges in the organization and also the status of the gauge, such as active, inactive, lost, defective, or obsolete.

One should use some of the following objectives in establishing a gauge-control system:

   a. Maintain measurement standards traceable to the National Bureau of Standards.
   b. Maintain working gauges traceable to the company's standards.
   c. Remove from our system gauges throughout the division that are worn beyond usable limits.

d. Inventory all company-owned gauges to eliminate purchase duplication and help meet emergency gauging requirements.
e. Train personnel on the importance of good gauge maintenance to better utilize gauging equipment available within the division.
f. Certify new gauging purchased by the division prior to installing it within our system.
g. Certify all gauges and tooling purchased by the division and assigned for use in a vendor's plant.
h. Maintain a usable, noncumbersome record system on all gauging within the system.
i. Become fully prepared to meet governmental standards for possible future government contracts.
j. Establish measurement credibility with outside suppliers of purchased items and contract manufacturing.
k. Assist in developing the technical climate, the necessary skills, and the understanding to cope with the higher precision requirements now being encountered.

2. Supplier Quality Performance

Details regarding vendor quality information have already been discussed in Chapter 8. Quality information regarding the vendor can be listed in the quality information system, stored, and then can be used in the following areas:

a. Incoming inspection
b. Returning material information
c. Vendor certification and rating
d. Statistical information analysis

3. Parts and Product Performance

Organizations generally keep a number of records on parts quality and product performance. Service industries do the same on the services they offer and their evaluation. Data is collected on part characteristics and about each phase of the manufacturing process. The information can also be collected on variable and attributable data. When historical part data is collected in an organizational manner, statistical analysis techniques can be applied to measure process capabilities and other statistical parameters.

Many organizations today are also trying to phase the input from CMM directly to the computers. This vast data input allows quick and efficient data analysis.

4. Statistical Analysis

One of the most popular uses of computers is to analyze vast amounts of data efficiently and effectively in a short time. While the Japanese learned the basics of statistics from Americans, they have absorbed the methods and are using them to constantly improve their quality. In the United States we neglected the basics behind the proper use and considered them a management tool. We can still improve performance with the help of computers. However, it is essential that organizations take interest and insist on the use of statistics as one of the management's as well as the workers' tools. Most management information systems were not designed to capture truly useful data about the manufacturing process. Process capability studies require knowledge about man-machine combinations, time of manufacture, variable data associated with the process, and most importantly, statistical techniques.

There are a number of statistical techniques that are useful in improving quality and productivity. Some of them are listed below:

a. Process capability studies (Cp and independent Cpk)
b. Tolerance analysis
c. Control charts
d. Multivary charts
e. Repression analysis
f. Precontrol

Other techniques are also listed in other chapters. (See Chapter 14).

Computer-aided quality systems also help to generate other graphical forms such as frequency tables, histograms, control charts, multivary charts, and quality costs. Data can be captured in real time and acted upon before scrap is generated. The graphic techniques help management to understand the underlying trends and make proper decisions based on facts.

5. Quality-Improvement Inspection Plans

Every company manufactures or purchases a number of parts. The necessary information must be given to the operators so the quality parts can be manufactured or purchased. Similarly, design changes or improvements should be processed immediately and the information transformed quickly to the operating leads through inspection plans. Properly implemented computer systems help tremendously in achieving these objectives.

6. Quality Management

This is another vast, fertile field where an effective quality-information system can help an organization achieve an on-line, red-line decision-making (management by exception) ability in order to manage the business effectively. Quality uses can be collected on red-line bars; failure data and other data can be corrected similarly to make ongoing, effective decisions. There is really no limit to what one can do in future effective computer use.

The following table briefly outlines the areas that one can use on various computer-aided quality-management systems.

APPLICATION AREA	BENEFITS
Quality costs	Manage quality improvement effectively Improve quality of products and services
Statistical process	High, predictable yield
Product monitoring and analysis	Lower production costs; reduced rework costs; lower scrap levels; reduced labor costs
Quality improvement plans and instructions	Respond to changes and improved communication
Product and services	Less defects
Testing	Optimize test procedures Improve purchased-part quality
Vendor quality Management	Reduce number of vendors Improved purchased-part quality
Gauge control	Less scrap Improved quality
Reliability analysis	Lower warranty costs
Process capability analysis	Less scrap Effective manufacturing operations
Quality Circles	Improve communication Improve quality

Key Considerations in Implementing Computer-Aided Quality Information Systems

Information Systems

The use of computers is still new; many people are not completely familiar with all phases of computer usage. You should keep in mind some of the following considerations in applying and implementing a quality information system.

1. Try to use menu-driven programs.
2. Plan for the total integrated quality information system. However, each unit should be independent and should run on its own without causing too much disturbance in the total operation.
3. Try to organize and plan for real time system.
4. Use graphs and charts as much as possible.
5. The system should be quick and should perform most of the mathematics.
6. The system should be able to receive many inputs from many different sources.
7. The system should be reliable.
8. The system should be compatible with a hardware/software package used with existing coordinating measuring machines and other measuring equipment in use in the organization.
9. System should be compatible with large-scale computers in use in the organization.
10. System and software should be from a source that has an established record and reputability in the business.

Keys to Effective Quality Information Systems

One should keep in mind the following key elements of effective quality information systems in designing new systems:

1. Use the KISS principle (Keep It Simple and Sweet).
2. Use graphs, charts, and trend lines. (People can read and grasp the reports quickly.)
3. Always review the quality reports and get rid of useless ones.
4. Expand use of computers.
5. Expand use of on-line, on-time reporting.

In short, one should always try to implement information systems quickly; they will help to satisfy the objectives discussed at the beginning of the chapter.

EVALUATE YOUR ORGANIZATION

		OK	AVERAGE	EXCELLENT
1.	How are quality costs reported and analyzed?			
2.	How are quality costs used?			
3.	How is the data collected? (Is an automated data-collection system used?)			
4.	How are information from field-product quality and customer complaints used?			
5.	How are the gauges and other data-collection systems checked (gauge control)?			
6.	Are the inspection instruction sheets useful?			
7.	How are the systems for poor-quality products (hold orders, engineering deviations, rework instructions)?			
8.	How are quality standards established? Are they revised?			
9.	How does the system measure quality level (quality index)?			

CAIR (Computer-Aided Inspection and Reporting Systems) has improved the productivity of our quality engineers. Our quality engineers are now able to analyze data of complex process studies in a few minutes instead of hours required with manual analysis techniques. This has resulted in a 15-fold increase in the number of capability studies in our factory units.

W. S. Grehner,
Quality Research Department,
Deere and Co., Moline, Illinois
(*Iron Age,* Sept. 5, 1983, p. 59)

Chapter Eleven
SERVICE QUALITY

Recently I happened to talk with a lady who had bought a foreign-built car. Even though the car was built properly, she faced the problem of a poor electrical connection, which caused her inconvenience for several months. The dealer was nice to her; and every time she complained he checked the car, cleaned it, polished it, and returned it to her without fixing the problem. The lady wrote to the main office in the foreign country. To her surprise, within two weeks she got a reply, then a company serviceman flew to her town. He finally detected the problem by finding a loose coil inside the door, which was grounding the electrical system. The lady told me this story proudly, praising the auto company. This is what is called *customer service*. Many times customers would like to complain, but either because of the time factor or apathy, people don't usually complain unless they have to. Things are beginning to change. Customers are more cost conscious, and in the buyer's market, they have more power and more choice than they did in the 1950s and 1960s.

It is necessary for an organization to see the customer as the most important person in its business. Customers are not generally dependent on one company any more; there are several choices for the customer, and an organization must uphold its reputation to earn repeat business. Many times organizations look at complaints as an interruption or a bother. They should realize that the customer is doing them a favor by calling and reporting the defects so that they can be corrected as soon as possible. The

FIGURE 11-1

Wheel diagram with O.Q.I. at center and segments:
1. Quality Planning and Policy
2. Quality Deployment
3. Quality for New Products (Quality of Design)
4. Vendor Quality Control
5. Manufacturing Quality Control
6. Computer-Aided Quality Systems
7. (unlabeled)
8. Service Quality
9. (unlabeled)
10. (unlabeled)

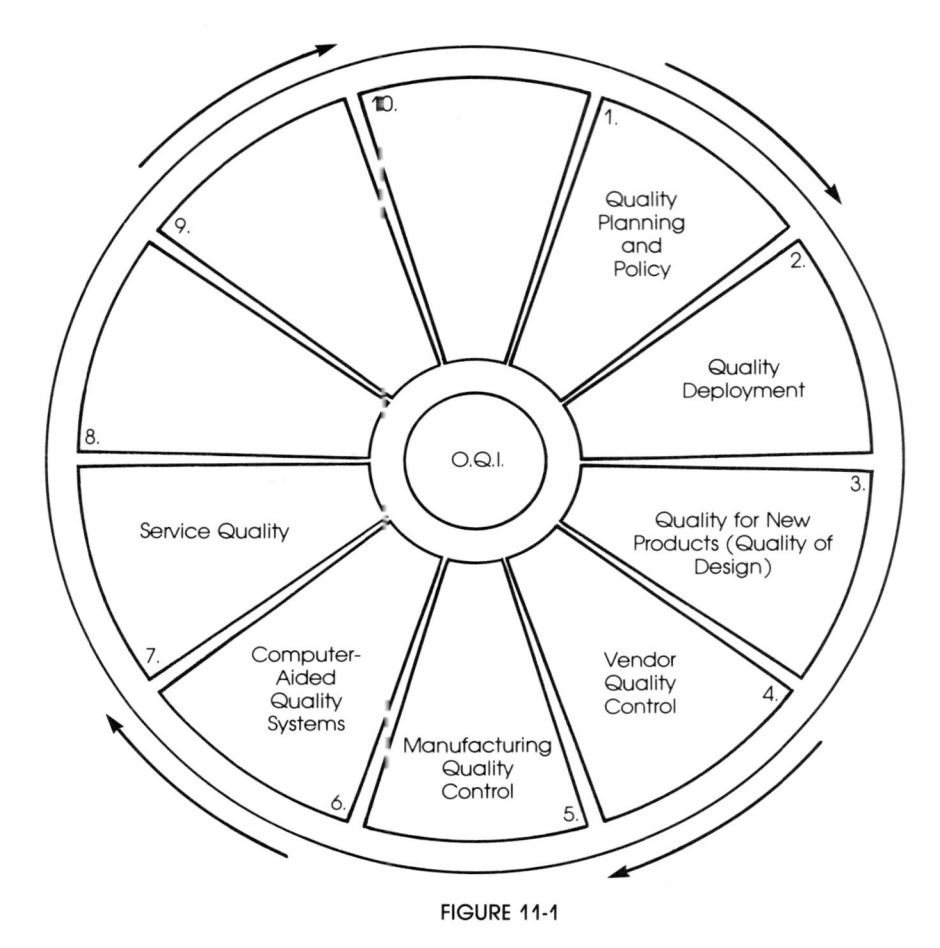

customer is the one who is creating a business through his or her needs; he or she indirectly pays the salaries of the employees. Hence, we have to realize that the customer deserves the most courteous attention—he or she is the supporter of the business.

Current Situation

When you look at the conditions that exist today, what you see is not too encouraging. About half of the organizations give importance to customer complaints, while the other half view customer complaints as a bother and handle them poorly. Sometimes extended warranties are encouraged, as they help an organization cover up defects. In the long run, however, they create problems, since many customers do not like to pay extra and will go somewhere else.

In general, customers are most unhappy with the following:

1. Defective products
2. Product not performing what was proposed
3. Late deliveries of parts
4. Poor or incomplete service
5. Costly service
6. Additional unnecessary service
7. No service for the products sold

You can add many other reasons to the list. People usually do not like to complain unless they are really unhappy and need someone's attention. All the reasons listed above do deserve attention. They are caused by poor manufacturing quality or design quality or incomplete testing of products and services. The differences that exist among the same products are due to variations caused by man, machines, methods, and materials, as well as many other communications or incomplete procedural problems. An organization must offer good services by minimizing complaints; this can be done by following some of the following steps to improve customer relations:

1. Make sure customer contact and treatment are the highest caliber, thereby establishing trust.
2. Reply immediately when failure occurs; be honest.
3. Analyze failures to prevent recurrence and to improve performance.
4. Always treat the customer like royalty.
5. Use customers' input to improve a new product or service.

Every organization should carefully study the following aspects of service quality:

1. Reliability analysis
2. Safety analysis
3. Product liability
4. Maintainability and availability analysis
5. Completeness of services

1. Reliability Analysis

The word *reliability* originally came into being to emphasize the need for satisfactory product performance over a period of time. Reliability is defined by AGREE (Advisory Groups on Reliability of Electronic Equipment) as follows: "Reliability is the probability of performance without failure of a specified function under given conditions for a specified period of time."

This definition indicates that reliability is a probability, and probabilities need to be defined based on the function, environmental conditions, and recognized operating time. Generally, reliability takes into consideration the various operating conditions that products face in the real world. Unreliable products cause downtime, inconveniences, increases in cost, safety hazards, and in some cases, lack of security. Reliability can be analyzed in four ways. Inherent reliability consists of reliability at the design stages. Predicted or estimated reliability is known as reliability of components. Assembly reliability is estimated through known reliability of the components and its effect on the assembly operation; finally, demonstrated reliability is the one that must be shown through hypothetical testing.

There are several books on this topic; you should study reliability very carefully to improve the quality of products in the operational area.

2. Safety Analysis

There is a considerable overlap between safety analysis and reliability analysis. In general, in systems safety, you are trying to build a product or service that is free from conditions that can cause death, injuries, illness, or damage to the equipment or human beings. Unsafe operation could take place due to operator error, poor design, or poor maintenance. In some cases, products or services could be misused by the end users, which could cause injuries or human or economic losses. Hence, it is essential that the safety aspect be considered in the early stages of product design and manufacture.

3. Product Liability

The American Insurance Association has observed that in 1963 there were 50,000 product liability suits countrywide. In 1971 the number of product liability suits rose dramatically to 500,000; and the prediction has been made that in 1985 there will be 1,000,000 product liability suits. Today there are thousands of product liability case studies that can be read or watched on television. Every day product liability costs are increasing due to consumer interest, demands for improved quality, publicity about lawsuits and large awards, along with the encouragement of the law profession. Companies are sued because of manufacturing defects, design defects, marketing deficiencies, or the inability to perform an adequate job due to product deterioration.

SERVICE QUALITY 165

There are a number of reasons for legal suits; however, they can be divided into two types: pure negligence or strict liability. In order to minimize the product liability suits, some of the following actions are recommended:

1. Management should define safety requirements.
2. Products should be reviewed from the point of view of safety.
3. Field feedbacks and analysis should be thoroughly analyzed and used in product tests.
4. Engineers should use injury data and adhere to safety standards for the product.
5. Manufacturing and quality control should provide good instruction sheets, collect information, record it properly, and maintain records for future use. (Good documentation helps to minimize the risk of large awards.)
6. Marketing should develop and insist on the use of safety and warning labels and should not publicize something that is not promised.

4. Serviceability, Maintainability, and Availability Analysis

It is necessary for an organization to understand the concepts of maintainability and availability of its products. Serviceability means the ease with which products can be repaired or assembled or disassembled. In maintainability and availability of its products. Serviceability means the ease consider the operational use of the equipment or product. Even though these three aspects are interrelated, each has different means and a different role in the product quality.

5. Completeness of the Service

Often, services are performed haphazardly. The customer expects a quality product and he or she also expects quality service. I have experienced, in some cases, taking back the same equipment three or four times before it is fixed properly. A customer should not have an unpleasant surprise when he or she receives the bills. Today, more than ever before, everyone is cost conscious; there is a need to watch all repair work very closely. However, this does not mean one should take share costs and make the customer unhappy with poor service in addition to having to pay for part of the expenses.

What Can We Do to Improve the Quality of Services

In the previous chapter I have already discussed some ideas in this regard. You can use the following additional suggestions as necessary in your operation.

1. Early Closed-Loop Complaint System

Customers generally complain in four different ways. Some write letters, some call on the phone, some come and see you, and some send the message through public media. It is necessary for an organization to collect all these details and sort them systematically. With the advent of computers (major ones as well as personal computers), large data banks can be handled effectively without too many delays. Once the data system is finalized, priorities and projects should be established based on data analysis, and work should be assigned to the proper personnel. Periodic reviews and reports are essential to keep track of what is happening to complaints; the objective should be to minimize complaints and eliminate repetition as much as possible.

2. Monthly Meetings

I have found it useful to hold monthly meetings with engineering, manufacturing, purchasing, and quality-control personnel. To conduct effective meetings, you must remember the following points:

1. Meetings should not last more than one hour.
2. The agenda must be published.
3. Work must be assigned.
4. Everyone should participate in the meeting.

3. Failure to Analyze Parts

When parts have failed or are defective, there is a general tendency to send new parts; the defective parts are discarded by the customer. Very rarely do organizations require defective parts to be returned and analyzed. This type of system not only creates misuse of parts, but the organization misses the opportunity to learn what went wrong with parts, hence the same problems keep recurring due to incomplete oral or written information that is sent to the organizational headquarters. Again, I would like to emphasize that it is essential to check defective parts and find the root cause of the problem through statistical analysis.

4. Use of Statistical Tools

To find the real causes of defective parts, I recommend that you learn statistical tools that will help you to locate them. The three statistical tools that are used most commonly in such analysis are:

1. FMEA. Failure mode effect analysis attempts to predict all possible effects caused by the failure of a component. This technique can bring to light unexpected product design weakness. You can use the following steps in analysis:

1. Collect data and prepare form.
2. List part name and number.
3. List all possible failures.
4. List all effects of failure.
5. List critical areas based on safety.
6. Look at the best correction and how to improve design.
7. Assign probability if possible.
8. Check cost value.
9. Prepare cost-benefit analysis if possible.
10. Select the most feasible corrections for improvement.

2. Fault tree analysis (FTA). This is the opposite of FMEA. It starts with the undesired event and works back to the possible causes of failure. This method becomes a shopping list of probable causes for each symptom of system failure. You can use the following steps in fault tree analysis:

1. Identify top event (a fault or failure).
2. Write other events in parallel.
3. Review analysis.
4. Determine where corrective action is desired.
5. Follow up to see if it helped to correct the fault or failure.
6. Repeat FTA if necessary. One can read the use of this technique in *Quality Circles Master Guide* (Prentice-Hall, Inc., 1982, p. 137).

3. Weibull analysis. This is another important statistical technique, which was discovered by Professor E. Weibull in the nineteenth century. This statistical method helps tremendously in analyzing failure data in general and predicting statistically the performance of products in actual use. The Weibull distribution is a generalized exponential function that determines the origin, mean, and frequency of a set of data. More details regarding its use and applications can be found in statistical books.

5. Visits to Customers and Dealers

Many times complaint data which may not be complete is received on the phone or by letter. In some cases the customer may not be able to describe the defect correctly. Hence, I feel that visits to customers or dealers should be an integral part of an ongoing quality-improvement programs. These visits can also be planned to dealers or distribution centers. This type of exchange of visits also helps to improve communication and goodwill with customers. Better relationships always improve the use of a product.

6. Visits by Quality Control Personnel and Product or Service Designers or Researchers

This is another useful and effective tool in improving the quality of products and services. Often new products are invented and designed without realizing their use, needs, and serviceability or maintainability. This type of visit by designers helps them to understand the other side and the customers' needs and expectations.

7. Quality Costs Analysis and Ongoing Programs to Reduce External Quality Costs

Organizations also need to collect cost information on failures. I have discussed the importance of quality costs and their analysis in Appendix B. Warranty costs are a part of total quality costs; they comprise the major share in most organizations. It is necessary that once the magnitude of warranty costs is realized, it is essential to devise a system to reduce them. Appendix B shows the step-by-step procedures that one can follow in this type of analysis.

8. Improve Perception of Quality

In order to improve the perception of quality by the customer, it is necessary for an organization to provide distribution channels in all kinds of support to perform professional distribution. The support may include timely responses to inquiries, descriptive product brochures, product samples, technical backup when required, training seminars, pricing, and other details.

Regular meetings should take place between sales, distribution, and warranty departments. Periodic surveys of products are necessary to obtain feedback, instead of waiting until a customer complains about the product.

These surveys could be formed; they could consist of comprehensive interviews. The results should be tabulated and distributed to all concerned parties. Another important aspect in improving customer relations is the quick settlement of small claims. This helps to create trust and better publicity through the customers' channel.

EVALUATE YOUR ORGANIZATION

1. Our organization performs periodic surveys on our products or services.	Rarely	Sometimes	All the time
2. Our organization involves engineers, financial personnel, or other personnel in resolving customer complaints.	Rarely	Sometimes	All the time
3. Our organization insists that failed parts or poor-quality goods be returned for further analysis.	Rarely	Sometimes	All the time
4. Our organization regards customer complaints as high priority; the complaints are seen as a source of valuable information.	Rarely	Sometimes	All the time
5. Our organization has established systematic procedures to handle product complaints and recalls.	Rarely	Sometimes	All the time
6. Our organization always work to reduce warranty costs.	Rarely	Sometimes	All the time
7. Our organization always tries to see from the customer's point of view.	Rarely	Sometimes	All the time
8. Our organization tries to improve customer service policies to satisfy the customer's complaints.	Rarely	Sometimes	All the time
9. Our organization has very good procedures to handle customers' complaints.	Rarely	Sometimes	All the time
10. Our organization has a well-established early warning system.	Rarely	Sometimes	All the time

Note: The author has developed more than 300 questions to analyze organizations.

On the average, a customer who has had an unpleasant experience with a business will tell nine or ten other people. And about 30% will tell more than 20 other people. This negative word of mouth can be very harmful to your business.

Direct Selling Education Foundation,
Washington, D.C.

Chapter Twelve
QUALITY AUDITS

Even though quality-control audits are common in Japan, they are still in the evaluation stage in the Western world. In many organizations you will find some kind of system for quality audits. However, their actual use and importance are questionable. Mr. Asaka has compared the quality-control audit and health management system very nicely. In health management, a person goes to a medical clinic, examines the system, checks for causes, gets the medicine, recovers from the disease, and keeps himself in good condition. Of course, one should also use preventive medicine such as exercise, good nutrition, and so on. Quality control and quality audits work similarly for an organization: Quality audits are conducted to check the causes of poor quality, action is taken for correction, the process is improved, and the organization is kept healthy and quality-minded at all times.

In the narrow sense, auditing is the process of checking and verifying records prepared by others. In the financial area it is used to check accounting records and profit-and-loss accounts—or in other words, to check the financial status of the company.

Quality audits generally are performed to investigate the following:

1. To find out if the quality policies of a company meet its quality standards adequately.
2. To check if the data found in performing quality audits represent the company's efforts in building quality products.

FIGURE 12-1

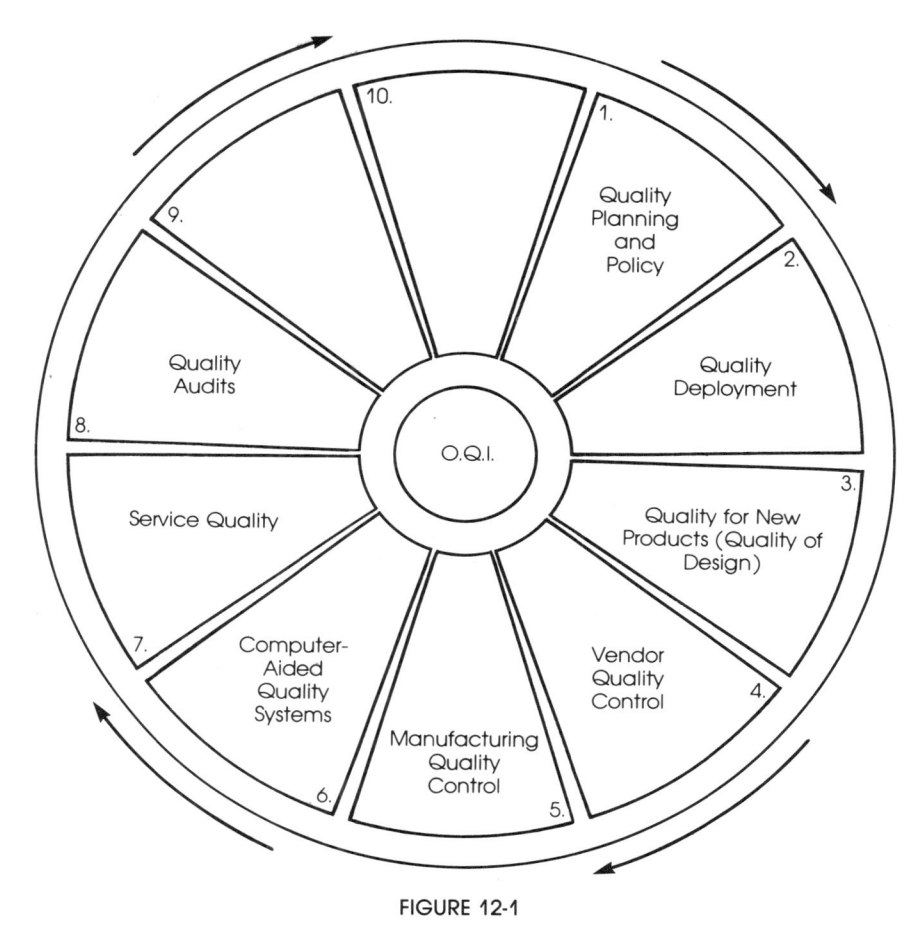

3. To make sure that products meet the specifications and insure that plans, systems, and procedures meet quality policies and goals.

Joseph Juran helps us with a general definition of quality audits in the *Quality Control Handbook*[1]: "Quality audit is an independent review conducted to compare some aspect of quality performance with a standard for that performance."

In line with traditional techniques of accounting, it may examine both methodology and results. It is not an alternative to inspection. Inspection is a function which must first be done by the individuals performing an operation and second by an independent individual. On the other hand, a quality audit reviews the effects of the actions of people and/or decisions made by the people involved in a product. It progresses through research, design, development, manufacturing, packaging, installation, and consumption

[1] *Quality Control Handbook, 2nd Edition.* New York, McGraw Hill, 1962.

stages. An internal quality audit generally involves such informal functions as the design, development, vendor control, manufacturing, and service of the products.

External Audits

External audits are more common in Japan. One of the first quality audits was established in 1951; the best organization was awarded the Deming Prize. Today, there are more than one Deming prizes offered for various areas of industries. Japan has also started another audit for those organizations that were awarded the Deming Prize, and the best organization in this audit is given the Japan Quality Control Prize. There is also another ex-

FIGURE 12-2

TYPES OF QUALITY AUDITS

There are a number of different types of quality audits used by various organizations. Some of these are called management system audit, process audit, product audit, vendor audit, external audit. This table shows the general outline of the quality audits.

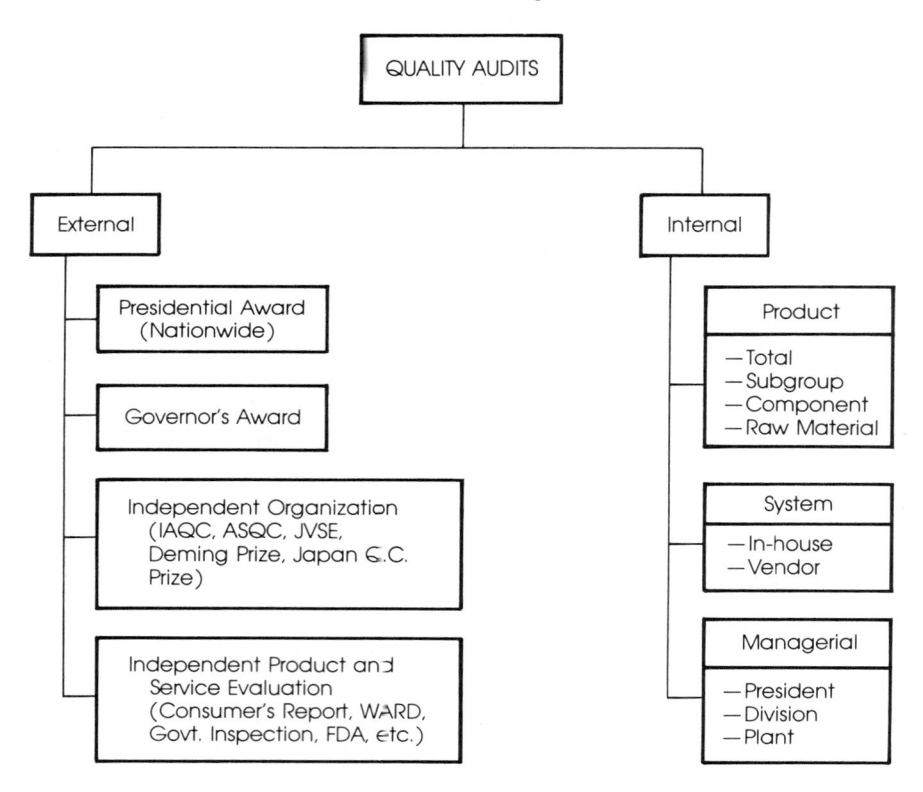

```
                         QUALITY AUDITS
                        /              \
                  External            Internal
                     |                   |
        ┌────────────┤                   ├──────────────┐
        │                                               │
  Presidential Award                               Product
   (Nationwide)                                    — Total
        │                                          — Subgroup
        │                                          — Component
  Governor's Award                                 — Raw Material
        │
        │                                          System
  Independent Organization                         — In-house
   (IAQC, ASQC, JVSE,                              — Vendor
    Deming Prize, Japan Q.C.
    Prize)                                         Managerial
        │                                          — President
  Independent Product and                          — Division
   Service Evaluation                              — Plant
   (Consumer's Report, WARD,
    Govt. Inspection, FDA, etc.)
```

ternal auditing system called the JIS Mark. This mark gives a national guarantee of quality to Japanese products, and the authorization is confirmed by a reexamination every three years for the purpose of improvement.

In the United States, external audits are performed in various organizations. Societies like IAQC (International Association of Quality Circles) and ASQC (American Society for Quality Control), try this on a small scale. But there is no widespread publicity or recognition given to the prizes or audits. Many products are evaluated independently by organizations such as Ward Reports or Consumer's Union.

Nationwide quality product evaluation is helpful in improving the quality of products on a large scale and in getting customers' attention immediately. In the United States we need to establish a system whereby external audits and recognition will be publicized widely, resulting in a keen, healthy quality-improvement competition across the nation. The author recommends the following system:

1. Presidential Award. This award should be given in each category of industry by the president of the company. A quality audit system should be established with the help of the commerce department. Those industries that have received awards from the state should be eligible for this award.

2. Gubernatorial Award. This award is similar to the Presidential Award based on quality audits within each state. Each state should give this award to industries by category, and the evaluation should be made independently.

More details can be developed by the governmental official. A similar award system can be established in each state. Award money should be split fifty-fifty with half the money going to the government and the other half to the participating industries. Participation should be voluntary, but publicity and recognition should be nationwide.

Internal Audits

Internal audits can be divided into three different categories, as listed here:

1. Systems audit
2. Product audit
3. Managerial audit

1. Systems Audit. System audits are performed to evaluate and confirm that all functions of the company are following its quality program policy. In addition, these audits insure the effectiveness of the quality procedures that make up the program. For the effective performance of a quality audit, it should be scheduled so that it is not pushed aside by day-to-day activities.

Two types of quality auditing methods are frequently used:

1. Auditing *a specific* quality procedure or system.
2. Auditing *all* the procedural activities by departmental function.

In the first method, auditing is done on a step-by step basis by reviewing the procedures in a sequence.

In the second method, each procedural activity is divided by departmental function and audit instructions are made for each. In short, it is "auditing by discipline."

Regardless of which method is used, specific, accurate instructions on how to perform the audit are necessary for it to be effective.

2. Product audit. A product audit is done mainly to let the management know how good the quality of their products is. The point of view of the customer is being used in this audit. Customers' opinions are used to evaluate the product, with customer surveys or input from sales or service personnel helping in this regard.

A product audit shouldn't be used to replace the final inspection procedure. It should be performed as if you are looking from the customer's point of view to see the various features the customer expects in a product. Customer satisfaction and needs should be evaluated based on product and service performance, reliability, and acceptable visual requirements.

To accomplish this, one can use various quality audit forms and analyze the product periodically. Such forms are discussed in other parts of this book.

3. Managerial quality/audit. This type of audit can be performed at three different levels:

1. Presidential audit
2. Divisional or plant manager audit
3. Departmental-head audit

An audit group comprised of executives (top managers) headed by the president of the organization visits each sales office to find out the degree to which the organization's policies and the promotion of quality programs are being carried out and to eliminate any obstacles. The head of each sales office carries out a quality audit in his or her office, and the department heads in turn do the same in their departments. To go a little further, it is recommended that quality audits be done also in the organizations of vendors who supply parts.

This managerial quality audit is usually begun when a quality program is in the introductory stage, but today many organizations make it a regular function; the number of audits is increasing tremendously. The detailed quality-audit forms for this type of analysis can be prepared by the quality auditor, using past experience and quality objectives and goals of the organization.

Quality Auditor

It is not easy to perform quality audits in any organization. No matter whether you perform a system audit, product audit, or managerial audit, the evaluation and implementation of results takes a long time and sometimes becomes impossible due to conflicts of interests between the various departments. It is crucial that an organization select the proper personnel to conduct quality audits. Some of the responsibilities of a good quality auditor are listed here:

1. He or she should be objective.
2. He or she should use judgment and some kind of approved index system.
3. He or she should recommend corrective actions.
4. He or she should possess good technical knowledge and a skill for asking proper questions.
5. He or she should understand human relations and be gentle but firm in expressing opinions.
6. He or she should realize that conflicts do take place between people as well as between different departments; he or she must be careful in handling delicate situations properly.

Robert Wachhiak, has listed Ten Commandments for Quality Auditors in his paper that was presented to ASQC's 32nd Annual Technical Conference in Chicago in 1978. They are:

1. Know the objectives.
2. Know the controls.
3. Know the standards.
4. Know the population.
5. Know the facts.
6. Know the cause.
7. Know the effect.
8. Know the people.
9. Know how and when to communicate.
10. Know the modern methods.

Some of the dos and don'ts that quality auditors should remember while trying to perform their jobs effectively are listed here:

Dos

1. Always be specific and discuss details related to the topic that is under audit.
2. Ask proper questions to learn the facts; make sure agreements are reached during the discussion. Do not leave subjects open-ended.
3. Compliment on a good job; keep it straightforward.
4. Use KISS principle (Keep It Simple and Sweet).
5. Review findings with the head of the area, location, or plant.
6. Be cautious about unnecessary wasted time and irrelevant discussion.

Don'ts

1. Don't argue based on your own opinion.
2. Don't assume information that is not shown and make remarks based on unknown facts.
3. Don't compare different plants or different locations or use them as part of the discussion.
4. Don't get upset if you are ridiculed.
5. Don't pretend that you know everything.
6. Don't pull any surprises in your final report.
7. Don't visit unexpectedly or change your visit without proper notification.

Major Function of the Quality Auditor

As previously discussed, quality audits can be performed at various levels by various groups. Systems must be organized effectively so that quality audits are used to their fullest extent. One way to achieve this purpose is through a two-man team responsible for divisional or companywide quality audit programs, reporting directly to the highest level. Generally, this team reports to the vice-president of quality, who is generally chairman of the quality council.

The major function of this two-man team is to perform and carry out all plans and objectives as directed by the quality council so as to constantly improve the quality of the products and productivity of the organization. The team collects the data on quality performance and compiles the results, which are presented to the quality council on a quarterly basis. The team performs quality audits throughout the organization. My experience indicates that unless some such system is implemented, quality audits and their use do not seem effective in the United States.

Major Responsibilities of the Quality Auditor

1. To establish and maintain a schedule of periodic evaluations, including all functions and facilities affecting the quality of the products made by the organization.

2. To develop a list of items to be audited for each facility and revise and update it at least once per year. This list must include all areas affecting the quality system—for example, design, manufacturing, purchased items, testing, inspection, quality reporting, service, customer relations, and so on.

3. To visit all facilities within the organization several times throughout the year and actively participate in auditing the total quality system.

4. To initiate and implement a rating system that is to be applied to the list in item 2, above, so as to formulate conclusions about the areas audited. This rating system must be consistent and flexible so it can be used in all areas of quality audits.

5. To develop and implement a format for reporting the results of the quality audits to management and the quality council.

6. To contact personally the manager or responsible person of each facility audited to go over the results of any audits that were performed in that facility and to solicit comments and corrective actions to be included in the final report to the quality council.

7. To establish and maintain histories of any and all audits performed. This history file will serve as a reference to show the direction of trends for that facility.

8. To update continually all of the above listed procedures at least annually.

9. To maintain a professional attitude at all times, for this position represents the whole division as an audit function.

How to Perform an Effective Quality-Control Audit

It is not easy to perform an effective audit unless the quality-control auditor plans and conducts his activities systematically. You can use the following steps in preparing for audits:

1. Planning—In this step, the auditor should schedule the visits, notify the proper personnel about the intention, and check for any conflicts.

2. Agreement—Agreement should be clear regarding the intention of the quality-control audits and checking procedure. One should also get agreement regarding corrective action procedure.

3. Verification—The quality-control auditor should visit the plants or locations personally, go through the agreed procedure, and then report the findings to the local management. Corrective action plans should be reviewed also at this stage.

4. Reporting—A written report should be issued to the concerned parties. A copy should be sent to the quality council for review, if necessary.

5. Follow-up—This step is important. Quality audits should not be an annual visit held sometime by somebody. A systematic follow-up is essential for the success of quality-control audits in any organization.

Keep the following key points in mind for effective quality-control audits:

1. Establish the proper atmosphere.
2. Obtain agreement regarding the quality-control audit procedure.
3. Avoid confrontation during visits.
4. Review quality-control audit results with local authorities.
5. Determine corrective actions.
6. Recommend corrective actions.
7. Issue a formal report and follow it periodically.

Case Study

The following quality audit system and procedure can be used as a guide in preparing a quality audit system for an organization.

S.Q.T. Company Quality Audit System (Purpose)

The purpose of the audit system is to assure that a sufficient quality plan has been established by each facility or function such that

1. If followed, it will produce quality products that are fit for use and safe for operations.
2. Defective products are properly disposed of or reworked to specified standards.
3. Where discrepancies are found, appropriate action is taken to prevent any such product from leaving the plant or to recall the product if that is necessary.

4. Information systems provide data necessary to identify problem areas easily and quantitively.
5. Corrective or preventive actions are taken where necessary and improvements are made as opportunities present themselves.
6. All products conform to print specifications, or a written deviation signed by the proper authority is available.
7. Proper procedures and special instructions are in written form and available to the concerned persons.
8. Quality improvements will be realized through training programs in
    a. job knowledge
    b. product knowledge
    c. Quality Circles
    d. leadership skills
    e. use of statistics

Procedure

I. Establish quality audit system policy-making structure
   A. Policy
   B. Objective
   C. Purpose
   D. Procedures
   E. Schedule and Agendas

II. Set up an annual schedule that will rotate three (3) times per year.

III. Make up an audit checklist for each facility scheduled that will compare it to the standards and directives of the quality council. Each facility or department is required to have its own quality plan, which will be used in the conformance audits.

IV. Develop a rating system for use on the checklist to serve as an indicator of what the degree of effectiveness is for each item. This will probably not be ready for at least a year, and then it is undecided as to what degree we should rate or whether or not to rate at all.

V. Send out announcements to the facilities of our scheduled audits and items that might be evaluated. These announcements will normally be sent out one (1) *month* prior to the audit, but never less than one (1) *week* without prior approval of the facility or department manager.

VI. Review previous reports with the facility manager.

VII. Perform audit.

VIII. Review current audit results with the facility or department manager.

IX. Make up a finished report for use in the next group quality council meeting.

X. Develop and maintain a record of all audits to establish any trends that occur through time.

XI. Review and upgrade the audit system through the direction of the quality council.

XII. Continue quality audits based on agreed schedules.

XIII. Audit plan:

Audits are conducted by the quality auditor, who may be assisted by a management person selected from a facility other than the one being audited. The audits are conducted on-site and cover two major areas.

A. Written Plan

Does the facility/function have a written plan and does it satisfy the requirements of the company policy on quality?

B. Implementation

Is the plan being followed in its entirety?

All areas of involvement must be checked: the shop, inspection, development, engineering, purchasing, marketing, and so on.

The quality auditor is responsible for making arrangements for audits, carrying out the audit, and filing a report on this quality audit policy and procedure.

XIV. Pre-audit:

Become familiar with approved area.

Review prior audit reports to be sure that the current audit includes a recheck of reported deficiencies.

Arrange visit—give at least four to five weeks' notice and advise of expected time involved. Set this up by phone and confirm with a letter. Be sure the plant manager, or whoever the top manager of the facility is, will be available for exit interview.

XV. During audit:

Arrange preliminary meeting with manager and quality control manager of function to be audited to explain audit procedure.

Meet with quality control manager and check quality plan versus implementing procedures. Tour facility and observe if procedures are actually being used.

Continue check of plan and procedures as necessary.

Prior to leaving, review findings with manager of quality assurance and other department heads who may have been involved with a discrepancy or to compliment them.

XVI. Post-audit:

Write report and distribute it as follows: Address it to general manager, with copies to the division general manager, quality-control manager, audit system file, and quality council.

The auditor is responsible for determining the requirements for copies. We do not encourage more than are necessary because they are confidential data and should be somewhat restricted as far as the plant manager is concerned.

XVII. Audit reports:

Audit reports will be based on the principles in the quality audit program. All items will be covered and identified as to the degree of implementation (poor, marginal, qualified, and outstanding). Comments should be objective, factual, and in perspective with the total activity. Recommendations will be included under the section or item to which they refer.

Comments relating to previously reported discrepancies will be included on the report along with current comments on a given plan element, not separated.

A summary statement can be included, if desirable, either at the beginning or end of the audit report. Should include request for 30-day reply.

XVIII. Quality training:

Training will be provided, through the quality audit system, in quality-related subject areas. Requests for such training are to be submitted to the division quality auditor, quality-control director, or the vice-president of quality circle.

Some of the subject areas are:
1. Quality Circle
2. QC mini-facilitator
3. Machine/process capability studies
4. Basic statistics
   a. frequency distributions
   b. use of sigma
   c. graphs
   d. $\overline{X}$ and R charts
5. Pareto diagrams
6. Sampling
7. Precontrol
8. Quality plans
9. Audit system

10. Total quality system
11. Design of experiments
12. Reliability analysis

Training in other areas can be made available through the quality audit system.

XIX. Sample quality audit report:

S.Q.T. COMPANY

AUDIT SUMMARY SHEET

PLANT_____ DATE_____

Quality Subsystems	Subsystem Score			
	Poor (0–59%)	Marginal (60–79%)	Qualified (80–89%)	Outstanding (90–100%)
1. Management of quality system				
2. New-product introduction				
3. Mfg. quality—casting division				
4. Mfg. quality-machining division				
5. Mfg. quality-assembly division				
6. Purchased-material quality				
7. Quality information				
8. Education and training				
9. Postproduction quality				
10. Quality circles				
11. Gauging and measuring equipment				
12. Special quality studies				
13. Reliability and testing				
TOTALS				

RECOMMENDATIONS:

1. Quality goals, achievements:

2. Quality cases, achievements:

3. Outgoing quality, achievements:

By _____ Date _____

ELEMENT WEIGHTING WORKSHEET

PLANT_____ DATE_____
QUALITY SUBSYSTEM 2. NEW-PRODUCT INTRODUCTION

Quality Element	P	M	Q	O	N/A	Observations	Comments
1. Product specification							
2. Product evaluation program							
3. Feasibility assessment							
4. Product build schedule							
5. Problem list and action plan							
6. Design reviews (I, II, III)							
7. Drawing sign-off							
8. Phase II bill of materials release by engineering quality control and manufacturing							
9. Plan for product acceptance in marketing							
10. Other areas (as required (prototype testing failure analysis)							
11. Quality tables							
12. Cost target control							
13. Process capabilities							
14. Statistical tolerancing							
15. Design of experiments							

184 QUALITY AUDITS

ELEMENT WEIGHTING WORKSHEET

PLANT_____ DATE_____
QUALITY SUBSYSTEM 4. MANUFACTURING QUALITY—MACHINING DIVISION

Quality Element	P	M	G	O	N/A	Observations	Comments
1. Process capability studies							
2. Process sheets							
3. Inspection instructions							
4. Identification							
5. Nonconforming material							
6. Material Review Board							
7. Equipment maintenance							
8. Gauging and calibration							
9. Quality information feedback							
10. Corrective action							
11. Fixtures							
12. Outgoing quality							
13. Quality audit							
14. Handling/storage							
15. Setup approval (use of precontrol)							
16. Visual aids							
17. Operator involvement							
18. Foremen commitment							
19. In-process checks							
20. Receiving inspection							

ELEMENT WEIGHTING WORKSHEET

PLANT_____ DATE_____

QUALITY SUBSYSTEM 8. EDUCATION AND TRAINING

Quality Element	P	M	Q	O	N/A	Observations	Comments
1. Training—operator							
2. Training—foreman							
3. Training needs identification							
4. Work-simplification training							
5. Education and training objective							
6. Inspection training							
7. Maintenance training							
8. Other work-related training							
9. Orientation program							
10. Statistical training (engineering)							
11. Statistical training (manufacturing)							
12. Statistical training (foreman)							
13. Statistical training (operator)							
14. Statistical training (administration)							

Deficiencies of the Quality Audit

Even though a quality audit seems simple and works toward improvement of the organization, in reality things do not happen that way. You may face many problems in conducting effective audits and in trying to implement corrective actions.

Here are some of the obstacles I have experienced in trying to implement quality audit systems in organizations:

1. It takes a long time to get the basic concept accepted in the organization. Many times local management feel that it's a "spying" action and do not cooperate completely.

2. A quality-control auditor is looked on as an outsider and sometimes treated below level, since local personnel think he or she is not capable of completely understanding operations.
3. Quality audits can be abused by the quality-control auditor.
4. Many times corrective actions are not implemented and the quality-control auditor does not receive proper support from top management.
5. Many times reports are incomplete and auditing notes are ignored. When this occurs, management sees the quality-control auditor as a burden, performing an unnecessary function. In bad times, this job is deleted due to ineffective operation and poor understanding of objectives by top management.

Advantages of the Quality Audit

There are several advantages of a properly used quality-audit system in organizations. Organizations that have implemented them for several years in foreign countries and in the United States have reported the following benefits:

1. External audits help to create nationwide quality improvement. (Japan has used the Deming Prize, JIS Mark, and Japan Quality Control Prize in this regard.)
2. Internal quality audits help to promote better understanding of the need for ongoing quality improvement in the organization.
3. Quality audits help to promote use at quality costs.
4. Quality audits also help to locate the weak quality areas in the organization.
5. Managerial quality audits help to establish team spirit in the organization, since management and employees discuss problems openly during quality audits.
6. Quality audits can also be used to measure quality performance in various plants or divisions.
7. Effective quality audits also create a systematic method for implementing corrective actions in the organization.

An effective quality-audit system can have a financial impact in the long run. Some of the financial measures are listed below:

1. Larger market share
2. Higher sales

3. Cost reduction
4. Better return on investment

I hope that in the future, every organization will look to quality-audit systems positively and implements them slowly but surely in order to improve the quality of products and services that are offered to the worldwide market.

EVALUATE YOUR ORGANIZATION

1. Our organization believes in the quality-audit system.

```
    0           5          10
    |-----------|-----------|
    No       Average       Yes
```

2. Our organization uses the quality-audit system effectively.

```
    0           5          10
    |-----------|-----------|
    No       Average       Yes
```

3. Our organization uses external audit input to improve quality of the products and services.

```
    0           5          10
    |-----------|-----------|
    No       Average       Yes
```

4. Our organization uses the corrective action system effectively.

```
    0           5          10
    |-----------|-----------|
    No       Average       Yes
```

5. Informal managerial audits are common in our organization.

```
    0           5          10
    |-----------|-----------|
    No       Average       Yes
```

Note: The author has developed 300 questions to analyze organizations for the quality-improvement process.

There are several other questions in sample case studies in this chapter that can be used to evaluate your organization with respect to effective use of the quality-audit system.

The purposes of Q.C. audits are to improve the office, branch office, workshop, and staff department. The basic Q.C. audit is usually begun when Q.C. is in the introductory state, but today, many companies make it a regular function and are increasing in number.

Tetsuichi Asaka, University of Tokyo

Chapter Thirteen
QUALITY CIRCLES: IMPROVING QUALITY THROUGH PEOPLE INVOLVEMENT

These days the consumer enjoys the freedom of choosing products made by different countries to a greater extent than ever before! Competing in the world market has put an extra burden on all industries; building high-quality products while keeping the production cost low is one of the biggest challenges today's industrial world is facing.

One effective way to improve quality and productivity is through participation of all the employees of an organization. There are many ways managers have used participation to improve the quality and productivity of their organizations. During the last several years I have come across different methods of "people participation" programs, as follows:

1. System management
2. Scanlon plan
3. Japanese management systems
4. Survey feedback
5. Managerial grid
6. Quality of work life
7. Union management cooperative efforts
8. Creation of favorable work climate

FIGURE 13-1

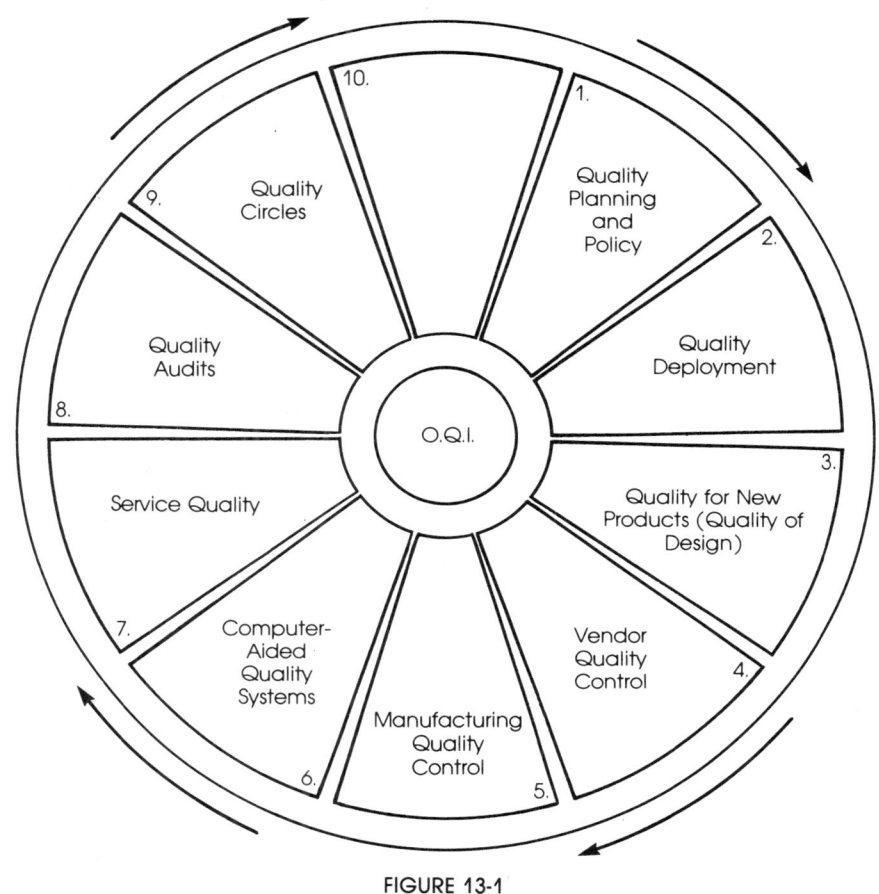

Wheel sectors:
1. Quality Planning and Policy
2. Quality Deployment
3. Quality for New Products (Quality of Design)
4. Vendor Quality Control
5. Manufacturing Quality Control
6. Computer-Aided Quality Systems
7. Service Quality
8. Quality Audits
9. Quality Circles
10. (center: O.Q.I.)

9. New plant design and redesign
10. Design of work in the eighties
11. Team building
12. Autonomous work groups
13. Positive reinforcement
14. Job enrichment
15. "Flexitime"
16. American productivity center work schedule
17. Product business teams
18. Quality Circles
19. Nominal group technique to generate productivity improvement
20. Management by group objectives

The method used most commonly today by more and more industries in the United States is called Quality Circles. We will discuss this fascinating "people-building" philosophy and its relationship to the OQI (Organizational Quality Improvement) program.

The belief behind the concept of Quality Circles is that the people who work daily a particular job know more about it than anyone else. So why not get input from these people to avoid, solve, and control problems that relate to their specific jobs! Nations like Japan are conquering the world market in electronics, automobiles, and many other fields. The reason behind these high-quality products is that Japanese organizations use their employees effectively. They not only employ their hands, but also their brains.

In 1974, upon carefully observing the Japanese participative management system called Quality Circles, Americans began to implement it in their own organizations. And today these pioneer industries—Honeywell, Lockheed, Westinghouse, Mercury Marine, and Hughes Aircraft Corp.—are enjoying the benefits of this people-building philosophy. During the following five years, the growth of this concept exploded. Today there are about 6,000 organizations—manufacturing as well as service industries—that are implementing this philosophy effectively.

What Are Quality Circles?

One of the ways to best define Quality Circles is as follows:

It is a small group of people doing similar work, meeting regularly to identify, analyze, and solve problems in their work area.

The participation in the circle program is strictly voluntary. The major characteristics of Quality Circles are:

1. Circles meet regularly at a scheduled time.
2. Participation is voluntary.
3. Problems are identified, analyzed, and solved as a group.
4. Suggested solutions are then presented to management for final action.

The reasons that I believe the Quality Circle process is so successful are:

1. It uses basic statistics.
2. It uses group solving methods.
3. It creates more job satisfaction.

Introducing Quality Circles in the Organization

Generally speaking, people resist change. It is a well-known fact that people spend 23 percent of their time at work. Hence, when a change in the work surroundings occurs hastily or without the full knowledge of the employees, negative rumors begin to circulate about the new change. Hence, even though the basic ideas of Quality Circles or employee participation programs are exciting and appealing, a sound, carefully thought-out implementation plan is necessary for effective introduction of the Quality Circle program in an organization.

A sound implementation plan should contain the following:

1. Time allowance for research and understanding of the concept
2. Selection of a two-person team
3. Actual attendance of a Quality Circle meeting to see the process in action
4. Making a decision to start
5. Selection of a facilitator/coordinator
6. Letting people form a steering committee
7. Developing plans and goals
8. Presenting the plan both to management and the union
9. Making sure one has adequate training materials
10. Starting training
11. Forming Circles
12. Checking monthly progress

1. Research and Understanding of the Concept

You should research and study available materials—books, audiovisual aids, magazine articles—on this subject before forming a suitable plan for your organization.

2. Selection of a Two-Person Team

A two-person approach has proved to be successful in various organizations. Two people supplement each other in work as well as in times of sickness or any other emergencies. More people can be added as the program grows bigger.

3. Attendance of Quality Circle Meetings

You should visit an organization and witness a Circle meeting. Seeing the actual operation of the Quality Circle is extremely helpful in planning and organizing the program.

4. Making a Decision to Start

The information gathered by a two-person team should be presented formally to the management before any decision is made about initiating the Quality Circle program in your organization. Such a presentation should include:

- Advantages and disadvantages—pros and cons of the Quality Circle program
- Funding required
- Training required
- Other implementation details

5. Selection of a Facilitator/Coordinator

This is a key position in the Circle program. A facilitator's responsibilities include planning and organizing the program, training the members and Circle leaders, attending all the Circle meetings, measuring the program's progress, and so on.

6. Forming a Steering Committee

The steering committee is generally made up of representatives from various departments in an organization. Representatives from each major department should be included.

7. Developing Plans and Goals

The planning phase involves planning for training, developing materials, and selecting areas that should initially get involved in the program.

8. Presenting the Plan to Management and the Union

An information session with middle management and union leaders should be planned once the goals and plans of the program are decided. This will familiarize them with what is involved in the program, and all the doubts and questions will be answered openly. This is important to get everyone's support for future program activities.

9. Adequate Training Materials

There are plenty of training materials available today in the marketplace. Books, audiovisual programs, computerized programs geared for members and facilitators, and leader training prepared by experts are all commercially available.

10. Starting Training

The facilitator should prepare a training plan after preparing a list of those (volunteer) individuals who wish to undergo training. Training is the heart of the Quality Circle program; it is essential for systematic functioning of the Circles.

11. Forming Circles

During the training period the facilitators should review the procedure of the formation of Quality Circles. Usually six to eight members should form a circle. The name and leader of the Circle should be chosen by its members.

12. Checking Monthly Progress

The steering committee must meet every week to review problems. Once a month a progress report of all projects undertaken should be evaluated to locate and solve difficulties.

Quality Circle Organization

Many companies operate within a formal organizational structure: A president is the chief officer and below that level are many department heads acting as vice-presidents. However, many problems surface when the company operates with rigid rules and strict departmentalization. Some of these problems are:

1. Poor communication
2. Superiority or inferiority feelings according to an employee's place on the authority ladder
3. Ownership
4. Department loyalty instead of organization loyalty

By implementing the Quality Circle process, these problems can be eased and a team spirit created in the company. As the company becomes more and more involved in Quality Circles, the structure for the process is established, much like the one shown in Figure 13-2. Let us take a look at each element (and some others) in detail.

Executive Committee

The executive committee is, in actuality, the top management of the company, which establishes and approves Quality Circle policies and programs. The executive committee also gives approval to start the program and offers basic guidelines so that Quality Circles can operate within the company's administrative policy. Once the executive committee approves the program, Quality Circle policy should be established so that guidelines can be set for the rest of the organization. Later it will be simple to get approval from the executive committee on major issues such as pay policy and recognition questions. Generally, the operating committee handles most of the Circle

FIGURE 13-2

INFORMAL QUALITY CIRCLE ORGANIZATION

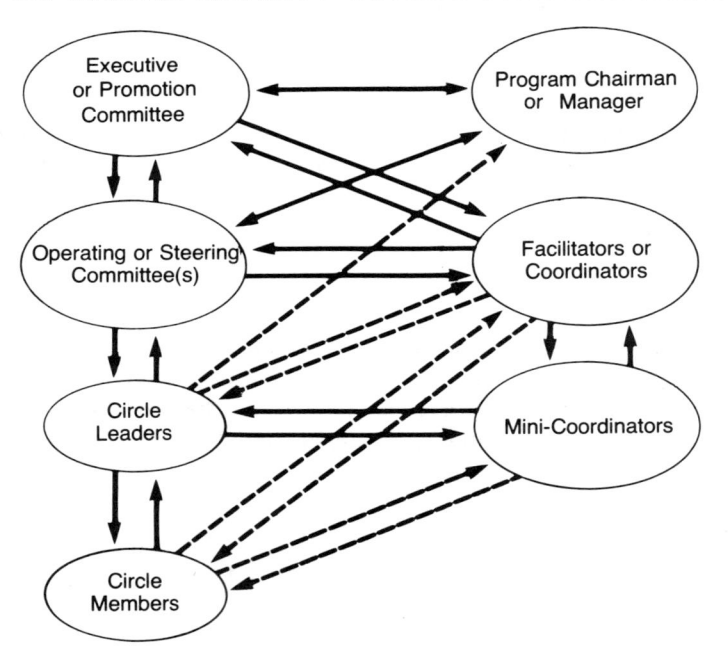

program. However, the executive committee performs the following functions:

1. Attends Quality Circle meetings frequently
2. Understands principles and techniques of Quality Circles
3. Suggests problems from time to time
4. Promotes Quality Circle programs in top- and middle-management levels
5. Promotes benefits and advantages of Quality Circles

Once the Quality Circle program is approved and the training started, it is wise to form an operating committee, known as a steering committee in many companies. The operating committee generally consists of the plant manager, quality control manager, industrial engineer, manufacturing manager, personnel manager, plant superintendent, facilitator, and one of the Circle leaders. The operating committee is really another informal Quality Circle that oversees the total Circle program to insure proper implementation of Circle projects and to promote Circle activities.

If there is more than one plant, each should have its own operating committee; all should work closely with one another. This will insure harmony and togetherness in the program rather than independent action.

The operating committee should also maintain records on cost savings, implementation expenses, project costs, and general Circle program progress. Operating committee members should also attend all Circle presentations. They should invite senior management personnel to attend who are instrumental in supporting and implementing the Quality Circle program. In summary, these key functions are performed by the operating committee:

1. Preparing objectives for the plant
2. Meeting with facilitator
3. Promoting Quality Circles throughout the organization
4. Attending meetings and constantly reviewing progress
5. Keeping program interesting and fun for members
6. Publicizing the program
7. Reviewing training material and program
8. Following up completed projects
9. Obtaining training material and adding new material to enhance knowledge of members

Quality Circle Leader

The Quality Circle leader is elected by Circle members. He or she is responsible for the operation of that particular Circle and is, therefore, responsible for the Circle's activities. The leader works closely with the facilitator (who is responsible for a number of circles) and receives much the same training.

The Quality Circle leader may be the supervisor, if that is the wish of the group. Otherwise, the supervisor can be a member of the Circle or may act as an aide to the group. The supervisor should be kept informed of all activities at all times. Quality Circles always utilize existing organizational activities as well as the existing structure, chain of command, and authority. Employees must sell their ideas to management. The advantage in the Quality Circle lies in the fact that all members learn to work as a team, analyzing and solving problems and presenting their solutions as a team to management.

The very heart of the Quality Circle concept is full participation by all members. Quality Circle leaders are not expected to do all the work; everyone shares in the task of getting things accomplished.

Some of the major functions a leader should perform are to:

1. Generate enthusiasm for Circle activities
2. Take care of operation of the Circle
3. Meet with the Circle once a week
4. Use facilitator for assistance
5. Be responsible for Circle records
6. Create coordination and harmony in the Circle
7. Be key link between members and management
8. Attend leadership training
9. Work closely with the supervisor
10. Seek advice and help if required
11. Keep the meeting on track
12. Enforce code of conduct
13. Maintain a good attitude about Circles
14. Give assignments
15. Start and end meetings for the Circle
16. Help get new members for the circle
17. Promote Quality Circle program
18. Visit other companies

19. Attend quality programs
20. Teach others useful material to better the society and surroundings

Quality Circle Members

The Quality Circle member is extremely important to the group, for without members there are no Circles and no program at all. Hence, the members are the heart of the program, and proper use of their untapped brainpower is the key to its success. Membership must be strictly voluntary, and anyone who wishes to join should be welcome. Each person must also feel free to decline membership—an active Circle will probably attract this person later. Experience has also shown that some members who join the Circle and decide to leave, frequently return at a later date.

Quality Circles can be formed in various areas. In Japan the original Circles started in manufacturing areas and then expanded into others. Even today, the majority of Quality Circles function in manufacturing. However, there is no reason why this philosophy cannot be expanded into many other areas. Banks, hospitals, insurance companies, and large retail stores are considering Quality Circles to improve services to their customers. At present, few Circles have been formed in such industries as engineering, maintenance, data processing, and finance.

There should be no restriction as to membership. Although the original Circles were formed mainly in one work area, there are different ways to group people in Circles to solve daily problems, and in the future there will undoubtedly be many changes in the way Circles are formed.

One of the key elements for Circle members is training. In Japan, basic quality-control techniques and statistical training are given in schools and colleges. Once the worker joins the company, he or she is trained thoroughly there. However, in other countries this is neglected. To implement a Quality Circle program, training has to be properly planned and managed.

Suitable training material should be developed. All members must go through training so they will understand the basic concepts and become familiar with the techniques. Without training there will be less cohesiveness in the group, and members may soon lose interest in the project due to lack of good guidance and understanding.

In general, Quality Circle members perform the following functions:

1. Attend all meetings (on time)
2. Learn statistical techniques
3. Follow the code of conduct
4. Stay within all Quality Circle policy rules

5. Promote the Quality Circle program
6. Enjoy the work
7. Help recruit new members for the Circle
8. Participate in solving problems

In short, Quality Circle members are the backbone of the program; their active participation makes the Quality Circle program successful.

Facilitator

A facilitator should have a good educational background, preferably a college degree. Such a background helps him or her train people to plan and organize work properly and to function effectively. A facilitator also needs a good working knowledge of manufacturing, quality control, statistics, and engineering. A facilitator works with a variety of people and problems and is the one to help the Circle in case of difficulties.

Since the facilitator must effect improved communication and cooperation, another key quality he or she should possess is the knack for getting along with people. A facilitator must be people-oriented. Most of the work carried out by the facilitator is concerned with people, and if he or she gets on well with them, many problems are easily solved. As we will see later, this program faces many problems having to do with human relations. Some people get upset very easily or become unhappy over certain remarks, and it is the facilitator who must investigate and resolve these differences. In general, the facilitator should be a dynamic human being who is interested in the growth of people.

Public speaking is another essential skill for a facilitator to possess. He or she must speak in meetings and must train people on a continuing basis. Skill in public speaking is an aid to implementing effective training. Without good training—getting the proper message across—Circle programs would grow very slowly or be lost completely.

The facilitator should also know different styles of speech. When working on the floor, he or she should use the language of the people on the floor; when working with office people, he or she may have to change speaking style to convince them. These two areas are different, and to achieve success and coordination the facilitator has to work closely with both. This can be achieved only by being sensitive to people and speaking their language so that they will accept the facilitator as an insider.

The facilitator should be bold but tactful. Solutions to many problems may depend on help and coordination from manufacturing, engineering, and other areas. Since many people from those areas may feel that Quality

Circles interfere with their work, getting their cooperation can sometimes be difficult. A facilitator has to find a way, talking with people or even contacting management, to keep the projects alive. This is not an easy task. There is often frustration, even unhappiness. However, as long as a variety of personalities is involved, such things are bound to happen. Patience and coolness are needed to guide people correctly.

In general, a facilitator should be pleasant at all times. He or she should carry the full responsibility of the Circle program and should thoroughly understand the basic philosophy of Quality Circles. He or she should, however, be willing to share with others the credit and success of the program so that expansion can be achieved smoothly and effectively.

The facilitator has a number of different responsibilities; they vary daily. Sometimes the facilitator might have to act as a teacher and train people; at other times he or she might work as a consultant and help a Circle with its projects. He or she must also act as a counselor, promoter, mediator, and public speaker.

If the company cannot easily find a suitable person for this position, it will be necessary to train such a person with the help of courses and materials. Following is a brief outline of requirements for the job of Quality Circle facilitator.

Requirements for the Job of Quality Circle Facilitator[1]

Thorough Knowledge of the Quality Circle Program

1. History
2. Communications
3. Group dynamics
4. Objectives and goal setting
5. Roles and functions of committees, leaders, and members
6. Statistical techniques and their uses
7. Progress evaluation systems
8. Problems in managing program
9. Leadership
10. Training techniques
11. Public speaking

---

[1] From *Quality Circles Master Guide* by Sud Ingle. Englewood Cliffs, NJ: Prentice-Hall, Inc., 1982.

Working Knowledge
1. Operation of the company
2. Statistics
3. Product service
4. Purchasing/vendor relations
5. Mathematics
6. Business management (accounting and budgeting)
7. Manufacturing processes
8. Quality control
9. Speech
10. Behavioral science

Education: B.S. in Education or Engineering
Experience: Three to five years in a related industry with manufacturing exposure

Duties of the Facilitator
1. Sits as an active member of the steering committee
2. Serves as Quality Circle program coordinator
3. Trains members, leaders, management
4. Coordinates Circles
5. Maintains Circle records
6. Arranges meetings with outsiders
7. Attends in-Circle meetings
8. Solves personal problems
9. Searches for new members
10. Works in the shop daily
11. Searches for new ideas
12. Publicizes the program
13. Spreads a good word about the program
14. Links all people in the organization
15. Prepares for presentation—invitations, papers, visual aids
16. Prepares new training material
17. Follows up on completed projects
18. Attends conferences
19. Reads outside materials
20. Organizes informal gatherings—invites outside speakers

Mini-Coordinators

Mini-coordinators are helpful in expanding the Quality Circle program a little faster without affecting enthusiasm. As mentioned before, mini-coordinators can be selected, requested, or volunteered from various departments.

One mini-coordinator is generally responsible for only one or two Circles. In Japan this type of work is carried out by foremen or other department heads. Mini-coordinators do not have to spend all of their time on Quality Circle activities; it is usually just one part of their routine work. However, it is a tremendous help to the company, since it serves a twofold purpose. During the initial stage the company can use this method without investing too much in the program. It also helps in the long run to develop additional facilitators for the company.

A mini-coordinator performs the following key functions:

1. Attends assigned Circle meetings
2. Contacts outside people if required
3. Works closely with the facilitator and conveys members' messages or needs that are necessary for the success of the Circle's project
4. Guides the Circles in their projects if required
5. Reviews training material with assigned Circles if required
6. Keeps unity in the assigned Circle operation
7. Watches for problems and calls for help
8. Reminds members to follow the code of conduct
9. Passes on interesting informative material; keeps the Circle rolling
10. Provides feedback on projects that are presented to the management

The idea of a mini-coordinator is new in the United States, and it will take some time for it to spread in industry.

Operation of a Quality Circle

The actual operation of a Quality Circle begins after the members' graduation. If a large group is trained at one time, it should be divided into smaller groups. However, the decision concerning group size should be left up to the members. The facilitator should help to prepare members for their work. Some groups will be large, some small—size does not make any real difference. It is recommended that the groups be formed by members who generally work in one area, but that is not necessary either. A key aspect of the formation of a Circle is to let members decide its membership.

QUALITY CIRCLE OPERATION CYCLE

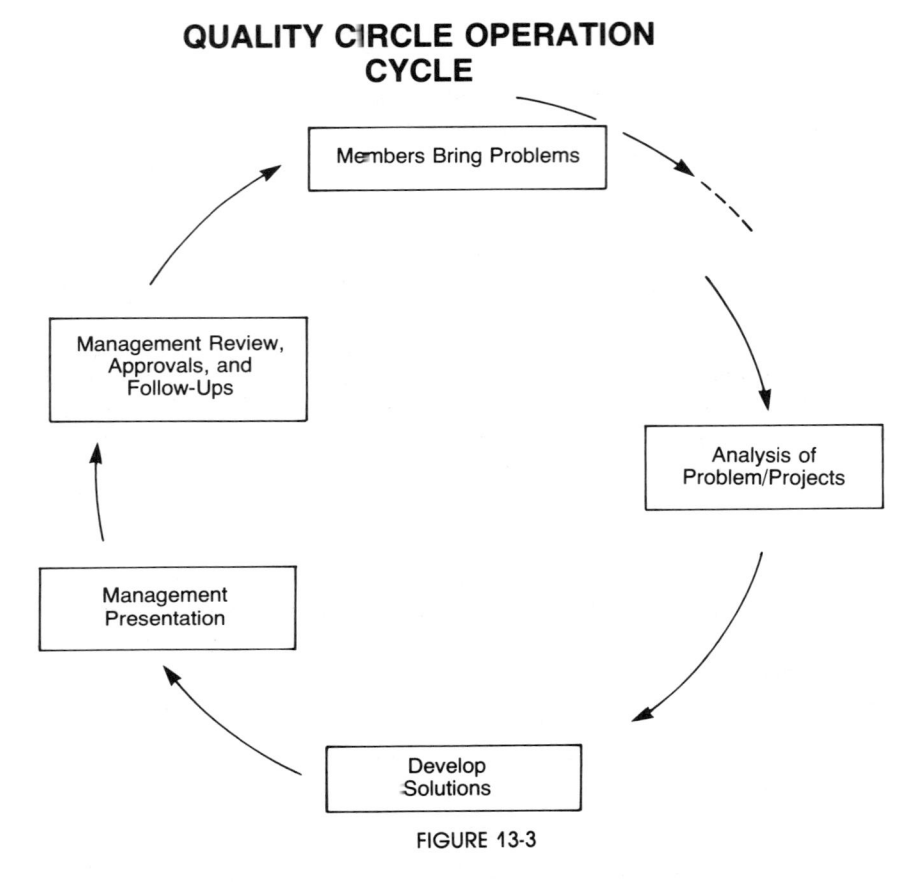

FIGURE 13-3

Steps in Operating Procedure

Step 1. Members bring potential problems. At the first meeting, the facilitator or coordinator generally provides the necessary organization kit describing the Circle's activities. This kit contains such basic tools as pens, pencils, paper, notebook, calendar, folders, and other useful articles that the members will need while working on a problem. The group then chooses a name for their Circle, a leader, and a secretary. The secretary takes care of the paperwork and other assignments.

When these formalities are completed, the Circle generally decides to prepare a list of all the problems that members wish to tackle. Once the list is prepared, a method must be devised to quantify or evaluate the severity of the problems. One way is to collect data by frequency of occurrence, by scrap or rework, by rejects, or in any other way that the Circle suggests to assess the depth of the problem.

Then assignments must be given to various members for the collection of data. Statistical techniques, check sheets, or graphs are useful at this time. The time period and collection of fresh data are very important, since some of the problems may already be solved by the time the Circle gets going, or a solution may be forthcoming. This type of analysis is also helpful to ascertain the actual existence of problems.

Even though the data collected are crude and cover a short period of time, a Pareto diagram can be prepared. A Pareto diagram will generally point out the important few and trivial many. Based on this analysis, members can decide which problems should be worked on collectively. With the Pareto diagram, the problem usually becomes so obvious that everyone agrees to tackle the one or two most important problems.

In some cases, problems might be so obvious that Circles do not wish to spend much time collecting and analyzing data. That should not stop the Circle from tackling any problem if most of the members agree to work on it. However, it is necessary to take precautions so that the Circle does not fall into a trap and waste its time on minor problems or on projects where solutions are already in progress.

Step 2. Analysis of problem or projects. Once the problem has been selected, the Circle can start analyzing it with the help of two important statistical tools—brainstorming and cause-and-effect diagrams (see Chapter 8). A cause-and-effect diagram is usually developed in which the effect is noted at the end and several major areas for causes are marked on the right-hand side. The idea-generating brainstorming techniques help to get all members involved so that various causes can be listed. The leader generally asks members for their opinions regarding causes and lists them on the sheet. With group consent, the key cause is picked for analysis, and another set of data is collected to verify the cause. If it proves that the Circle has picked up the key cause, members can generally proceed further to seek the solution. However, if the data do not show sufficient evidence, the Circle will have to search for another problem cause and collect new data for verification. Sometimes this process might have to be repeated two or three times, until the true cause is found. Once the major cause is discovered, the Circle will generally proceed to develop a solution.

Step 3. Development of solution. Once the cause is verified, Circle members get together, put their brainpower to work, and start proposing solutions. One member might think of a change in a fixture, another might suggest a change in material, and other members may make different suggestions. Since most of the members face these problems every day, their solutions generally remedy the problem permanently, provided any other necessary changes that will affect the solution take place at the same time.

Once the Circle arrives at a method to fix the problem, a plan should be prepared for implementation. Approval to test the solution on a small scale should be obtained through the foreman or facilitator. This test will help to verify the solution. A small-scale pilot run, rather than a full-scale implementation of the wrong solution, saves time, money, and energy. This early stage is an important phase of Circle operation, and it might vary in length from two or three weeks to two to three months. The Circle should not have to finish the project within a certain time period, nor should the Circle be rushed to finish the project. That type of pressure generally discourages Circle activities and is not fruitful. On the contrary, management should extend outside help without interfering in the daily operation of the Circle.

To maintain an effective Circle, weekly meetings must be held, ranging from 30 to 45 minutes in length, depending on the need. This helps to maintain good communication, create new solutions, and keep harmony in the Circle. Suggested solutions can be tested on a small scale through Circle work also. A preventive system should be devised to make sure that the problem remains solved. Without a good preventive program, solutions are effective for only a short period. Circle members should also review all other aspects of the problem and see if the solution can be implemented in other areas where similar problems exist. This helps to avoid duplicate efforts and eliminates waste quickly. After a certain period, when the Circle arrives at an effective solution, the facilitator must arrange the next phase—showing management the results of the work.

Step 4. Management presentation. A presentation for management is an important form of recognition for the Circle. The conscientious endeavors of Circle members need to be recognized by management if Circle morale is to be sustained. It is most important that the facilitator arrange for such a presentation for each project, whether or not it is successful. It is possible that new information might show up in the middle of a Circle project, indicating no further need to continue work on the project. The facilitator or mini-coordinator should review the situation at that time and suggest that a member of the Circle present an interim report to management. This helps both sides. Circle members feel that their work was not in vain, and management gets to hear some aspect of a project that they might otherwise have overlooked.

A lot of hard work goes into preparing a presentation. However, it is enjoyable for most members, who must prepare short talks, reports, visual aids, and in some cases even small samples to prove their point. Each presentation is different; all are interesting. Quality Circle members may have to learn to operate a slide projector, movie projector, or other visual-aid equipment to put on an effective presentation. The Circle works as a team of professionals as they prepare and present evidence of their achievements.

Questions are always asked about arrangements for management presentations. First, the facilitator or mini-coordinator reviews the project with all Circle members present. Once an agreement has been reached, a rehearsal is arranged with all necessary equipment. It may take more than one rehearsal to be certain that everyone knows his or her part.

A management presentation helps Circle members to become assertive and learn how to talk in front of others. The facilitator has to make arrangements for the place, date, and time of the presentation. He or she should make sure that all of these things are suitable for management as well as for Circle members. A meeting room should be found that is large enough for everyone to be comfortable in. It should be quiet enough for people to be able to hear the talk easily. These are small matters, but they do count in the evaluation and effectiveness of the program.

Another important aspect of the presentation is the invitation. Facilitators should review the project and make certain that all concerned parties are invited. This will include the plant manager, industrial engineers, manufacturing engineers, quality control personnel, and other people. Remember that good communications help to build a successful company, and the more people who know what is going on, the better the results.

Step 5. Management review and follow-up. After Circle members have presented the solution to management, it is management's duty to review the suggestions and solutions thoroughly. People from quality control, industrial engineering, and manufacturing engineering should be asked to evaluate the impact of the work, or to provide any help to complete the project. Generally, when management presentations are given, the advantages are also discussed. Most of the work is already completed by then, unless a large amount of financial help or additional manpower would be required. Management has to review these aspects as well as time factors in certain areas. The steering committee must assume this responsibility in each plant.

After the presentation, a discussion should take place for approval or disapproval of the suggestions. A follow-up program should be prepared for future use. The Circle should be informed about any decisions so that the communication is completed and members know the outcome of their efforts.

At a later time, the steering committee should see that the work is completed, and the facilitator should make sure that Circles are informed about the program.

Basic Techniques for Service Industries

People voluntarily sign up for Quality Circle training, which generally lasts eight to nine weeks. The following basic techniques are most useful for service industries at the beginning:

1. Introduction: why and what
2. Teamwork
3. Brainstorming
4. Pareto analysis
5. Cause-and-effect analysis
6. Data-collection methods
7. Activity analysis
8. Process analysis
9. Problem-solving process
10. Presentation skills

Today many service industries implement Quality Circles, using more than the above basic techniques. There is always room for improvement, and a program should be modified or changed according to need. Do not copy blindly.

Introduction: What and Why

Actually, the orientation to Quality Circles is not a technique, but once people join the program, it is necessary to train them. In the introductory session, the following information should be covered:

1. History of Quality Circles
2. Problems today (inflation, low productivity and quality, and so on)
3. Need to recognize brainpower of the people
4. Quality Circle operation
5. Quality Circle organization
6. What goes on in a Quality Circle?
7. Keeping the organization number one

People should become familiar with the history and operation of Quality Circles. This is essential before anyone can commit to the process.

Teamwork

Teamwork is the foundation of the effective and successful Quality Circle. People need to know how important it is that they work together for the common cause—that is, keeping customers satisfied by quality services and products and staying in business.

Brainstorming

Brainstorming is a technique for generating the greatest possible number of solutions to a problem for evaluation and development. Characteristically, certain things occur during brainstorming. The problem to be addressed is clearly stated and understood by all members of the group. All suggestions are recorded. Each member is given an equal opportunity to express his or her ideas. All suggestions, good or bad, are encouraged. At no time are any suggestions or possible solutions criticized.

Pareto Analysis

A Pareto diagram combines two of the common forms of graphs, a column graph and a line graph. The column graph is characterized by the arrangement of the columns in descending order of length. The horizontal axis does not contain the numerical scale; it is simply a baseline for the columns, one column for each of a set of independent categories, and occasionally an "other" column for a group of the least significant categories.

Cause-and-Effect Analysis

Cause-and-effect analysis was first developed by Kaoru Ishikawa of the University of Tokyo in the early 1950s. His first application of the technique was in the Fulsai Ironworks in 1953. Since the final form looked like a fish, some people called it the *fishbone diagram;* it is also referred to as the *Ishikawa diagram.*

Three types of cause-and-effect diagrams are in use today. They are:

1. Cause enumeration: This is the most commonly used; it is also called the "basic cause-and-effect diagram."
2. Dispersion analysis: The complete diagram looks like the enumeration type except that its construction is approached differently.
3. Process analysis: This is described in detail below.

Data-Collection Methods

The following data-collection methods are useful for Quality Circles.

1. Check sheets
2. Graphs
3. Sampling
4. Computers
5. Surveys

Details can be found in reference books.

Activity Analysis

Service industries such as banks, hospitals, or government agencies employ many technical and professional people, and many operations include a lot of paperwork. The use of active analysis can be most helpful in finding unnecessary work steps and in making many operations effective.

Activity analysis means analyzing an operation or task step by step and charting it carefully to find out productive and nonproductive work procedures. Generally, the following symbols are used to analyze the operation:

- ● Productive operation
- ○ Nonproductive operation
- ◐ Partially filled-in circle indicates required but nonproductive operation
- ☐ Inspection or review

After listing all the activities and their corresponding symbols, careful study should be made by the Circles, and some important questions should be asked: What is the purpose of this activity? Can it be done better? Who can do it best? Should it be done at a different time?

These questions cover the basic who, what, when, where, why, and how inquiries introduced earlier in Quality Circle training. Through use of the activity analysis chart, the Quality Circle finds better procedures and eliminates ineffective and unnecessary ones. Once a new way is found, the chart shows the difference between the old and new methods.

Process Analysis

Many times problems can be found in one department or one area, but the source(s) of the problem could lie somewhere else. One of the most useful tools in such a situation is the process or flow process analysis. Process analysis is generally performed with the help of a flow process chart. The flow process chart is a detailed record of the sequence of events in any process.

1. Write down the activity being studied, breaking the job down into different types of activities.
2. Choose the subject to follow; stick with this subject. Pick a person, material, or paper form, depending on which goes through the entire process you are working on.
3. Pick starting and ending points to be sure you cover the ground you want.
4. Put your initials and the date on the form.

In the body of the form, write a brief description of each detail. List each step that occurs, no matter how small or seemingly insignificant. Every time something happens to the subject, whether material or person, each time there is a move, it should be recorded exactly the way you see it being done.

Applying Symbols

Symbols help to simplify the job of analyzing details. The description you have written down determines the symbol you will use. The symbols used in charting are:

○	Operation:	Use the circle to show that an action or operation is taking place (typing a letter, filling out a form, picking up an object).
⇨	Transportation:	When something is moved from one place to another, use the arrow to show transportation.
D	Delay:	When the subject is interrupted or delayed in its flow (an interference), use the letter *D* (a letter in an outgoing box, a carton awaiting transportation).
▽	Storage:	When an object is kept and protected against unauthorized removal, use an inverted triangle to denote storage (goods in warehouse or stockroom).
□	Inspection:	When something is checked or verified but not changed, use a square to denote an inspection (proofreading a letter).

Presentation Skills

When Quality Circle members prepare to show their solutions to management, they must present their story effectively and appropriately so that management will accept the proposals without delay. To do this, Circle members need many different skills. Some of them are represented in:

1. Oral preparation by the members
2. Preparation of the project report
3. Use of video and audio equipment
4. Visual aids
5. Group assignments in project presentations

Ten Steps to a Successful Management Presentation

1. Maintain a schedule, start and end on time.
2. Use a large enough room with plenty of seating.
3. Have a chairperson or coordinator present to keep the meeting under control.
4. Use an agenda with subjects and speakers outlined; leave room for taking notes.
5. Use visual aids such as slides, charts, graphs.
6. Do not discredit other departments or people.
7. Use positive points as accomplishments.
8. Invite all interested parties.
9. Do not ask for additional funding or people.
10. Do not ask for on-the-spot decisions.

Key to a Successful Quality-Control Program

In order to have a successful and effective quality-control program, you should keep the following key points in mind:

1. Proper atmosphere for the program
2. Support from top management
3. Effective steering committee
4. Enthusiastic facilitator

5. Systematic training
6. Slow, systematic growth
7. Good follow-up and evaluation system
8. Recognition

How to Avoid Quality Circle Failures

Based on our experience with more than 200 organizations, we would like to discuss some of the factors that can contribute to the failure of the Quality Circle program.

1. Poor communication
2. Closed policy
3. Inadequate training
4. No follow-ups on projects
5. Poor middle-management support
6. "Lip service" from the management
7. No union involvement

Other deterrents to a good program are too many Circles, too many projects, expecting overnight success, lack of financial support, and changes in the management. Remember, Quality Circles are not the answer to all the problems all the time.

Benefits of Quality Circle Process

Many organizations that implement Quality Circles successfully have observed the following benefits:

1. Improvement in quality
2. Improvement in productivity
3. Improvement in interdepartmental communication
4. Less absenteeism
5. Safety improvement
6. Job satisfaction
7. Cost reduction
8. Waste reduction—less scrap, efforts, time
9. Team spirit
10. Return on investment (average 6 to 1)

Successful Case Studies

Case Study Number 1

Subject: To improve the use of a telephone system in a bank.

Case Study Number 2—
People Helping People Leads to Quality

Cal Winget, an assembler in Plant #15 and leader of the MERC "Trim Power" from Department 568, was asked by a friend to assist in installing an outboard power trim un t on his boat. Cal thought, Why not; as I assemble them every day I should be able to do it.

After completing the installation without any problems, he discovered they had two parts left over, a hose clamp and a plastic harness binder. Where did these go?

Back at Mercury, Cal asked his foreman and also checked with service repair as to where these parts were to be used. No one seemed to know the answer. Cal made a personal visit to one boat dealer, telephoned three others, and had contact with product engineering. Still no one knew. By now this unusual situation had become the project of Cal's MERC Circle. After several weeks of investigation, the "Trim Power" Circle made a management presentation in which they recommended the following: In view of the obvious lack of need for these parts and the resultant waste involved, supporting elements of Mercury such as service repair, dock auditing, lake testing, and so on should be required to give proper notice when they receive obsolete parts no longer used with any unit.

The engineering department involved with these units took immediate action to have them deleted from the bill of material when they were made aware of it. This mutual cooperative effort between management and the assembly workers to solve this problem was started because of Cal's persistence, initiative, and sincere desire to correct an obviously undesirable condition. By assisting his friend, Cal assisted everyone at Mercury.

Case Study Number 3:

Problem: Employees of the boxing line are frustrated in the performance of their duties by large percentages of defective wood boxing components. They require considerable additional effort to assemble

	and often result in an inferior package being sent to the field.
Suggested solution:	Implement a vendor in-house inspection program.
Results:	Those wood components received from vendors who have had in-house inspection implemented have shown a reduction in defective units of from 60–100 percent defective down to 0 percent.

Case Study Number 4

Problem:	Lack of knowledge and effective means of communicating quality problems to assembly people.
Suggested solution:	Construct, install, and maintain a large defect identification poster to create an awareness of and consciousness for improving the quality of the assembly.
Results:	Many of the original 17 defects, as reported by results of a Pareto analysis, have been eliminated; others are greatly reduced in frequency of occurrence.

Future of Quality Circles

We live in a society that is very fast moving. It is true that a stagnant society cannot progress and stay on top in today's competitive world. However, due to ongoing changes and new technology, management is always looking for new ways to progress and improve the position of the organization in the world.

Sometimes changes take place out of some of the old system ideas. In other cases, old ideas take shape and better systems emerge through the combination. Hence, Quality Circles, although built on the people-building philosophy, may not last long because management may want to find better ways to improve quality and productivity. Experience indicates that Quality Circles have limits in their contribution to the total quality improvement of an organization. Hence, I feel that although the name Quality Circles as such may not remain after a certain number of years in any organization, the process will impact management styles of many organizations and will slowly but surely establish the participative management system that is badly needed in an organization.

FIGURE 13-4

Case study #1:
Shortening customers' telephone waiting time

This is the story of a QC program that was implemented in the main office of a large bank. An average of 500 customers call this office every day. Surveys indicated that the callers tended to become irritated if the phone rang more than five times before it was answered, and often would not call the company again. In contrast, a prompt answer after just two rings reassured the customers and made them feel more comfortable doing business by phone.

1. Selection of a Theme

Telephone reception was chosen as a QC theme for the following reasons: (1) Telephone reception is the first impression a customer receives from the company, (2) this theme coincided with the company's telephone reception slogan, "Don't make customers wait, and avoid needless switching from extension to extension," and (3) it also coincided with a company-wide campaign being promoted at that time which advocated being friendly to everyone one met.

First, the staff discussed why the present method of answering calls made callers wait. Fig. 1 illustrates a frequent situation where a call from customer B comes in while the operator is talking with customer A. Let's see why the customer has to wait.

At (1), the operator receives a call from the customer, but due to lack of experience, does not know where to connect the call. At (2), the receiving party cannot answer the phone quickly,

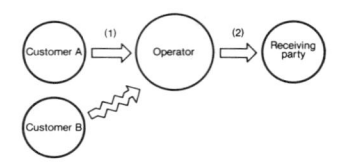

Fig. 1. Why customers had to wait

perhaps because he is unavailable, and nobody can take the call for him. The result is that the operator must transfer the call to another extension while apologizing for the delay.

2. Cause-and-Effect Diagram and Situation Analysis

In order to fully understand the situation, the circle members decided to conduct a survey regarding the callers who waited for more than five rings. Circle members itemized factors at a brainstorming discussion and arranged them in a cause-and-effect diagram. Operators then kept check sheets on several points to tally the results spanning twelve days from June 4 to 16.

Cause-and-effect diagram

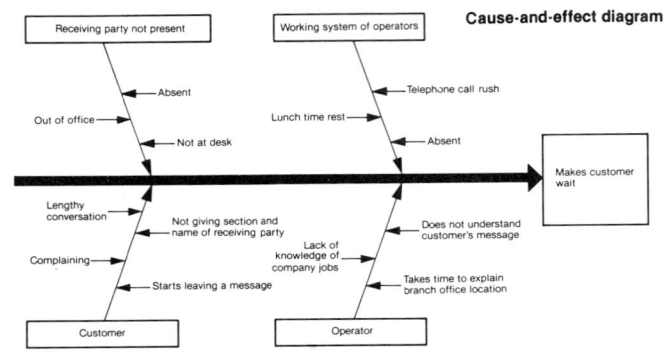

Fig. 2. What makes customer wait

3. Results of the Check Sheet Situation Analysis

The data recorded on the check sheets unexpectedly revealed that "one operator (partner out of the office)" topped the list by a big margin, occurring a total of 172 times. In this case, the operator on duty had to deal with large numbers of calls when the phones were busy. Customers who had to wait a long time averaged 29.2 daily, which accounted for 6% of the calls received every day.

4. Setting the Target

After an intense, but productive discussion, the staff decided to set a QC program goal of reducing these waiting callers to zero. That is to say that all incoming calls would be handled promptly, without inconveniencing the customer.

5. Measures and Execution

(1) Taking lunches on three different shifts, leaving at least two operators on the job at all times.

Up until this resolution was made, a 2-shift lunch system had been employed, leaving only one operator on

214

the job while the other was taking her lunch break. However, since the survey revealed that this was a major cause of customers waiting on the line, the company brought in a helper operator from the clerical section.

(2) Asking all employees to leave messages when leaving their desks.

The objective of this rule was to simplify the operator's chores when the receiving party was not at his desk. The new program was explained at the employees' regular morning meetings, and company-wide support was requested. To help implement this practice, posters were placed around the office to publicize the new measures.

(3) Compiling a directory listing the personnel and their respective jobs.

The notebook was specially designed to aid the operators, who could not be expected to know the details of every employee's job, or where to connect his incoming calls.

6. Confirming the Results

Although the waiting calls could not be reduced to zero, all items presented showed a marked improvement as shown in Table 3 and Fig. 3. The major cause of delays, "one operator (partner out of the office)," plummeted from 172 incidents during the control period to 15 in the follow-up survey.

Table 1. Check sheet
Designed to identify the problems.

Reason\Date	No one present in the section receiving the call	Receiving party not present	Only one operator (partner out of the office)	Total
June 4	\\\\	卌 \	卌 卌 \	24
June 5	卌	卌 \\\	卌 卌 \\\	32
June 6	卌 \	\\\\	卌 卌 \\	28
June 15	卌	卌	卌 \\\	25

Table 2. Reasons why callers had to wait

		Daily average	Total number
A	One operator (partner out of the office)	14.3	172
B	Receiving party not present	6.1	73
C	No one present in the section receiving the call	5.1	61
D	Section and name of receiving party not given	1.6	19
E	Inquiry about branch office locations	1.3	16
F	Other reasons	0.8	10
	Total	29.2	351

Period: 12 days from June 4 to 16, 1980

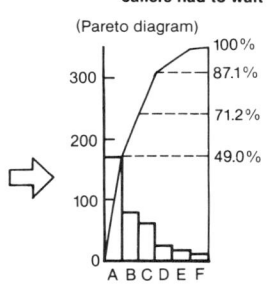

Table 3. Effects of QC (comparison of before and after QC)

	Reasons why callers had to wait	Total number Before	Total number After	Daily average Before	Daily average After
A	One operator (partner out of the office)	172	15	14.5	1.2
B	Receiving party not present	73	17	6.1	1.4
C	No one present in the section receiving the call	61	20	5.1	1.7
D	Section and name of receiving party not given	19	4	1.6	0.3
E	Inquiry about branch office locations	16	3	1.3	0.2
F	Others	10	0	0.8	0
	Total	351	59	29.2	4.8

Period: 12 days from Aug. 17 to 30.

Problems are classified according to cause and presented in order of the amount of time consumed. They are illustrated in a bar graph. 100% indicates the total number of time-consuming calls.

Fig. 3. Reasons why callers had to wait
(Pareto diagram)

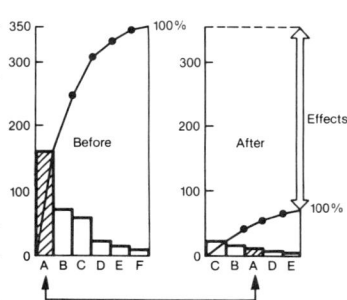

Fig. 4. Effects of QC (Pareto diagram)

Evaluate Your Organization

A review of the following questions will help your organization to understand organizational readiness for implementing Quality Circles systematically and successfully in your organization.

Organizational Readiness

1. What is the most important asset of your company?
2. What kind of training programs exist in your company?
3. How do you train employees?
4. How is communication in your company?
5. What kind of activities do you engage in for employee recognition?
6. To what extent is teamwork used in your company?
7. Do employees offer suggestions to improve performance?
8. How are problems solved in your company?
9. How much do you think it costs to implement Quality Circles?
10. What is involved in maintaining Quality Circles?

FIGURE 13-5

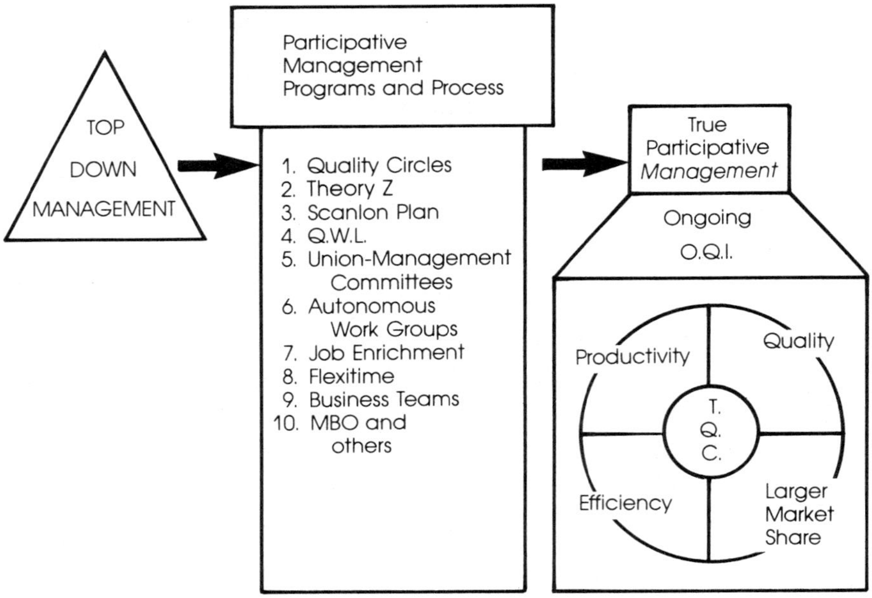

TOP DOWN MANAGEMENT → Participative Management Programs and Process

1. Quality Circles
2. Theory Z
3. Scanlon Plan
4. Q.W.L.
5. Union-Management Committees
6. Autonomous Work Groups
7. Job Enrichment
8. Flexitime
9. Business Teams
10. MBO and others

→ True Participative *Management*

Ongoing O.Q.I.

Productivity — Quality — Efficiency — Larger Market Share

T.Q.C.

FUTURE OF QUALITY CIRCLES

We, therefore, see the need for management to present these people with organizations and jobs that capitalize on this new work ethic. One that may be best suited for these hard times when American industry has to make giant leaps forward to catch up with other producing nations.

Management will have to get in step by replacing:

Control by some with creativity by all.

Consumption as a pacifier with a commitment to produce.

Confinement of talents and aspirations with a community in which everyone is eager to deliver all he or she can.

Editorial, *Industry Week,*
May 10, 1981

Chapter Fourteen
RECOMMENDED TRAINING PROGRAMS FOR OQI

Why Train the People?

An effective and successful training program for OQI (Organizational Quality Improvement) is the heart of improving the quality of organizations. In the United States, the work force is ingenious, but this brainpower needs training in statistical techniques. In the last decade, very little attention has been given to training the work force properly. I feel the most important task for management is to make sure that this training phase of the program is carried out smoothly. Trainers and quality-improvement managers play a critical role in training the people in an organization.

Is there any need for elaborate training of OQI? Why not start a program the right way? If employees were just called into a large meeting and told that the company would start quality-improvement teams tomorrow and that they were expected to join the group and participate in solving problems, what do you think would happen?

Many programs in the past may have been started in this way and many have worked effectively. However, I have seen in my experience that this old method does not always work. You must be careful and go about introducing OQI programs slowly in a company for the first time.

Training is a very important phase that has not been taken care of in the United States for a long time. People need more information. The more they know about a product or its costs, the wiser the decisions they will

---

RECOMMENDED TRAINING PROGRAMS

1. Basic training in statistics

2. Top management training

3. Middle management training

4. Supervisors and foremen training

5. Operators and grass root training

6. Engineering, manufacturing engineers, and Quality Control engineers training

7. Training for vendors

FIGURE 14-1

reach. Similarly, statistics has been considered useful only in offices or in colleges, but few people have taken the time to demonstrate how simple statistics can work for shop areas. Hence, most of our work force is ignorant in statistics. In the absence of training, confusion about and dislike of the quality-improvement program may easily be created among its members. Therefore, it is important to teach statistical techniques to all members and show them their use. Once the people in an organization grasp the basic concepts, there is no problem getting them to use the techniques effectively while they collect and analyze data.

Basic Training in Statistics

I have discussed in detail basic statistical techniques that are useful in any organization (Chapter 4). These techniques must be understood and used as necessary in the various programs described in the next few pages. Most of the description of statistical techniques is made simple so that those who do not have a background in statistics can still grasp the concept easily. It is essential that we teach this subject in a relaxed manner, because we want people to use the methods and they are going to use them only if they understand the concept.

Some of these improvement topics in statistical methods are listed here.

1. Pareto analysis
2. Precontrol
3. Process capabilities and use of Cp and Ck indices C,P,np,4V
4. Stem-leaf chart
5. Multivary chart
6. Red X theory
7. Process and activity analysis
8. Scatter diagram
9. Stratification
10. Control charts ($\bar{x}$.-R,C,P,U,np)
11. Sampling
12. Force-field analysis
13. Cum-sum charts
14. Cause-and-effect analysis using data-collection methods
15. Systematic problem solving through statistical techniques (Chapter 4)

Recommended Training Programs

Let us review the types of training recommended for implementing OQI properly in an organization.

1. Top management training (one day)
2. Middle-management and department heads training (three days)
3. Supervisors and foremen training (three days)
4. Operators and grass-roots training
5. Engineering, manufacturing engineers, and quality-control engineers
6. Vendor training

7. Other useful skill-block training programs
8. Recommended courses for vocational schools and colleges

1. Top Management Training for Quality Awareness (One Day)

Objective   To learn organizational quality-improvement tactics and planning

Topics
1. New quality era
2. Managing OQI
3. Quality Wheel analysis
4. Statistical thinking
5. Functions of quality control and quality audits—new product development
6. Management of quality
7. Roles of top management in quality control
8. Quality council
9. Quality promotions
10. Case studies
11. Self-analysis
12. Leadership
13. On-hand experience in SQC (statistical quality control)
14. Importance of design of experiment
15. Presentation skills and simulations
16. Implementation plans
17. Practical statistics for nonstatisticians (Chapter 18)

2. Training for Middle-Management and Department Heads

Objectives
1. To make them understand the principles of OQI
2. To practice OQI
3. To analyze organization for project selection

Topics
1. New quality era
2. Principles of OQI
3. Quality Wheel and self-analysis
4. Quality Wheel analysis
5. Functions of quality achieved

6. Operations of quality systems and quality costs
7. Role of middle management and department heads in OQI
8. Statistical principles
9. Case studies
10. Team-building—group dynamics
11. Industrial statistics
12. Time management
13. Looking at processes
14. Improving processes
15. Charting processes
16. Quality Circles
17. Problem solving through statistical methods
18. Cost-benefit analysis
19. SPC (statistical process control)
20. Design of experiment
21. Putting it all together—implementing OQI
22. Practical statistics for nonstatisticians

3. Training for Supervisors and Foremen

Objectives
1. To make him/her show how to solve problems through statistical methods
2. To make him/her understand OQI and Quality Circles
3. To make him/her show how to improve quality and productivity of processes of products and services

Topics
1. New quality era
2. Why OQI and Quality Circles?
3. OQI industrial statistics
   — Looking at processes
   — Improving processes, Red X Theory
   — Charting processes
   — Cost-benefit analysis
   — Problem solving through statistical methods
   — Quality costs, data collection
   — Quality audits, vendor-customer relations
   — Methodology and quality information systems
   — Annual quality improvements

4. Quality Circles
   — Group dynamics
   — QC techniques
   — Operation of QC
   — Case studies
   — Practicing QC
5. Leadership Training
   — Leader's groups and individuals
   — Conducting meetings
   — Conflicts
   — Stress
   — Communications
   — Promotional achievements
   — Data collection
6. Practical statistics for nonstatisticians
7. Other training such as automation, robotics, and so forth

4. Operators and Grass-Roots Training

The author recommends two types of training in this area:

A. Basic Quality Circle training (6–8 hours)

Topics
1. Why QC?
2. Teamwork
3. Brainstorming
4. Pareto analysis
5. Cause-and-effect analysis
6. Data collection
7. Activity analysis
8. Process analysis
9. Problem-solving methods
10. Management presentation

B. Statistical process control (6–8 hours)

Topics
1. Why use statistics?
2. Statistical methods
   — Precontrol
   — Multivary charts and histograms
   — Rum chart—cum-sum chart

- Stem-and-leaf chart
- Control charts ($\bar{x}$-R,C,P,U,np)
- Stratification
- Scatter diagram
- Force field and cost-benefit analysis
- Quality costs and how to analyze them

5. Engineering, Manufacturing Engineers, and Quality Control Engineers Training

Objectives
1. To understand OQI
2. To practice OQI
3. To improve processes and designs of new products and services
4. To choose new projects for improvement

Topics
1. Principles of OQI
2. Operation and implementation of OQI
3. SPC
4. Methodology
5. Control charts, Red X Theory
6. Statistical thinking
7. Looking at processes and improving processes, components search patterns
8. Cost-benefit analysis
9. Design of experiments
10. Reliability, maintainability, availability
11. Process capabilities (cp and ck)
12. Production management
13. Evolutionary operations
14. Reliability
15. Nondestructive testing
16. Organizing for OQI
17. Cost standards and similarity practices
18. Practical statistics for nonstatisticians

6. Training for Vendors

Objectives
1. To make vendor understand organizational needs
2. To create close bond between the organization and the vendor

RECOMMENDED TRAINING PROGRAMS FOR OQI   225

                3. To build confidence in vendor's products
                4. To improve quality of the vendor's products and services
                5. To make vendors use SPC and design of experiments

Topics
1. New quality era
2. Vendor evaluation and certification
3. Statistical process control
4. Inspection process
5. Process improvements
6. Process analysis
7. Methodology
8. Nondestructive testing
9. Quality Circles
10. Implementing OQI and Quality Circles
11. Statistical thinking
12. Problem solving through statistical methods
13. Specifications and standards
14. Quality cost and quality audits
15. Practical statistics for nonstatisticians
16. Other important topics important for the organization

7. Other Useful Skill Block Training

Iron Age magazine recently published a supervisory training program that is being conducted at the Nissan Plant at Smyrna, Tennessee. The program indicates a thorough, systematic training before a supervisor is ready for the job. Many other organizations also offer ongoing training to improve employees' skills in various areas so that they became better employees.

I recommend that the following types of programs be offered to anyone in an organization. With the advent of video equipment, it is not necessary to have a full class of 15 to 20 students. Each employee, on his or her time, can attend these classes or training and use videotapes. Some of the common and useful courses (six to eight hours) are as follows:

1. Job-instruction training
2. Personal computers and their uses
3. Specifications and standards
4. Communication training
5. How to conduct a meeting

6. Managing charge
7. Leadership
8. Team building
9. Time management
10. Delegation role, expectations
11. Specific industrial courses in electricity, pneumatics (i.e., machine tools, casting, assembly, processes, welding, inspection, etc.)
12. Industrial safety
13. Paperwork simplification
14. Word processing and telecommunications
15. Principles of decision making

8. Recommended Degree Course in Quality Management for Vocational Schools, Junior Colleges, and Universities

Today many colleges offer degree courses in statistics, engineering, industrial engineering, or manufacturing engineering. I believe that higher education institutions should start offering degrees in quality management.

The following topics are recommended in this regard:

1. Managing total quality program (OQI)
2. Quality Wheel analysis
3. Human factors and motivation
4. Quality audits
5. Quality cost analysis
6. Probability
7. SQC
8. Design of experiment
9. Quality Circles
10. Reliability
11. Vendor relations
12. Manufacturing processes
13. Customer-based quality
14. Variance analysis—variation research
15. Value analysis and engineering
16. Work simplification methods
17. ASTM, military, and other standards

18. Employee motivational programs
19. Integral logistic support
20. Materials testing (general)
21. Holography testing
22. Computer-aided quality control (programming, CAD/CAM)
23. Automation
24. Robotics
25. Flexible manufacturing systems
26. Management practices
27. Maintainability
28. Supervisory and leadership training
29. Product safety, product liability
30. Blueprint reading
31. Nondestructive testing
32. Communications (verbal and nonverbal)
33. Conducting quality training programs
34. Quality information systems
35. Methodology and inspection

One can add many other topics that are related to quality management. There are a large number of books available in various areas. All that has to be done is to adopt these types of courses to the engineering or business-management area.

9. Ongoing Training Methods

Organizations that believe in quality work and are interested in improving productivity generally believe in ongoing training. There are programs for all levels of management and all levels of workers. It is not enough to train people when they join the organization or train them when they are in trouble. It is essential for an organization to establish training departments that would coordinate training achievements with the local college or vocational school campus, so that ongoing training of employees can be carried out smoothly at all times.

Some of the common methods that are used today for ongoing training are:

1. Monthly meetings
2. Company newsletters
3. Videotapes

4. Films, cassette tapes
5. Evening classes at vocational schools and colleges
6. In-house training by quality experts (2-3 days)

Training—A Never-Ending Job

We must all remember that training is a never-ending job. New knowledge is being used every day; new inventions create more information every second in this information explosion era. People leave and join new organizations. With such employee turnover, training the new employee is very important so that he or she becomes thoroughly acquainted with the working of the organization. Such training makes a new employee a productive member of the team.

New products and services are constantly being introduced in various organizations at different times. In order to keep good quality standards, it is essential that those who have to deal with the new products and services know what is involved with it in order to do a good job. New methods and procedures of operation also play an important role in improving productivity. Again, those who are involved should be well informed of the change.

Another factor that should be given consideration is the understanding and retention level of various human beings (employees). No matter how much or how little is taught, there is always a tendency for people to forget a part of the training; if it is their first exposure, there is a good chance that only 10 to 20 percent is understood at the beginning! However, very few people will admit their ignorance and will keep working without asking questions. Ongoing training helps an employee to retain material, as it follows up the training that was given. This way, everyone is involved in learning new material or reviewing old knowledge without expressing their ignorance to others and without feeling shy.

Effective leadership, organization-wide, rarely happens by chance. Rather it is the result of an organization's determination that all of its supervisors/managers will be:

- *active rather than passive.*
- *goal oriented rather than crisis motivated.*
- *people oriented as well production oriented.*
- *future oriented rather than wedded to the past.*

Hence the need for a planned and organized effort to train and develop organizational members.

"Supervisory/Management Training"
published by BNA Communications,
Rockville, Maryland, 1984

Chapter Fifteen
OQI IN SERVICE INDUSTRIES

In the United States today there is a variety of service industries. These service industries differ in their nature and the scope of their operations, and they face different types of problems than do manufacturing industries. However, labor is common to both industries. In order to run any business, we need people. We also need customers to buy the products or use the services. Because people are involved in giving the service and people are the ones who use that service, they certainly contribute to the quality of the services of an organization.

It is a well-known fact that more than half of American businesses are run by a large variety of service industries; the number is increasing daily. Following are the key industries that play an important role in the United States economy.

1. Health care
2. Finance
3. Transportation
4. Utilities
5. Department stores and food supermarkets
6. Insurance
7. Education

8. Government agencies—federal, state, and local
9. Hotels, motels, and restaurants
10. Nonprofit organizations

In the United States, public service institutions, government agencies, and other service organizations have grown much faster than have manufacturing industries. The service staff in manufacturing industries has grown much faster than the operating units.

In general, the performance of most of these service industries is considered to be poor. Some of the popular explanations for this are:

- Managers are not businesslike
- They may need better people
- Their objectives and results are intangible

General Operation of Service Industries

Even though service organizations do not manufacture any tangible goods, they still need to satisfy customers. All these organizations are established with a specific purpose in mind; if the purpose is not properly strived for, customers will start looking around. Hospitals, for example, need to give patients better health care at reasonable costs. Banks and savings and loan institutions need to offer the people the required financial services conveniently and at a reasonable cost. Public transportation systems must do the same. Even educational institutions cannot afford to raise tuitions as they might like any more or offer courses just for the sake of someone's interest. The rapid change in customer satisfaction has created a new challenge for all service industries alike!

Standards and procedures are used commonly in service industries just like blueprints in manufacturing operations. In service industries it is essential to update procedures and use them effectively for quality operations and services. The quality of the process needs to be analyzed and evaluated through constant internal and external checks. This can be accomplished through the following steps:

1. Data collection
2. Data analysis through manual system or computer
3. Corrective actions
4. Ongoing monitoring
5. Periodic review

One of the key elements in improving organizational quality improvement in a service industry is to establish this system and use it effectively. Measurements such as length or diameter can be used as they are in manufacturing operations. In service industries data must be collected on errors, delays, waste, storage, and transportation; this data should be minimized with the help of control charts, histograms, process charts, activity charts, man-machine charts, and by using principles of motion economics effectively.

The final outcome of service industries is generally measured using the following indicators:

1. Efficiency
2. Productivity
3. Budget requirements
4. Quality and operation
5. Customer satisfaction
6. Reputation

Sample Case Study[1]

Quality Assurance in Hospitals

Health and well-being are probably the most important concerns of an individual. For that reason, the quality of patient care is extremely important in the health-care setting. The mission statement of every hospital reflects this and refers to the high quality of care the hospital intends to provide.

Hospitals have monitored the quality of care for a long time. Initially these efforts were done mainly through the medical staff. All hospitals have medical staff committees for various specialties. The peers of a physician review the quality of patient care through those committees. They also suggest solutions if problems existed.

There have been numerous cases in which courts have ruled that hospitals are responsible for the quality of patient care delivered in the hospital. There was also a malpractice insurance cost crisis in the seventies. These insurance costs increased very rapidly because of the numerous claims and large awards made. In some locations medical staff refused to take patients because of high insurance costs or the unavailability of malpractice insurance. For these reasons, hospitals became even more interested in monitoring the quality of patient care.

---

[1] From A. M. Salvekour, assistant administrator, St. Cloud Hospital, St. Cloud, Minnesota.

In the early 1980s the Joint Commission on Accreditation of Hospitals issued a new standard for quality assurance. This standard recognized that the quality-assurance efforts of hospitals were fragmented, unorganized, and inconsistent. Previous to the issuance of this standard, the Joint Commission required a certain number of quality-assurance audits for each hospital. It was subsequently found that this numerical requirement did not adequately monitor or improve the quality of patient care; instead, it became a paper exercise to meet the Joint Commission standards.

The principle used in developing the new Joint Commission standard is as follows:[2]

The hospital shall demonstrate a consistent endeavor to deliver patient care that is optimal within available resources and consistent with achievable goals. A major component in the application of this principle is the operation of a quality-assurance program.

The standard itself states[3]:

There shall be evidence of a well defined, organized program designed to enhance patient care through the ongoing objective assessment of important aspects of patient care and the correction of the identified problems.

The interpretation of this standard by the Joint Commission states that the governing body of the hospital is responsible to establish, maintain, and support, through the hospital's administration and medical staff, an ongoing quality-assurance program that includes effective mechanisms for monitoring and evaluating product care, as well as an appropriate response to findings. A written quality-assurance plan must be prepared. The responsibility for quality assurance must be delegated to proper individuals or committees. The mechanisms for assuring accountability of the medical and other professional staff for the care they provide must be described in the plan. The quality-assurance program must be comprehensive and it should be flexible enough to permit innovation and variation in assessment approaches.

A sound quality-assurance program is expected to include the following:

1. Identification of important or potential problems or related concern in the care of the patient.
2. Objective assessment of the cause and scope of problems or concerns, including determination of priorities for both investigating and resolving problems.

---

[2] *Accreditation Manual for Hospitals, 1984.* Joint Commission on Accreditation of Hospitals, Chicago, Illinois, 1983.

[3] Ibid.

3. Implementation of actions that are designed to eliminate the identified problem.
4. Monitoring activities designed to assure that the desired results have been achieved and sustained.
5. Documentation that reasonably substantiates the effectiveness of the overall quality assurance program.

The quality of a product may be easier to define because of its tangible nature. It becomes more difficult to define quality in the case of a service. In the health care setting it is extremely difficult to define quality of patient care because of its intangible nature and the uncertainty of opinions. The Joint Commission allows the hospital to define quality through its unique situation. Written criteria are used that relate to essential or critical aspects of patient care and are generally acceptable to clinical staffs. These criteria should be clinically valid in that, when applied to actual practice, they can be expected to result in improved patient care or clinical performance.

As quality-assurance evaluations are undertaken using these written clinical criteria, pertinent findings are reported to the medical staff, the chief operating officer, and the governing board. The Joint Commission standard states that the quality-assurance activities should be integrated and coordinated to avoid any duplication of effort. Also, in the interest of consistency, terminology used or methods employed are expected to be defined in the plan.

The quality-assurance program itself is expected to be reappraised at least annually. The reappraisal should identify components of the quality-assurance program that need to be instituted, altered, or deleted.

As hospitals began to implement this quality-assurance standard, they typically developed some goals related to it. Examples of the goals are:

1. Patient care is maintained at optimal achievable levels of quality within available resources.
2. Patient care is delivered in an efficient, effective, and safe manner.
3. Patient-care practices and professional performance are regularly and reliably evaluated.
4. Evaluation results are incorporated in hospital and medical staff policies and procedures.
5. Assure that the hospital environment and equipment meet standards of safety for patients, employees, and visitors.

The quality-assurance program is usually designed in various functions:

1. Systematic collection of data
2. Analysis and evaluation of data

234 OQI IN SERVICE INDUSTRIES

3. Corrective action to effect change
4. Oversight to assure that all components are performing properly.

Collection of Data

Typically, hospitals organize a quality-assurance department. Effort is made to eliminate duplication of effort and to preserve confidentiality of data. All relevant sources of information are used. These include medical records; hospital statistical reports; reports from external agencies like the Joint Commission, insurance agencies, and licensing organizations; patient surveys and complaints; incident reports; insurance claims data; observation of staff members; studies undertaken to identify problems; and so on. The information generated yields the following type of analysis:

1. Mortality review
2. Morbidity review
3. Surgical case monitoring
4. Pharmacy and therapeutics review
5. Antibiotic and other drug monitoring
6. Blood-use review
7. Infection surveillance
8. Medical records review
9. Identification and analysis of adverse patient outcomes attributable to medical management
10. Hospital services review
11. Surveillance of proper and safe use of medical equipment
12. Review and evaluation of effectiveness and efficiency of the medical and other professional staff
13. Delineation of credentials and confidentiality based on objective performance data
14. Continuing education programs based on documented need for knowledge or skill.

Data Analysis

Collected data is analyzed so that it will help in quality-assurance activities. The purposes of such an analysis are:

1. To establish range of acceptable practice, performance, and outcome.

2. To identify and substantiate cases and patterns outside these acceptable ranges.
3. To make recommendations for further investigation and/or corrective action.

Use of Findings and Follow-up

The analysis leads to recommendations that should be acted upon. Usually a higher authority must take that corrective action. If the recommendation is for medical staff, it is acted upon through the organizational structure of the medical staff. On the other hand, if the recommendation is for the hospital department, it is implemented by the hospital administration. On some occasions the authority of the governing board may be needed to implement a certain corrective action.

Oversight

According to the Joint Commission standard, the governing board is responsible for this function. Oversight assures that all components of the quality-assurance program are functioning in a proper manner. It makes sure that:

1. Data-gathering activities are valid, reliable, and comprehensive.
2. The findings are properly derived.
3. Actions taken are appropriate to the findings.
4. The impact of problem-solving efforts is being monitored and documented.

Risk Management

The primary goal of a risk management program is to preserve the resources of the hospital and its staff from avoidable financial loss due to claims against it. Quality assurance is related to risk management. Quality assurance can reduce the professional liability from the identified corrective action. On the other hand, a risk management situation can lead to a corrective action that improves quality of patient care. In many hospitals these two functions report to the same administrative person.

Incident reports, which include patient falls, medication errors and other undesirable outcomes, patient complaints, and other information are used by hospitals for risk management. However, it was found that these reports deal with only "environmental" issues. The other dimension of risk management is that of "clinical" loss prevention. Clinical loss prevention involves identifying those patient management events that could potentially lead to liability for the hospital and its staff. National malpractice experience demonstrates that it is in the clinical or patient management area that a hospital stands to suffer its greatest potential dollar losses due to professional liability. For these reasons, many hospitals have started an occurrence screening system. Typical objectives of such a system are:

1. Identifying events which are unexpected in the course of an unexpected hospitalization
2. Enabling early analysis of such events to determine whether they could result in liability
3. Enabling the gathering of information on those events with liability potential as close to the time of event as possible to assist the hospital or its professional staff in minimizing the likelihood of a claim
4. Enabling early action to minimize the likelihood of subsequent claim and financial loss
5. Assisting in determining how liability exposure can be minimized currently and in the future
6. Increasing the involvement of medical staff members in loss-prevention efforts
7. Identifying additional sources of information in quality-assurance activities

The concepts used in occurrence screening were first developed as a part of the California Medical Insurance Feasibility Study conducted in 1976 by the California Medical Association and the California Hospital Association. Their study was conducted in response to the medical malpractice crisis in the 1970s. The principal investigator of this study was Don Harper Mills, M.D., J.D.[4]

Design of the occurrence screening system, also known as the generic outcome screening system, can vary from hospital to hospital. Basically, occurrence screening is designed as a criterion-based review system. The patient-care events being screened for are usually identifiable from patients' medical records. An individual screens a medical record against the occurrence screening criteria and ifentifies events that need further investigation. These events are reported to proper authorities and further action may be taken.

4. Ibid.

A number of criteria can be used; they can be grouped in a number of categories.

1. Unexpected health impairment
2. Unexpected medical intervention
3. Unexpected intensity of service
4. Unexpected hospital-incurred incidents

Some examples of occurrence screening criteria are given below:

1. Admission to hospital or return to ER/OPD (Emergency Room/Outpatient Department) within three months following ER/OPD management for condition related to or suggestive of adverse results or complication of such prior management
2. Readmission within six months for a condition representing either a complication of treatment or incomplete treatment of a problem present on previous admission to this hospital
3. Hospital-incurred incident—for example, a fall, medication reaction, or similar
4. Unanticipated transfer to another acute-care facility
5. Organ failure (heart, kidney, liver) not present on admission
6. Significant neurosurgery or functional deficit or intractable pain not present on admission
7. Laceration, perforation, tear, or puncture of an organ or body part occasioned during an invasive procedure and requiring surgical intervention for repairs
8. Unexpected return to the operating room on the same admission, or transfer to operating room following delivery
9. Unplanned removal, partial removal, or repair of a normal organ or body part during an operative procedure
10. Operation for removal of foreign body left in operative site

Each hospital can assess its need and add, subtract, or modify these kinds of criteria.

In conclusion, hospitals have been monitoring the quality of patient care for a long time. The subject is quite complex in the health care field, but noticeable progress has been made. New Joint Commission standards and concern for malpractice losses have intensified these efforts recently. New fiscal pressures through restricted reimbursements from government and other payors will also encourage greater focus on quality assurance at the lowest cost.

Problems in Service Industries

There are many problems that one can list in managing a service industry. It is not possible to list all of them here and suggest solutions on how to handle them, nor do I claim to help show how to manage a business effectively in such a short section of this book. However, it is necessary to understand some of the problems that service industries face in managing business so that if management decides to implement OQI, they can be aware of these situations beforehand and try to plan the necessary corrective actions early in the game so the OQI program will run smoothly.

I would like to list some of the major problems in service industries that I have observed over the last several years.

1. Variety of objective. When you work with service industries, improvements in quality may not make sense easily. Some organizations like to see improvements in efficiency, while others like to show improvements in productivity. In some cases, productivity is a bad word; some agencies rather see effective operations within budgetary limits! Hence, it is my opinion that each service organization should decide its objectives and do what is needed to achieve those objectively and should not try to copy other organizations.

2. No tangible products. Another major problem in service industries is the final product evaluation. There is no such thing when you are working in a service organization. Customer satisfaction and customer complaints are the two main resources you must depend on for evaluation. Service industries really don't deal directly with the making of a product, hence it is difficult to evaluate their quality operations.

3. Branch operations. Many service organizations such as banks, colleges and universities, or department (chain) stores operate small branches where you cannot use the essential OQI concepts. You need to modify the approach and get small branches involved in major operations of the organization.

4. Shift operations. In many organizations such as hospitals and banks, operations are carried on a shift basis. This creates problems in the formation of quality or productivity improvement teams and managing the OQI process.

5. Education levels and variety of interests. Most service organizations generally employ personnel that are well qualified, but trainers may face problems in training these people in the OQI process due to diversity in their education levels. Trainers need to know the process thoroughly so they can answer all kinds of questions from different employees regarding OQI.

6. No competition. In some service organizations there is no competition for the services they offer. In such cases, I have found that it is very difficult to establish quality goals and convince the management to work on quality improvement. In such cases it is necessary to concentrate on budgetary achievements or improvement in the worker-management relationship.

Quality Wheel for Service Organizations

On various occasions I have experienced that service industries would like to differentiate themselves from manufacturing industries due to differences in operations, activities, and the basic nature of the business. I would like to propose a different type of Quality Wheel for service industries. The following items should be included in this wheel:

1. Quality policy and planning
2. Market research and surveys
3. New service introduction
4. Vendor quality
5. In-process quality performance
6. Data collection systems
7. Service testing
8. Special study using statistical methods
9. Quality information and measurement system
10. Customer complaints and feedback evaluation

Figure 15-1 will show the Quality Wheel based on the above-listed spokes. I recommend that service organizations should pay special attention to the following key areas in the self-analysis of the Quality Wheel:

1. Government standards and regulations
2. Quality costs
3. Quality audits
4. Office automation
5. Proper work reduction

QUALITY WHEEL FOR SERVICE ORGANIZATION

1. Quality Planning and Policy
2. Market Research and Quality Deployment
3. New Service Evaluation
4. Vendor Quality Evaluation
5. In-House Quality Performance
6. Quality Systems Evaluation
7. Services Evaluation
8. Special Studies and Quality Evaluation
9. Quality Information
10. Customer Complaints and Feedback System

FIGURE 15-1

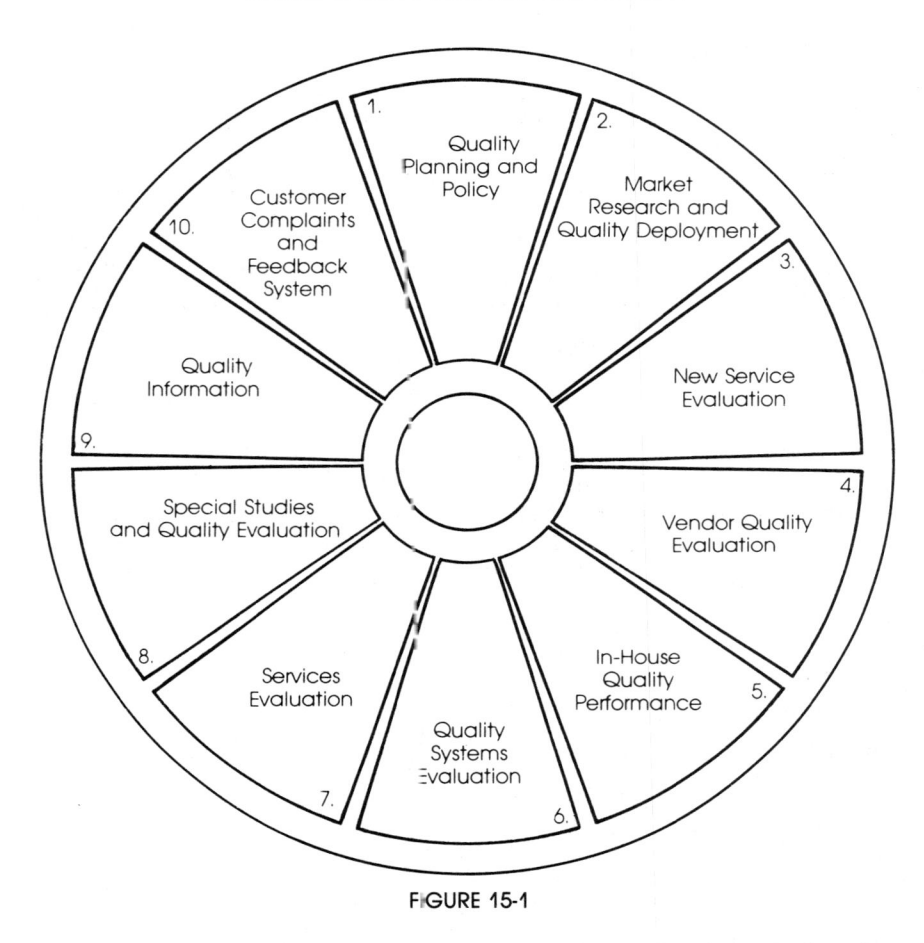

In order to achieve these goals, one should follow the implementation plan recommended below.

OQI Implementation Plan

Many times service organizations are structured differently and you may wonder whether it is necessary to change the implementation plan described here. Based on my experience, I feel that it is not essential to change the basic structure of the implementation plan dramatically. However, you will need to make minor changes to suit the needs of service industries.

One of the recommended plans for a service industry is listed here.

1. Introduction to top management
2. Approval to start
3. Formulation of quality council
4. Selection of the members
5. Three-day training for OQI
6. Project collection
7. Project presentation
8. Project approval
9. Project solution
10. Three-month review
11. Six-month review
12. Annual banquet
13. Ongoing OQI
14. Ongoing training
15. Ongoing quality and productivity improvement process

OQI Training for Service Organizations

We have discussed various OQI training features in Chapter 14. However, this training must be modified for service industries due to their needs. The following training program is recommended for OQI training in service industries.

OQI Training (Three Days)

Topics to Be Included

1. Why OQI?
2. Operational aspect of OQI
3. Group dynamics of OQI
4. Charting and analyzing processes (activity analysis, process analysis, man-machine analysis, principles of motion economy)
5. Self-analysis of Quality Wheel
6. Quality audits and quality costs
7. Improving results through time management, goal setting, interviewing

8. Quality Circle techniques
9. Statistical problem-solving techniques
10. Nominal group technique, force field analysis
11. Cost-benefit analysis
12. Data collection and analysis system
13. Managing with self-esteem
14. Product deployment
15. How to run productive meetings
16. PC—personal computers
17. Stem-and-leaf charts
18. Early warning system
19. Stratification, control charts, scatter diagram
20. Putting it all together

Advantages of Implementing OQI in Service Industries

I have already discussed in detail the advantages of OQI in other parts of this book. However, I will add the following advantages that can be related to service industries.

1. Improved images. Many service industries such as governmental agencies, city or county government units, and so on are looked upon as unnecessarily expensive. However, these service organizations can be run efficiently and effectively to improve their image.

2. Improved productivity. Productivity is generally associated with manufacturing industries. However, productivity is really a measure of output and input; it should not necessarily be confined to manufacturing operations. You can use this measure to improve the productivity of service operations also.

3. Reduced expenses. This is one of the most important aspects for service industries. Service organizations like banks, hospitals, and governmental agencies need to cut costs and reduce expenses. The OQI program helps to review the total operation and cut down on waste.

4. Improved communication. As the organization grows in size, effective communication becomes harder and many people wonder about the integrity of the system. Many new communication channels can be opened through the use of OQI.

5. Improved relations between management and workers. This need is common to all—manufacturing as well as service industries. It is essential that the management and workers work as a team or else face the problems of obsolescence.

6. Larger market share. Service organizations need to expand their market also. Banks, hospitals, or airlines cannot be content with what they have today. A larger market share is essential for long-range survival and to cut down the operating break-even point. One can expand the market with an OQI program since the team can review the overall needs and can come up with new ideas for future markets.

7. Improved profits or budgets. Profits are again associated with manufacturing industries; profitability is not looked upon favorably by the workers. However, you must understand that without profits, an organization cannot survive. Profits are essential for new research, new products, new equipment, new facilities, and many other things. In some service industries—government, for example—you can look to work within budgets instead of seeking a profit. Today, many governmental operations are running under a deficit. Through programs such as OQI, you can cut down unnecessary cost, reduce waste, and try to make a zero-deficit budget a reality!

These are some of the additional advantages that one can relate to service organizations.

EVALUATE YOUR ORGANIZATION

1. Our service organization has established quality policy or quality statement.

   1   5   10

   No   Maybe   Yes, definitely

2. Our organization has quality-improvement teams to improve the quality of services and programs to cut down costs and complaints.

   1   5   10

   No   Maybe   Yes, definitely

3. Our organization evaluates new services, procedures, and standards systematically that are released to use in our organizations.

   1   5   10

   No   Maybe   Yes, definitely

EVALUATE YOUR ORGANIZATION (continued)

4. Our organization collects and analyzes data systematically and performs quality audits periodically, using them to improve quality and efficiency of the organization.

1	5	10
No	Maybe	Yes, definitely

5. Our organization understands the concept of the Quality Wheel and uses it effectively.

1	5	10
No	Maybe	Yes, definitely

6. Our organization involves people in solving problems in a participative way.

1	5	10
No	Maybe	Yes, definitely

7. Our organization offers ongoing training programs for employees.

1	5	10
No	Maybe	Yes, definitely

8. Our organization constantly works for customer satisfaction; customer complaints are handled immediately.

1	5	10
No	Maybe	Yes, definitely

9. Our organization understands and uses statistical methods effectively.

1	5	10
No	Maybe	Yes, definitely

10. Our organization constantly looks for new services based on customer surveys and customer needs.

1	5	10
No	Maybe	Yes, definitely

Note: The author has developed more than 300 questions of this type for analysis.

Service Industries need to think of their own specific functions, purposes and missions. They need efficiency as well as effectiveness. Few service institutions today suffer from having too few administrators; most of them are over-administered and suffer from a surplus of procedures, organization charts and management techniques. What has to be learned is to manage service institutions for performance.

Peter Drucker,
Management: Tasks, Practices, Responsibilities,
New York, Harper, 1974

Chapter Sixteen
NATIONWIDE QUALITY IMPROVEMENT

Any nation interested in improving quality and productivity needs to understand the need for total quality commitment in the country. This quality commitment does not happen overnight, nor does it happen without quality and productivity today, and every year they gain superiority in a quality and productivity today; and every year they gain superiority in a new field. During the 1980s Japan is aiming at achieving the number one position in the electronics and machine tool industries. The results that we admire today are the outcome of nationwide quality commitment that started 20 years ago!

In order to understand the concepts of national quality commitment, we must know more about the present intrastructure of the government that exists in any nation, as well as the working of industries in that nation.

Roles Played by Different Parties in National Quality Commitment

Government. In democratic nations, the government is formed by elected members of a party. The majority of electoral candidates determines the ruling party. In the United States there is presidential rule; every four years, there is a possible change of government. Naturally, in most democratic countries, the ruling government is most interested in strengthening their party; building the nation is a secondary aim!

The ruling government usually tries to favor multimillionaire companies so that the government will get good support by way of funds and/or votes. It is observed in the United States, Great Britain, India, and many other democratic countries that the ruling party holds the upper hand and gives concessions either to the management or the workers, either to the landlords or the farmers, either to the majority caste or to the minority caste, as the situation may be, and tries to swindle as many votes as possible, thereby gaining a majority and forming the ruling party for the next term.

However, in all activities, the government shows very little foresight in building the nation in general. Wide publicity is given to the government's aims and goals and what it can achieve during the next term; however, very little is achieved after the elections.

Management. The management of an organization is also vigilant about changing the attitude of the government, as the management aims at all times to make a maximum profit for the organization. At times the management may even try to do favors for the government so that governmental rules and regulations can be relaxed. This results in saving money in various ways (tax reductions and so on) and maximizes profit. The profit made by an organization is generally invested, and not enough is spent on improvement of the quality of work life. As in government, management changes are very common in different organizations. Generally, management is interested in quantities and costs first. Quality is generally of secondary importance. When the question of poor quality arises, management is generally interested in banded (quick, short) fixes and in getting rid of the product as quickly as possible. It seems that instead of quantity and quality going hand in hand, they are treated as two controversial entities, with quality usually being sacrificed for quantity. Similarly, due to short-term positions given to high-level executives (usually presidents of organizations) short-term high returns are prioritized rather than the long-term interest of an organization, such as quality commitment.

Unions. In many countries unions are strong; they always keep watch on the activities of the management. When they find that there is any adverse activity that will hamper the interest of the workers—either monetarily or otherwise—union leaders immediately raise their voices and try to safeguard their rights and the workers' rights. The attitude of the union leaders in such cases prevents the program of the organization, thereby becoming a stumbling block in trying to achieve a national quality commitment.

Financial institutions. Everything needs money—new plants, new equipment, new employees, anything the organization would like to start. One of the critical constraints is the amount of financial support they can get. Financial institutions play a significant role in the organization and government operations. In various countries, financial institutions operate in a different manner; it is not possible to cover all the aspects in this book. However, I would like to add a comment here so the reader can get a clear picture of the interest rates in Japan versus the United States. In 1970 the interest rate for businesses in Japan was 4-5 percent, whereas the prime rate in the United States had climbed to 21-22 percent.

It is clear that the unhealthy relationship between these four areas (government, management, unions, and financial institutions) would not be healthy for a national commitment to quality. It seems that each member of this group is interested in its own interest rather than in the spirit of cooperation that can exist between government, labor, and management of the organizations.

Due to these attitudes, the final results can be summarized as follows:

1. There is a poor relationship between the three parties.
2. Management cannot work efficiently.
3. Workers remain usually unsatisfied.

The big question is how to avoid all these complications and obtain a nationwide, ongoing quality improvement. I believe one of the best ways is to promote national quality-improvement programs. These types of programs should create more interest in quality nationwide and also create a national quality commitment that we need badly today. Some of these programs have been successful, some of these are new, and some have already passed the infant stage in the United States and other countries.

National Quality Commitment Programs

I will list here ten programs that I feel will help to improve quality and productivity of products and services on a nationwide basis. More and more new ones will be added as time goes on.

1. Nationwide emphasis on quality. Rigorous attempts should be made to impact the minds of people that the quality of their work must be the best in all aspects. Quality of the product does not come simply by improving technology or methods or equipment. These factors are no doubt helpful to improve quality, but what is essential is the attitude of the people toward the work they conduct. If the worker is performing his or her work drowsily, and with a lethargic attitude, no matter how hard he or she seems to be working, the final result will always be below high quality standards. Hence, emphasis on quality is a key factor in national quality programs.

One of the best ways to promote quality is through a "quality month" in the nation. In the United States, different weeks are noted for different promotions, such as Safety Week, Education Week, and so on. I feel that a week is not enough to make a noticeable impact on people's minds. I recommend that the month of July should be proclaimed as a quality month. We celebrate the Fourth of July as Independence Day—why not promote quality to keep us free from economic collapse in the world! High-quality products and services will definitely do that (Figure 16-1).

We need more organizational conferences in all nations to emphasize quality. Some of the conferences can be as follows:

1. Quality conference for top management
2. Quality conference for middle management
3. Quality conference for supervisors and foremen
4. Quality conference for operators

These types of conferences can be arranged on a statewide basis and later on a national level with the help of governments. Many organizations today hold conferences in specialized fields. Only experts or special people usually attend these conferences and try to carry the message back to the organizations. In a "Quality Congress" we find quality managers and quality engineers in attendance. What we need is more involvement, more exchange

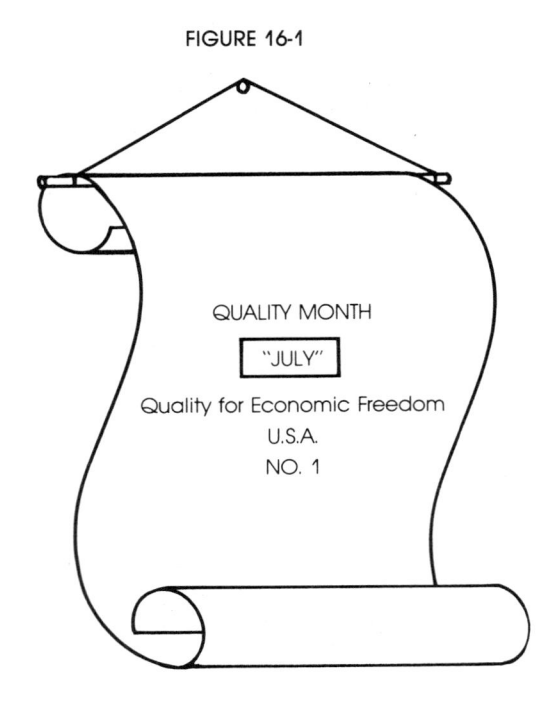

FIGURE 16-1

QUALITY MONTH

"JULY"

Quality for Economic Freedom
U.S.A.
NO. 1

of ideas by a wider cross section of employees of various organizations of a nation. This will help to emphasize quality nationwide.

2. Mass quality training through TV, radio, and newspapers. Today, mass media such as television, radio, and newspapers play an important role in everyone's life. National quality education can be enhanced if these media will help the nation promote quality rather than just criticizing the problems. Most of these media are in operation around the clock. They are useful in relaying news and information about events as well as sports, movies, and so on to the common man. These mass communication media should be profitably utilized to educate the masses in order to improve the quality of products and services in the nation. Mass media could become good vehicles to transport ideas of quality to the common man. Training in statistics and quality control should be offered as ongoing activities on these media.

3. "United for Quality" by government, labor leaders, and management. We discussed previously the poor relationship and apathy toward quality by these parties—government, labor leaders, and management. It is about time we promoted cooperative activities between these parties. I believe that the government should take the initiative and form committees to invite the key leaders from various manufacturing and service organizations to try to establish quality goals and objectives on a national level. These activities should be published through mass media so that everyone in the country knows about them.

4. "United for Quality" by industry. In Japan, MITI (Ministry of Trade and Industry) plays a significant role in promoting quality and capturing new markets around the world. I believe we need to unite by industry and try to face the foreign competition. Industries like automotives, electronics, computers, and the like can unite and share their common knowledge to improve industry as a whole. We need to be more open and understand the future competition between nations rather than between just a few key organizations. In recent years there has been such a movement in the computer industry and the automobile industry. However, progress has been too slow.

5. Annual presidential and state awards. I feel that annual awards should be established for organizations to recognize good quality work and quality improvements. This has to be done systematically, with proper planning and establishment of rules. It will give good publicity to organizations and institutions and will provide incentive for others to learn the good quality professions.

Presidential awards should be given through the White House; however, eligibility for the awards should be funneled through the states. Each

FIGURE 16-2

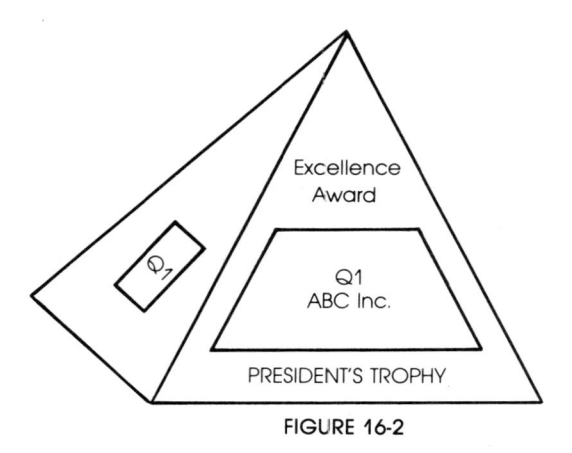

state should establish a similar system, and those who win state awards should be eligible for the presidential awards (Figure 16-2).

6. Emphasis on statistical thinking. Day to day, work in industries is generally directed by supervisors and management; they are generally responsible or involved in quality of the products and services. This process can be improved easily by adopting the use of statistical thinking to analyze and solve quality problems. Japan has shown the importance of statistical thinking and statistical methods to the rest of the world. In fact, Edward Deming, the world-renowned American statistician, says, "In Japan, statistics is a second language!"

7. Quality training centers. There are productivity centers in the United States and many other countries. However, I believe we need to establish quality training centers in the nation. The government should establish the centers and offer training in quality, statistics, and related topics. We have discussed more details in Chapter 15.

8. Independent quality evaluation centers. We need to establish these types of quality evaluation centers, which should be sponsored by the government and industries. Consumers, industries, and others should have easy access to the information. Computers should be used for storing and disseminating data to businesses and consumers. We have consumer reports, but the information is not used effectively. We need to use this information through mass media, and business should use it to improve the quality of products and services.

9. New training programs in educational institutions. We need to revise our vocational and college education systems. There should be greater emphasis on science and mathematics. We need to add training in quality management and quality engineering. The government should help educational institutions to develop these programs and emphasize their importance. I discussed the details of this in Chapter 14, page .

There are many experts on quality, myself included, who would be glad to work with those educational institutions interested in developing new curricula in the areas mentioned above.

10. National quality policy. There are pros and cons regarding developing a national quality policy. *Industry Week* (November 14, 1984) recently published both views on a similar topic. We do not want to establish rigid rules so that each and every organization must follow what is being dictated by National Quality policy. However, I feel that the government should guide the country and recommend expectations regarding quality. Let me quote remarks from the *Industry Week* article which seem appropriate here:

If we get back to focusing on broad government policies to improve our utilization of physical capital, human capital and technology—in conjunction with improved management policies—we can go a long way toward putting ourselves back on the track of being the first-rate industrial power that we were in most of the postwar period.

What we need is a good, broad guideline from the government on national quality commitment and quality training.

Desired Role of Government, Management, and Unions in Building National Quality Commitment

The discussion thus far has revealed that there are several factors involved in promoting and obtaining national quality commitment from all parties involved. It cannot be done by one individual or one organization, nor can it be achieved by a few. It should be a cooperative effort of everyone in the nation.

The attitude of the government plays an important part in building this concept on solid ground. Regardless of any governing party, there should be a common goal before any nation—that is, to build quality products and offer quality services in the nation. The suggestion offered in this chapter must be followed rigorously by any party that comes in power. This type of ten-point program should be sketched out by the eminent politicians who are the leaders of the various parties.

Government should also show a parental attitude toward industrial organizations as well as labor. It cannot hold a grudge or be biased toward any party. Government should establish guidelines for both groups to contribute to improvement, quality, and productivity of the nation.

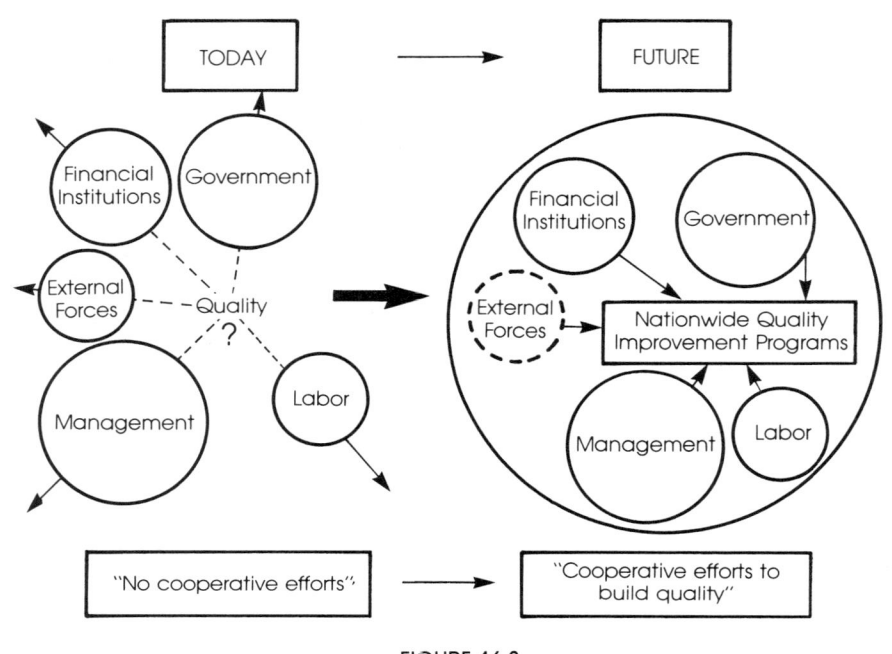

FIGURE 16-3

I also believe it is about time that management and labor join hand in hand to improve the quality and productivity of an organization, then share the fruits of their labors. Companies should think of long-range survival, not short-range profits for stocks and shareholders. If companies commit to building quality products, they will make profits and will not have to worry about survival. Figure 16-3 shows the future need of any country—the relationship between the three groups that should be achieved.

Importance of a National Quality Program

It is essential that each country develop promotional quality activities on a nationwide basis. It is not enough that each organization works on quality improvements alone. In the United States the work force is mobile. Many times during the year people change jobs, move from one plant to another, move from one part of the country to another part of the country, and in some cases, from one nation to another. Hence, it is necessary that there be good guidelines for quality expectations (that are common to all) on a national level. Many times industries become obsolete while using new inventions. New companies get formed (sunrise industries) and it is foolish to adopt old quality standards in a new quality era. Therefore it is necessary to update national quality standards constantly. Similarly, consumers need to be heard and listened to in deciding quality standards, because they are the final inspectors of the product. It is also necessary that some of the complaints be discussed on a national level to improve safety-related problems.

Finally, today many countries face the problem of budget deficit. In the United States it is expected that the budget deficit is increasing and there is no end in sight yet. We can help our nation to improve various public sectors by committing to quality improvement so that we can eliminate waste, be careful in what we are buying, and systematically organize the government sector by promoting teamwork.

You can see that it is not easy to achieve national quality commitment. There are many angles, many different views, many different interests, and many obstacles just to start something on such a broad scale. However, we must start today, before it is too late to change the destiny of our nation. What we really need today is training, determination, cooperation, and finally, the willingness to do something today and not wait until tomorrow for someone else to change our destiny.

And so, my fellow Americans, Ask not what your country can do for you, ask what you can do for your country.

President John F. Kennedy,
Inaugural Address,
January 20, 1961

Chapter Seventeen
WHY JAPAN IS AHEAD

This book cannot be completed unless we discuss modern Japanese quality control and the various manufacturing techniques that have made Japan so successful. There are thousands of articles and hundreds of books published about Japan today. I do not plan to repeat the details in this chapter. I have listed references at the end of this chapter for use, based on my visits to various industries in Japan and observations to salient features related to quality and productivity improvement.

In 1979 I visited the Japan Productivity Center in Tokyo. I discussed Japan's superiority in quality products with Yukio Suzuki and Tunji Naguchi, planning manager of the Research and Development Department, Union of Japanese Scientists and Engineers (JUSE), Tokyo. During this discussion, Mr. Naguchi clearly stated that quality is not a dream that comes true by waving a magic wand. Japan has worked for the past three decades to get to the top, and it is going to be almost impossible for any other nation to reach that point now. What did Japan do to achieve this undisputed number one place? For the last 12 years, Japan has adopted a six-point program to create, maintain, and improve its quality image. The six-point program includes the following:

1. Quality audits
2. Companywide quality control

3. Quality training and education
4. Application of statistical methods
5. Quality Circle activities
6. Nationwide quality-control promotional activities

1. Quality Audits

There are two kinds of quality audits performed on products:

a. Internal quality-control audits by executives
b. External quality control

In internal audits, top management, middle management, and quality-control people get involved in checking the quality performance of products and services of the organization. These types of audits have helped top management to understand the quality problem firsthand and to solve them more effectively. Direct communication between top management and working through supervisors also helped to create teamwork in the organization. This teamwork has helped to improve quality and cut down the cost of products.

External audits are carried out independently by JUSE and other organizations. The Deming Prize was established in 1951 to honor Edward Deming. There is the Deming Prize for an individual who has contributed to the development of quality control in Japan; the other is the Deming prize for an enterprise, and it is further divided into three categories. Another prize is called the Japan Quality Control Prize. This was established in 1970, and it is awarded to the organization that continues the steady effort of companywide quality control and produces the best effects after winning the Deming Prize.

2. Companywide Quality Control (CWQC)

The key feature of CWQC is that all departments—such as the decision department, manufacturing department, sales department, QC department, and the purchasing department—participate and execute quality control. There are a number of activities carried out in the company to execute CWQC through the use of statistical thinking and the statistical way. These activities are aimed to produce and supply good products and services for customer satisfaction. Everyone is involved in achieving this goal. Quality activities are oriented toward products and services and also for administrative and procedural work of the company.

One of the companies in Japan defines CWQC (companywide quality control) as follows:

Quality control does not bear fruit unless the whole company cooperates in carrying it out. Hence, TQC (total quality control) stands for a system under which all people in each echelon of a firm cooperate in pushing quality control from a company-wide point of view, while engaging in their respective assignments.

It is easy to promote the philosophy. However, in practice, one faces many problems. But nothing is easy in this world.

3. Quality Training and Education

Japan has made tremendous progress in promoting quality training and education all over Japan. This training is divided into five categories:

1. Training in schools and colleges
2. Training courses by JUSE
3. Internal training
4. Training through conferences and visits
5. Nationwide training through television and radio

The literacy rate in Japan is almost 100 percent, so it is easy to study the textbooks of quality control and statistical methods. There are numerous books and articles written on these subjects. If one wants to get a better education or better job, there is keen competition in schools and colleges as well as in companies. People are always interested in learning more, and, as mentioned by Dr. Deming, "Statistics is a second language in Japan." In general, there is a high emphasis on quality training and education all over Japan.

4. Application of Statistical Methods

It is said that the systematic introduction of modern quality control into Japan started as the application of statistical techniques. The initial training was offered by Edward Deming in 1950. The use of basic and advanced statistics has grown tremendously in Japanese manufacturing companies. Engineers, manufacturers, and quality-control managers generally use high-level statistics, whereas people in the shop use basic statistical techniques.

5. Quality Circles

Junjo Noguchi states that the spectacular performance of Quality Circles and the important role they play in improving quality and productivity is astonishing. It is estimated that in Japan between $20 and $25 billion is saved every year as a result of the creative activities of Quality Circles. Mr. Noguchi stressed that Japan has successfully harnessed people's brainpower through Quality Circles. It is extremely important that human beings and their jobs be respected, no matter how big or small they are. The Japanese believe that everyone contributes something to the betterment of the society and the world.

Quality Circles involve people in solving problems and tap their brainpower effectively. Joi Asahi, the managing director of the Japanese tire manufacturer, Bridgestone, once said, "Through everyone's participation, we will become the best." At present, it is estimated that more than ten million people have participated in this program and have helped to build a superior quality program in Japan. Japan has shown the rest of the world that productivity can be improved not only by using new equipment or more people, but also by tapping human brainpower and working together in companies.

People and their brains are the most precious resources we have. We want to improve our productivity not at the expense of our people, but at the expense of wasted time, lost motion, unnecessary work, and products of poor quality. Our most valuable aids in cutting waste are the people on the production floor who know their jobs better than anyone else. We want the involvement of their minds as well as their hands. When we can achieve this effectively, we will have the greatest team in the world, one that no one will be able to compete with.

6. Nationwide Quality-Control Promotional Activities

Japan has done a marvelous job of promoting quality control on a nationwide basis. One of the key features of nationwide quality control is Quality Month (the month of November), during which the importance of quality is emphasized all over the nation through a number of public lectures, as well as conferences and promotions held for top management, middle managers, foremen, and consumers. Simultaneously, posters, banners, and flags are distributed in all the factories throughout the country. Even mass media such as television and radio are used for wide publicity. Many large corporations hold their own meetings and conferences on quality programs. Special international symposiums are held also. Many companies in Japan also send quality-control managers and Quality Circle leaders to other countries such as the United States and Europe to learn and to improve their knowledge about what is going on around the world.

Based on my reading of many articles and books on Japanese management, it seems that the Japanese quality-control process has gone through many changes. In brief, I see the four stages as follows:

1. Inspection-oriented quality control
2. Control charts and basic statistical methods dominated quality control

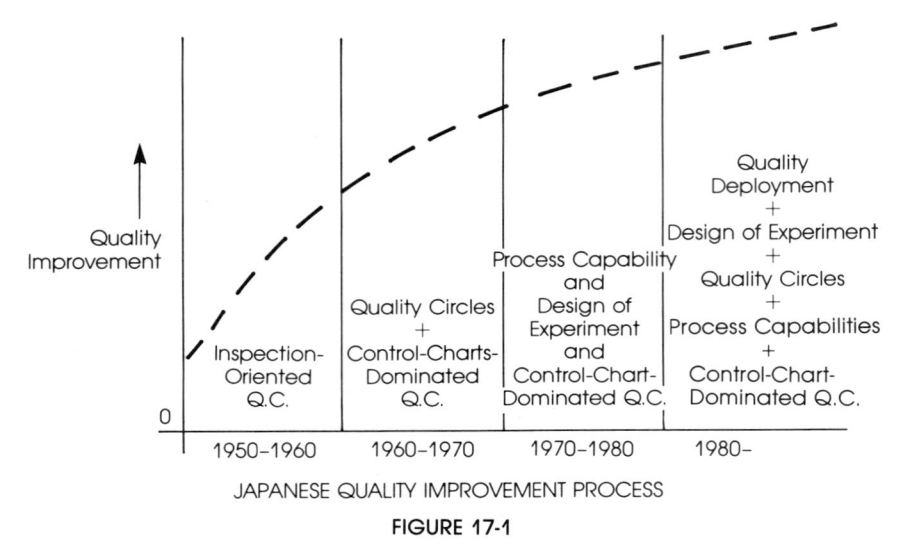

FIGURE 17-1

JAPANESE QUALITY IMPROVEMENT PROCESS

3. Quality Circles and process-capability-oriented quality control
4. CWQC product deployment and design of experiment-oriented quality control

So as one will see, quality-improvement methods have gone through many changes, and there will doubtless be more ongoing changes as time goes on! (Figure 17-1). That is why we must realize that quality improvement is a never-ending job.

Japan's modern quality control is not the only reason for its new higher productivity and quality. Various manufacturing methods also contribute to this phenomenal success. Let us review these key techniques.

1. JIT Purchasing

"Just in time" purchasing is very common in Japan. Companies do not order supplies to last for six to eight months. Most of the material is ordered for two or three days' supply. In some cases, it can be only for three or four hours. JIT purchasing helps to keep vendors quality-conscious and helps to cut down inventory. Problems with rejected material become minimal.

2. JIT Production (Kanban System)

"Just in time" production is another important method used to keep inventory down and improve quality of in-house products and assemblies. When a company does not have a large volume of parts, problems become obvious soon, and rejects cannot be hidden. People are involved immediately and try to solve problems as a team so that production lines won't stop. This way, quality is emphasized and everyone is conscious of doing a good job. Many companies have heard about the Kanban system, which is commonly used by Toyota.

There were doubts regarding the effectiveness of the JIT system in the United States at the beginning, as distance and a long order time played an important role in U.S. production. However, today many companies are committed to the use of this philosophy and it is working very well.

3. Use of Robotics and Automation

The general philosophy in Japan is that people should be used where brainpower is required, and that most of the repetitive work should be performed by automation and robots. Today in Japan, more than 50,000 robots are in use, whereas about 10,000 to 15,000 robots are in use in the United States. (One should remember that robots are an American invention.) It is necessary that we use robots for dirty, hard, repetitive work, but the introduction and use of robots has to be planned carefully so that people will be willing to accept the change rather than resent it.

4. Group Technology

There is a vast difference between manufacturing systems in Japan and those in the United States. In Japan, one man runs more machines, while in the United States, departmentalization is common, which can cause delays and unnecessary transportation of products.

5. Minimizing Setup Time

In Japan, setup time is considered waste; every organization tries to get rid of as much setup time as possible. There are reports that auto industries reduced their setup time from 24 hours to 8 hours to 4 hours. (The most recent setup time that was reported was less than 20 minutes.) One may think these are fairy tales. However, I observed the same changes in the United States, where setup time was reduced from 8 hours to less than 20 minutes. We need to use creativity, simple changeover methods, and do it!

6. Uniform Plant Loading

This principle helps to minimize delays and unnecessary storage of parts (warehouse space) in an organization. U-shaped lines are very common in Japan, and gravity-shoot principles are used for easy transportation. Tow motors are rarely seen within a plant.

7. Use of Good Cost-Control Procedure

As soon as new products are designed, engineering is given the responsibility to design a cost-control system. Each and every part is watched closely and the cost target is measured so that unnecessary costs don't get added in the new products.

8. Good Procedures and Standards

I observed the existence of good procedures and standards in many organizations in Japan during my recent visit. It was not only obvious that these were in existence in all phases, but were also used effectively. Instructions for the operators on how to carry on the operation properly were posted on the walls throughout the shops and assembly areas. I also noticed that standards and procedures were not written just to be kept in a folder or just for the use of engineering or management personnel.

9. Open Eyes, Open Minds

The Japanese usually keep an open mind while listening to others. The "People and Productivity" film produced by Encyclopedia Britannica in 1981 describes this trait very well in detail.

10. Lifetime Employment

Management changes in Japan occur infrequently. People are scrutinized rigorously when they are hired. However, once they are given a job, most of them stay a long time with the company. Most work at a variety of jobs before they are assigned to one department. Promotions on the job are watched closely. People tend to work hard when they know they will be in one company for a long time. (However, recent reports indicate the new generation is changing their attitude toward "lifetime employment" because there are more jobs, more flexibility and more attraction to the large cities where more is offered for the younger generation. The major effect is less loyalty to the company and less interest in the quality of good work.)

11. Effective Use of Buffer System, Overtime, and Female Work Force

Many companies in Japan use these three aspects more effectively when production goes up or down. Instead of hiring and firing personnel, these methods can be less troublesome.

12. Union Influence

Unions in Japan are not very powerful. Few are strong on a national level; most of them are local. It is reported that even though some of them go on strike, these strikes are not severe and do not last long. There is a more cooperative nature between union and management to build quality products. Work rules are not overly strict, and people can be observed helping each other in factories.

13. Vendor-Vendee Relationship

Most of the companies' vendors are just extensions of the major companies. Many of them work at sister plants. Incoming inspection is kept at a minimum; in some cases, there is no inspection at all. It is reported that purchased parts are received and sent directly to the assembly lines without any inspection. If defects are found, the vendor is liable to lose all future work.

14. Evidence of Use of Statistical Methods on Shop Floor

Going through a number of companies in Japan, the use of Pareto analysis, cause-and-effect analysis, check sheets, control charts, histograms, and other high-level statistics such as design of experiments was evident. In one company I noticed the use of computer reports as scratch paper to draw Pareto diagrams and cause-and-effect analyses.

15. Departmental Relationship

Japanese companies use more open space. Many department heads have open desks and areas alongside their subordinates' offices; the atmosphere is more informal. When problems occur, people from various departments get together to solve the problems instead of trying to pass the buck. In one factory, I observed a group of engineers and managers working on the shop floor after six o'clock to solve a gasket problem.

16. Product Deployment

We have already reviewed this concept in other chapters. It seems the Japanese are very much concerned with customer satisfaction and the customers' interest. New products are developed to satisfy more and more customers and thus capture bigger markets.

17. Effective Failure Analysis

Another area that is being used more effectively in Japan is failure analysis. More and more reports are published regarding reliability analysis and use of techniques such as failure mode-and-effect analysis and failure tree analysis, while in the United States failures are considered warranty costs and not analyzed critically to a large extent. How can quality be improved if we don't know what's happening in the field?

18. Attitude Toward Workers

Very informal relationships exist between workers and supervisors in Japan. People were not afraid to ask questions that exposed defects in parts. In one instance, I observed that the defective parts were sorted by workers and supervisors working side by side. It seemed that management respected workers and their brainpower and utilized them effectively.

19. Self-Inspection

You will find very few inspectors in many Japanese plants. Most of the inspection responsibility is given to each operator. Good gauging and clear instructions can be seen in all operations; generally, operators are responsible for the quality of products.

20. General Comments

It seemed that Japanese management used more common sense and practiced what they preached. The use of participative management was obvious, and everyone seemed to follow the principle, "Do it right the first time."

What Are the Results?

One can analyze the results of all these activities in five ways:

1. Quality
2. Productivity
3. Cost
4. Customer satisfaction and quality costs
5. Market share around the world

The following figures will show the difference between the two countries.

FIGURE 17-2

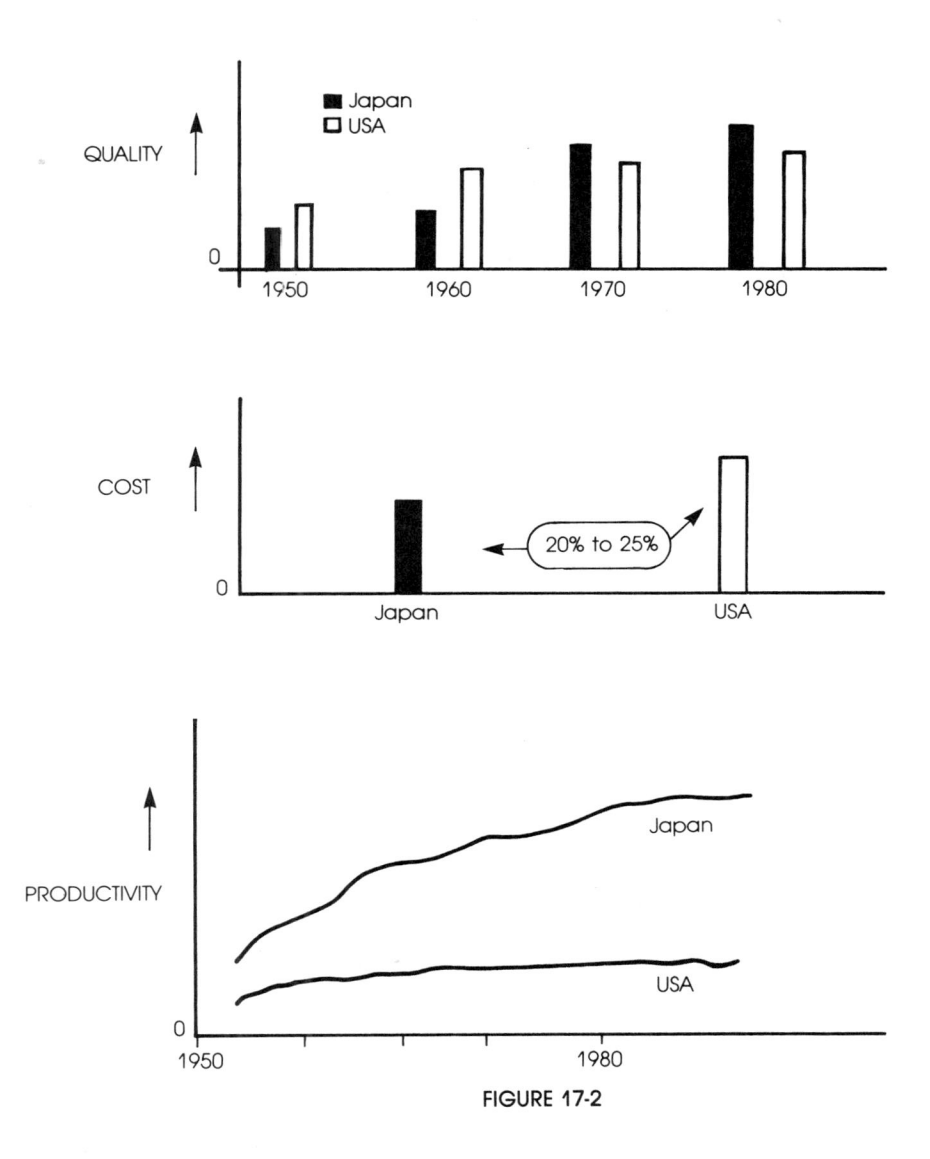

Is There Anything New?

The answer to this question is "yes and no." There are no new techniques, no new methods in what Japan has done to improve quality and productivity. But they have adopted and modified old techniques and methods and put them into practice. Japan has shown the rest of the world the effective use of the following:

263

1. Use of the four M's—methods, materials, man, and machine.
2. Effective cost-control methods.
3. Use of customer-based quality (product deployment).
4. Cooperation between union, management, and government.
5. Nationwide commitment to quality.
6. Importance of ongoing training.

You can probably add still other reasons to this list.

Lessons We Must Learn

1. Total quality commitment and involvement from top to bottom.
2. Customer-oriented quality process (product deployment).
3. Stick to basics and follow them religiously. (There is no use in reinventing new methods if the old ones are working effectively. Use common sense and the KISS principle—Keep It Simple and Sweet.)
4. Practice what we preach.
5. Do it right the first time.
6. Participation and recognition of workers.
7. Use of statistical methods.
8. Dynamic ongoing self-analysis of the organization.
9. Constant striving for improvement.
10. Ongoing massive and systematic training programs.

References on Japanese Management

The following sources will be useful for those who would like to know more about Japanese quality control and manufacturing methods:

1. "Japanese Manufacturing Method—Showa Case Study" (videotape), Quality Circle Services, P.O. Box 812, Fond du Lac, Wisconsin 54935.
2. Theory Z by Bill Ouchi. Reading, MA; Addison-Wesley, 1981.
3. "If Japan can, Why can't we?" (NBC Whitepaper). NBC-TV (June 24, 1980).
4. "People and Productivity" (film), Encyclopedia Britannica, 425 North Michigan Avenue, Chicago, Illinois 60611.

5. Ezra Vogel, *Japan as Number One.* Cambridge, MA: Harvard University Press, 1979.
6. Richard T. Pascale, Anthony A. Althos, *The Art of Japanese Management.* New York: Simon & Schuster, 1981.
7. Robert Hayes, Steven Wheelwright, *Restoring Our Competitive Edge.* John Wiley & Sons, 1984.
8. Richard Schonberger, *Japanese Manufacturing Techniques.* New York: The Free Press, Division of Macmillan Publishing Inc., 1982.

The goal is zero defects. ... It is difficult. But we have to get rid of the idea that we can permit some leeway simply because total elimination of defects is so difficult. We should not speak of this issue in percentage. For instance, if a customer came across a defective product, which happens to be 0.01 percent of all the goods produced at the factory, as far as that customer is concerned, there is a 100 percent defect record.

Masuharu Matsushita, president,
Matsushita Company, 1970

Part Two

Chapter Eighteen
BASIC INDUSTRIAL STATISTICS FOR NONSTATISTICIANS

In this chapter I will explain some of the concepts of quality-control statistical applications without getting into all of the technical terms and computations. The best way I know to do this is through practical examples.

The first thing to do in statistical quality control is gather data. This is a relatively simple but very important step. I will go through some practical examples to help demonstrate these concepts.

Suppose you are the quality-control supervisor in a factory that makes high-speed printers. One of the important dimensions is the length of the bracket that holds the paper roller.

When collecting data, it is important to keep track of the time and sequence of events. Knowledge of the product and the process helps in determining whether there are any unique characteristics that should also be documented. Such is the case with our printer bracket—we are going to record the straightness of the bracket.

Another important consideration that must be made is the frequency of checks. This depends on many things, but for the most part it is a decision made by good common sense. Consideration must be given to the rate of production, the type of check, available manpower and equipment, and so on. The main thing is that we take action as soon as possible and not be afraid to make a mistake. Experience has shown that people in industry tend to get hung up on technical details and are afraid they will make a mistake. Consequently, they do not get the job done. The best way to master the use of these statistical quality-control techniques is through experience; that simply means get out there and start practicing.

There are many ways to record data. To start with, pick the most convenient way to get all the data you need. Figure 18-1 shows a possible format for our printer bracket length data.

FIGURE 18.1 DATA COLLECTION

Check Number	Date/Time	Piece Number	Dimension	Straightness	Comments
1	May 9 8:00	1 2 3	12.157 12.156 12.155	.002 .012 .008	
2	9:00	4 5 6	12.157 12.153 12.154	.011 .008 .012	
					Break
3	10:00	7 8 9	12.158 12.156 12.157	.007 .010 .006	
4	11:00	10 11 12	12.157 12.155 12.155	.011 .007 .010	
					Noon Hour
5	1:00	13 14 15	12.158 12.156 12.155	.012 .014 .007	
6	2:00	16 17 18	12.157 12.158 12.159	.011 .014 .006	New Tool
7	3.00	19 20 21	12.156 12.156 12.154	.014 .006 .011	
8	May 10 8:00	22 23 24	12.156 12.153 12.155	.014 .006 .007	
9	9:00	25 26 27	12.158 12.155 12.156	.011 .018 .012	Changed Coolant
					Break
10	10:00	28 29 30	12.154 12.154 12.156	.006 .014 .009	
11	11:00	31 32 33	12.155 12.156 12.158	.011 .008 .009	

FIGURE 18.1 DATA COLLECTION (continued)

Check Number	Date/Time	Piece Number	Dimension	Straightness	Comments
					Lunch
12	1:00	34	12.158	.010	
		35	12.157	.014	
		36	12.156	.011	
13	2:00	37	12.158	.012	New Tool
		38	12.156	.013	New Lot of Parts
		39	12.156	.009	
14	3:00	40	12.154	.011	
		41	12.156	.008	
		42	12.155	.016	
15	May 11 8:00	43	12.158	.009	Recalibrated Gauge
		44	12.156	.015	
		45	12.157	.012	
16	9:00	46	12.157	.013	
		47	12.156	.010	
		48	12.156	.009	
					Break
17	10:00	49	12.155	.007	
		50	12.155	.010	
		51	12.154	.012	
18	11:00	52	12.158	.011	
		53	12.156	.013	
		54	12.157	.010	
					Lunch
19	1:00	55	12.156	.011	
		56	12.157	.008	
		57	12.154	.006	
20	2:00	58	12.157	.010	Stopped: Ran out of parts
		59	12.156	.005	
		60	12.155	.011	

You should continue to collect data until you have made about 15 to 20 checks. It is a good idea to be looking at your data all through the collection process for clues and indications of possible places for improvement.

Almost all of the statistical techniques will start with some form of data collection or use of previously collected data. Keep in mind that the data can in some instances be consecutive parts, but usually this will not be the case. You will most often be working with small samples taken periodically over a certain time span.

In the case of our printer bracket, we chose to check three pieces (bracket length) every hour for three days. This could have been any number of days or even shifts. We arbitrarily picked this frequency because it seemed logical considering our machine runs at a rate of 50 pieces per hour, one shift per day.

One thing you will find extremely helpful is to record comments. Keep a type of diary on the process being studied. The people involved should be instructed to write down any events that happen while the study is being taken. In our example, I would list things like delays in the process or breaks. Record as many details as you can even though they may not seem significant at the time. Your comments should always be recorded by time of day. Notice the Comments section in Figure 18-1.

The next significant step after all the data has been collected is to organize it into formats that allow you to analyze what's going on in your process.

Once again, as with data recording, there is no one way that is best to organize your data. In fact, experience has shown that the best approach is to organize the data in several different ways to allow you to see it from different viewpoints.

One of the first ways you will want to try is a *run chart*. This is simply plotting your data on a graph in time sequence. This technique can sometimes be used as a first step for collecting your data. (See Figure 18-2.) This run chart technique will give you great visibility to see what your process is doing over time. It quickly identifies trends, spikes, and patterns in your process or simply tells you that there aren't any noticeable indicators at this time. The run chart is one of the simplest of the charting techniques and also one of the most effective.

I would like to emphasize this point of simplicity. It has been my experience with statistical quality-control techniques that the greatest benefits are realized through good use and application of the simpler techniques. As I mentioned before, I continue to see people in industry getting bogged down trying to learn and apply high-level statistical techniques when good use of the simpler ones will do the trick and usually is faster. The whole point here is not to underestimate the power of these apparently simpler techniques.

Another very effective technique is the frequency distribution or histogram. (See Figure 18-3.) This technique ignores the time element and looks at the frequency of a particular reading or result. It is nothing more than a bar graph of the number of times each event or reading occurs. The bars usually go vertically but it is perfectly all right to run them horizontally. The frequency distribution tells you where your readings start and stop, where the majority of your readings are, and the shape of your distribution, which is important. I will be discussing the significance played by the shape of the distribution later in the chapter.

Two characteristics of the frequency distribution (histogram) are (1) the point where the majority of the readings are gathered and (2) the points

FIGURE 18-2

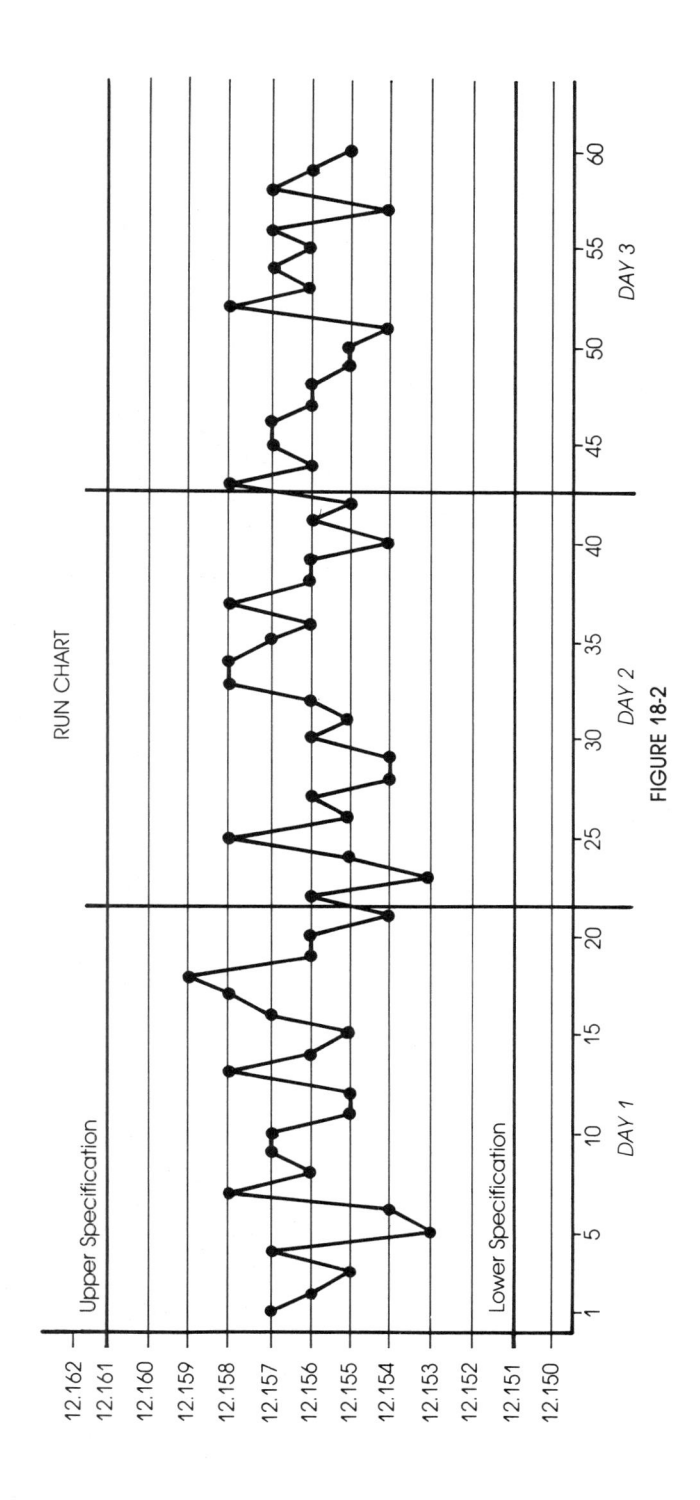

FIGURE 18-3

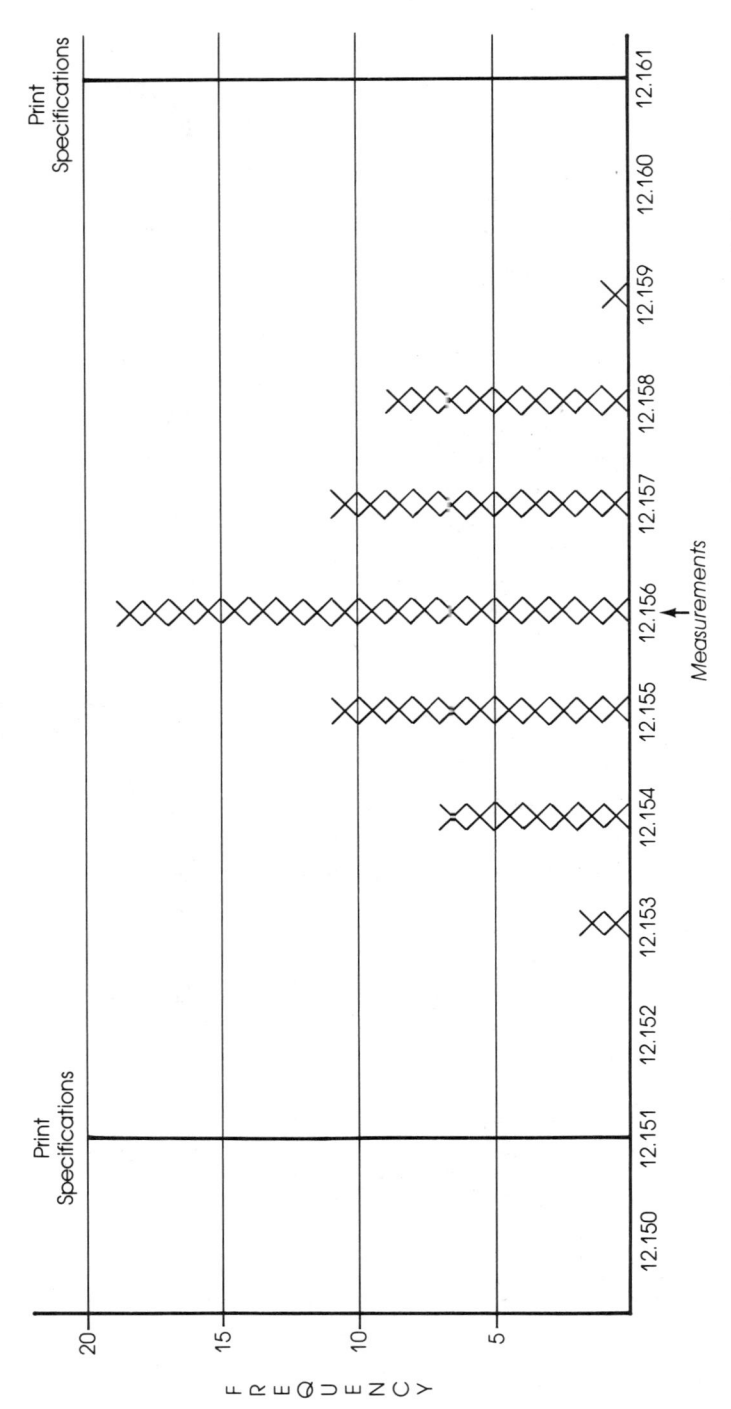

FREQUENCY HISTOGRAM (↑ marks the mean value)

BASIC INDUSTRIAL STATISTICS FOR NONSTATISTICIANS (SPC) **275**

where the readings start and stop (highest and lowest readings), which bring us to our first calculations.

The first characteristic of a frequency distribution that we mentioned, the point where the majority of our readings are gathered, is referred to as the *average point*. By definition, the average is a number that is typical of a group of numbers. Any time you have more than one number you have an average value. There are several ways of arriving at an average value, but two are most frequently used in quality control work. They are the *mean* and the *median*. The mean, the most common, is obtained by adding all the data values together and dividing by the number of data points you have. Figure 18-4 shows an example of how the mean is calculated. The mean is sometimes thought of as the balance point. If you look at the frequency distribution (Figure 18-3) you will find that the calculated mean value is the point on the bar graph (histogram) that seems to be the balance point for all the figures, similar to the balance point on a seesaw.

The second type of average that we mentioned, the median, is the middle number in a set of numbers. The median of a set of numbers can be found by putting the numbers in rank order—that is, from lowest to highest—and finding the number that is in the middle. That is the number which has as many values above it as below it. See Figure 18-4 for some examples of how the median is found.

FIGURE 18-4A. Examples of Averages

A) Find the *Mean* of a set of data

```
Data:   1) 6.5         STEP 1: Add up the data
        2) 7.1
        3) 4.3
        4) 5.7
        5) 7.8
          31.4 ← STEP 1
```

STEP 2: Divide the sum of the data by the number of
31.4 ÷ 5 = 6.28 ← STEP 2   pieces of data. In this example we have 5.

The mean of this data is 6.28.

B) Finding the *Median* of a set of data

```
Data:   1) 6.5         STEP 1: Put the data in rank order; that is, arrange
        2) 7.1                 them from lowest to highest.
        3) 4.3
        4) 5.7
        5) 7.8
```

In
rank
order —
```
        1) 4.3                STEP 2: Find the number that falls in the middle.
        2) 5.7                        This is the median.
        3) 6.5      STEP 1
        4) 7.1
        5) 7.8
STEP 2
```

6.5 is the middle number and the *median*.

Sample data from our printer bracket example:

SAMPLE NO.	PIECE NO.	DIMENSION	
#1	1 2 3	12.157 12.156 + 12.155 ——— 36.468	← STEP 1: Add up the data in each sample group.
	36.468 ÷ 3 =	*12.156*	← STEP 2: Divide the sum of each sample group by the number of readings (dimensions) you have in each sample group (subgroup). In our example we have (3) in each sample. *12.156* is our sample group average (subgroup #1).
#2	4 5 6	12.157 12.153 12.154 ——— 36.464	Note: Round your answers where necessary.
	36.464 ÷ 3 =	12.155	← Sample group average (subgroup #2)
#3	7 8 9	12.158 12.156 12.157 ——— 36.471	
	36.471 ÷ 3 =	12.157	← Sample group average (subgroup #3)

Do this for all subgroups (20 in the case of our printer bracket data) unless you are using the median technique.

FIGURE 18-4B. Calculating the Average (Mean) of Each Sample Group

In statistics the average, mean, and median are indicative of what is referred to as the *central tendency*. There are two fundamental measures of a set of data in statistics: they are (1) the central tendency, and (2) the dispersion. We have already talked about central tendency, but what is meant by dispersion?

Dispersion has to do with the spread of our data. Earlier we listed two characteristics of a frequency distribution. The first was the point where the majority of the values are gathered, which we now know to be the average or central tendency. The second was the point where the readings start and stop (highest and lowest values). This second characteristic is the dispersion of our data. More precisely, the amount of spread between all our values is what we use to determine the dispersion.

There are several ways to express dispersion, just as there were several ways to express the central tendency or average. The simplest, most frequently used method is called the *range*. The range is simply the difference between the highest and lowest or biggest and smallest readings. Figure 18-5

Sample data from our printer bracket example:

SAMPLE NO.	PIECE NO.	DIMENSION
#1	1	12.157
	2	12.156
	3	+ 12.155

STEP 1: Put the numbers in RANK ORDER; that is, list them from lowest to highest.

    1) 12.155
    2) 12.156 ←*Median* (middle number)
    3) 12.157

STEP 2: Find the middle number (median)

Note: In most cases where the sample group's size is small, such as our printer bracket data (subgroup size of 3), the ranking can be done mentally.

				RANK ORDERED
	4	12.157		1) 12.153
#2	5	12.153		2) 12.154 ←Middle number
	6	12.154	MEDIAN (Subgroup #2)	3) 12.157
	7	12.158		1) 12.156
#3	8	12.156		2) 12.157 ←Middle number
	9	12.157	MEDIAN (Subgroup #3)	3) 12.158

Do this for all subgroups (20 in the case of our printer bracket data) unless you are using the mean method.

FIGURE 18-4C. Finding the Average (Median) of Each Sample Group

FIGURE 18-5. Finding Ranges

Sample data from the printer bracket example:

SAMPLE NO.	PIECE NO.	DIMENSION	RANGE CALCULATIONS
	1	12.157	12.157 Highest
#1	2	12.156	−12.155 Lowest
	3	12.155	0.002 RANGE
	4	12.157	12.157 Highest
#2	5	12.153	−12.153 Lowest
	6	12.154	0.004 RANGE
	7	12.158	12.158 Highest
#3	8	12.156	−12.156 Lowest
	9	12.157	0.002 RANGE

Do this for all 20 subgroups (printer bracket data).

shows how the range is found on our bracket length data. One range alone is not a very good or accurate measure of dispersion. Usually what is done is to figure the range for each of our small sample groups (three, for example) and then find the mean of these sample ranges. To find a mean, if you recall, we add up the individual sample ranges and divide by the number of sample ranges we had. Figure 18-6 shows the calculation of the average (mean) range of our bracket data.

In actual practice it is common to collect our data in small samples at a time (perhaps three to five pieces) every hour. These sample groups are often referred to as subgroups. Then find the range and average (mean) of this subgroup right away. After you have gathered about 20 of these sample averages and ranges, find the average (mean) of the ranges and the average (mean) of the averages. This average of the averages is referred to as the grand average. If you used the median technique for finding the central tendency or average of each of your subgroups, you will find the grand average by calculating the mean of these median values. Figure 18-7 shows how all of this looks for our bracket length data.

FIGURE 18-6. Calculating the Average (Mean) Range

Sample data from the printer bracket example:

SAMPLE NO.	PIECE NO.	DIMENSION	RANGE
#1	1	12.157	
	2	12.156	.002
	3	12.155	
#2	4	12.157	
	5	12.153	.004
	6	12.154	
#3	7	12.158	
	8	12.156	.002
	9	12.157	

STEP 1: Add the ranges.

SAMPLE NO.	RANGES
#1	.002
#2	.004
#3	.002
	.008 ← STEP #1

STEP 2: Divide the total of the ranges (.008) by the total number of ranges added (3)

.008 ÷ 3 = .0027 →THE AVERAGE RANGE

The average range for the first (3) sample checks of our printer bracket is .0027.

Do this for all 20 subgroups (printer bracket data).

FIGURE 18-7. Calculating the Grand Average

Sample data from the printer bracket example:

SAMPLE NO. (Subgroup)	#1	#2	#3
	12.157	12.157	12.158
	12.156	12.153	12.156
	12.155	12.154	12.157
Sum →	36.468	36.464	36.471
Average →	12.156	12.155	12.157

STEP 1: Add up all the sample group (subgroup) averages. Note that the average value used can be either the *mean* or the *median*.

```
Subgroup
Average  #1) 12.156
         #2) 12.155
         #3) 12.157
             36.468  ← STEP 1
```

STEP 2: Divide the total by the number of subgroups averaged. In our practice example above we used 3 subgroups.

$$36.468 \div 3 = 12.156 \longrightarrow \text{GRAND AVERAGE}$$

Note: This grand average is actually the average (mean) of the average value calculated from each sample group (subgroup).

Do this for all subgroups (20 in the case of our printer bracket data).

You will find that it becomes very difficult and time-consuming to work with long numbers, such as those used in our example, that have many digits. To simplify working with numbers like these, we use a technique called *coding*.

Coding is simply letting one number represent another. One application of coding is when only the last one or two digits change, and the rest of the digits always remain the same. This can be seen in our sample data (Figure 18-8). Our nominal dimension is 12.1560, and the first four digits are always 12.15. Our coded numbers in this case are simply the last digit, such as 6 is the coded number for 12.156, 1 is the coded number for 12.151, and so on. Notice in the example in Figure 18-8 that after the calculations are completed, you simply uncode the data and the answers are exactly the same as in our earlier examples. There is no accuracy lost in coding the data if done properly.

Another frequently used form of coding is accomplished by coding the center number (nominal) with a zero (0) and showing all the other numbers as + or − numbers from that zero. This can be shown by using our sample data. In this case our nominal number is 12.156, which we represent in coded data as zero (0) and all of the remaining numbers are represented by a + or − number by how far they are away from our nominal. An example

FIGURE 18-8. Coded Data

SAMPLE NO.	PIECE NO.	DIMENSION	CODED
#1	1	12.157	7
	2	12.156	6
	3	12.155	5
	Sum	36.468	18
	Average	12.156	6
	Range	.002	2
#2	4	12.157	7
	5	12.153	3
	6	12.154	4
	Sum	36.464	14
	Average	12.155	5
	Range	.004	4
#3	7	12.158	8
	8	12.156	6
	9	12.157	7
	Sum	36.471	21
	Average	12.157	7
	Range	.002	2

GRAND AVERAGE (CODED)

SAMPLE NO.	
#1)	6
#2)	5
#3)	7
	18

18 ÷ 3 = 6 ⟶ Uncoded = 12.156

AVERAGE RANGE

SAMPLE NO.	
1)	2
2)	4
3)	2
	8

8 ÷ 3 = 2.7 ⟶ Uncoded = .0027

NOTE: The uncoded values are exactly the same as was previously calculated in earlier examples using the uncoded data.

of this is: 12.153 = −3, and so on. This technique works especially well where we have a gauge that reads in + and − figures. (See Figure 18-9 for examples.) Once again, be assured that nothing is lost in the calculations when using coded data, provided it is done accurately and that you uncode it when you are all done.

The material we have covered thus far forms the basis for what we refer to in statistical quality control as the *average and range chart*. The average and range chart is just one of many kinds of control charts, but it is by far the most commonly used. Control charts are the basis of what is currently referred to as SPC (Statistical Process Control). We will be discussing some of these other types of control charts later in the chapter.

There are many symbols used in statistical quality control. A few of these symbols are commonly used and you should become familiar with

FIGURE 18-9. Coded Data

Sample data from the printer bracket example:

The nominal dimension is 12.156 ±.005

CODING SCHEME

12.156 = 0

Record all other dimensions as + or − values from the nominal dimension.

Examples:
    12.157 = +1
    12.155 = −1
    12.159 = +3
    12.151 = −5
    etc.

NOTE: See Figure 18-10 for an example of this coding scheme used on our sample printer bracket data.

them. The average (mean) is represented by an $\overline{X}$, pronounced "x bar," and the average of the ($\overline{x}$'s) averages (grand average) is represented by an $\overline{\overline{x}}$, pronounced "x double bar." The range is represented by an R, and the average of the ranges is represented by an $\overline{R}$, pronounced "R bar." It is for this reason that the average and range control chart is often referred to as the $\overline{X}$ and R chart.

Figure 18-10 shows a typical average and range chart filled out with our sample data in coded form. Notice that the bottom portion of this format has two graphs. One graph is for plotting the subgroup averages ($\overline{X}$'s) and the other is for plotting the subgroup ranges (R's). A solid line is drawn through the center of each of the graphs, representing the grand average ($\overline{\overline{X}}$) and the average range ($\overline{R}$), respectively.

The purpose of the control charts is threefold. First, they will determine if the process we are studying is in a state of control (I will discuss this more later); second, they determine our process capability; and third, they monitor the process as an early-warning device to detect changes in centering and/or variability.

The unique part of these control charts is the control limits. Figure 18-10 shows an $\overline{X}$ and R chart with these control limits shown as dotted lines equally spaced above and below the center lines ($\overline{\overline{X}}$ and $\overline{R}$). The control limits are spaced in such a way as to tell us, when a point goes beyond these dotted lines, that a change has occurred in our process. Any points that go beyond the control lines should be investigated thoroughly to determine the cause and correct it. Both charts, the average ($\overline{X}$) and the range (R) charts, have these control limits. The range chart oftentimes has only an upper control limit (UCL) due to the fact that the lower control limit (LCL) falls below the zero point. You cannot ever have a range lower than zero.

VARIABLES CONTROL CHART ($\bar{X}$ & R)

PART NAME (PRODUCT)	Printer Bracket	OPERATION (PROCESS)	Milling Ends (#30)		PART NO. 123-456	CHART NO. 1
OPERATOR	Tony (#431)	MACHINE Mill	GAGE Height Stand	UNIT OF MEASURE .001	SPECIFICATION LIMITS 12.151 – 12.161	ZERO EQUALS 0 = 12.156

DATE	5/9						5/10						5/11						
TIME	8:00	9:00	10:00	11:00	1:00	2:00	5:00	8:00	9:00	10:00	11:00	1:00	2:00	3:00	8:00	9:00	10:00	11:00	1:00	2:00

SAMPLE MEASUREMENTS

#																				
1	+1	+1	+2	+1	+2	0	-2	+2	-1	+2	-1	+2	-2	+2	+1	-1	+2	0	+1	
2	0	-3	0	-1	0	0	-3	-1	-2	0	+1	0	0	+1	0	-1	0	+1	0	
3	-1	-2	+1	-1	+3	-2	-1	0	0	+2	0	-1	-1	+1	0	-2	+1	-2	-1	
4																				
5																				

SUM	0	-4	+3	-1	+1	+6	-2	-4	+1	-4	+1	+3	+2	-3	+3	-4	+3	-1	0	
AVERAGE, $\bar{X}$	0	-1.3	+1	-.3	+.3	+2	-.7	-1.3	+.3	-1.3	+.3	+1	+.7	-.7	+1	-1.3	+1	-.3	0	
RANGE, R	2	2	2	2	3	2	2	3	3	2	3	2	2	2	2	1	2	3	2	
NOTES																				

AVERAGES

UCL$_{\bar{X}}$ = 2.34
$\bar{\bar{X}}$ = .035
LCL$_{\bar{X}}$ = -2.27

RANGES

UCL$_R$ = 5.79
$\bar{R}$ = 2.25

FIGURE 18-10

BASIC INDUSTRIAL STATISTICS FOR NONSTATISTICIANS (SPC)   283

The formulas for calculating control limits are often printed on the reverse side of the $\overline{X}$ and R charts. Figure 18-11 shows these formulas and tables as printed on the reverse side of the American Society for Quality Control (ASQC) form. (See reference at end of chapter.)

Figure 18-11 shows this calculation work sheet filled out for our sample data. The control-limit calculations were based on subgroups 1 through 20. We then go through the calculation for $\overline{\overline{X}}$ and $\overline{R}$ as described earlier. The next calculation on the work sheet, $A2\overline{R}$, is the formula that determines the spacing on either side of the center line ($\overline{\overline{X}}$). The $A2$ number is a constant from the table in the lower right portion of our form, titled "Factors for Control Limits." The factor to be used under the $A2$ column for our sample is the one next to $n = 3$ column. The n column is the number of readings in each of our subgroups. In our case we were using subgroups

FIGURE 18-11

CALCULATION WORK SHEET

CONTROL LIMITS

Subgroups included 1 Through 20

$\overline{R} = \dfrac{\Sigma R}{k} = \dfrac{45}{20} = 2.25 \qquad = 2.25$

$\overline{\overline{X}} = \dfrac{\Sigma \overline{X}}{k} = \dfrac{.7}{20} = .035 \qquad = .035$

OR

$\overline{X}'$ (MIDSPEC. OR STD.) = $\qquad$ =

$A_2\overline{R} = 1.023 \times 2.25 = 2.30 \qquad \times \qquad = 2.30$

$UCL_{\overline{X}} = \overline{\overline{X}} + A_2\overline{R} \quad .035 + 2.30 = 2.34 \qquad = 2.34$

$LCL_{\overline{X}} = \overline{\overline{X}} - A_2\overline{R} \quad .035 - 2.30 = -2.27 \qquad = 2.27$

$UCL_R = D_4\overline{R} = 2.574 \times 2.25 = 5.79 \qquad \times \qquad = 5.79$

LIMITS FOR INDIVIDUALS
Compare with specification or tolerance limits

(UNCODED)

$\overline{\overline{X}} \qquad\qquad = (12.156035)$

$\dfrac{3}{d_2}\overline{R} = 1.772 \times (.00225) = (.00398)$

$UL_x = \overline{\overline{X}} + \dfrac{3}{d_2}\overline{R} \qquad = (12.1600)$

$LL_x = \overline{\overline{X}} - \dfrac{3}{d_2}\overline{R} \qquad = (12.1520)$

US $\qquad\qquad\qquad = 12.161$

LS $\qquad\qquad\qquad = 12.151$

US − LS $\qquad\qquad = .010$

$6\sigma = \dfrac{6}{d_2}\overline{R} \qquad\qquad = .0080$

MODIFIED CONTROL LIMITS FOR AVERAGES

Based on specification limits and process capability.
Applicable only if: US − LS > 6σ.

US $\qquad\qquad$ = LS $\qquad\qquad$ =

$A_M\overline{R} = \qquad \times \qquad = \underline{\qquad}A_M\overline{R} \qquad =$

$URL_{\overline{X}} = US - A_M\overline{R} \qquad = \qquad LRL_{\overline{X}} = LS + A_M\overline{R} \qquad =$

FACTORS FOR CONTROL UNITS

n	A_2	D_4	d_2	$\dfrac{3}{d_2}$	A_M
2	1.880	3.268	1.128	2.659	0.779
3	1.023	2.574	1.693	1.772	0.749
4	0.729	2.282	2.059	1.457	0.728
5	0.577	2.114	2.326	1.290	0.713
6	0.483	2.004	2.534	1.184	0.701

of three each time, so our $A2$ factor is 1.023. We now take and multiply our $A2$ times $\bar{R}$ (1.023 × 2.25).

To determine the control limits for our $\bar{X}$ chart, we now add and subtract this figure from our $\bar{\bar{X}}$ number of .035. Referring to our work sheet, we fill in the number for UCL and LCL. Our upper control limit, X-bar (UCL), is equal to $\bar{\bar{X}}$, which is .035 plus ($A2 \times \bar{R}$), which gives us an UCL of 2.34. The lower control limit X-bar (LCL $\bar{X}$) is figured by taking our $\bar{\bar{X}}$ and subtracting ($A2\bar{R}$) of 2.30, giving us −2.27. Looking back at Figure 18-10, we can see that these numbers agree with the dotted lines on the $\bar{X}$ chart.

In a similar manner, we calculate the control limits for the range (R) chart. Looking at our work sheet, we see that the formula for the upper control limit range (UCL R) is equal to the factor $D4$ times our average Range $\bar{R}$. Looking at our table "Factors for Control Limits," we see the factor $D4$ is the third column from the left. Going down the n column to 3, which was our subgroup's size, we see that our $D4$ factor is 2.574. We can now fill in our work sheet for UCL R, $D4$ multiplied times our R of 2.25 equals 5.79. Comparing this figure for UCL R to our chart (Figure 18-10), we see that it agrees with the dotted line on the range (R) chart. Also notice that there is no lower control limit on the range chart. This will always be the case for subgroup sizes of six or less, and for that reason our work sheets do not even show a calculation for it.

Now that we have constructed an $\bar{X}$ and R chart with the control limits, we can determine our "state of control." If all points fall within our control limits (dotted lines), we say that this process is currently operating in a "state of control." If any points fall outside these limits we must work on the process to find the problem and then rerun the chart until all points are within the limits.

Once in a state of control, we can determine our process capability. Keep in mind that up until now we have been working with averages. This is a very important point. The $\bar{X}$ and R chart and the control limits are all based on average values and cannot be directly compared to our specification limits. In order to compare our process data to the print specifications, we must go to our work sheet on the reverse side and work through the formula, Limits for Individuals. (See Figure 18-11.) Looking under this section of the work sheet, we see that it starts out by listing the grand average $\bar{\bar{X}}$, which we already figured in the previous section. For the example, our $\bar{\bar{X}}$ is equal to 12.156035. The next formula to be calculated is ($3/d_2\bar{R}$). Here we look up in our Factors for Control Limits to find ($3/d_2$). Going down to $n=3$ and across to $3/d_2$, we find 1.772. Once again, the reason we went down to $n=3$ was because each of our 20 subgroups was a sample of three pieces. Now, finding that our average range ($\bar{R}$) from our previous section was .00225, we multiply it times our $3/d_2$ factor of 1.772, giving us .00398. We fill this in on our work sheet as shown in Figure 18-11. Now we are ready to compute our upper and lower control limits for the individual readings. The upper limit for our individuals (ULX) is equal to our $\overline{\overline{X}}$ + .00398, which was the $3/d_2 \times \overline{R}$. Similarly, we compute the lower limit (LLX) by subtracting $3/d_2 \times \overline{R}$ from our grand average ($\overline{\overline{X}}$). Here we get 12.152, which we fill in on our work sheet. Next we write down our print specifications. US refers to our upper specifications; LS refers to the lower specifications. By subtracting the lower spec (LS) from the upper spec (US), we obtain our total tolerance spread (US−LS). Finally we compare our process spread to our print tolerance spread. The formula given for calculating our process spread ($6/d_2 \times \overline{R}$) looks difficult but really isn't. The (6σ) stands for 6 sigma. The symbol (σ) is the small Greek letter s or sigma, and it is widely used to denote standard deviation, which is a statistical term to measure variation or spread. Don't be overly concerned at this time with knowing all of these terms. The remainder of this formula can be computed quite simply. First you look up the factor for d_2 in the table Factors for Control Limits. Once again, for our sample data we go across from the 3 under the n column to the d_2 column, where we find the factor 1.693. We then insert this into our formula, which says: Divide 6 by 1.693 (d_2) and multiply this quotient by $\overline{R}$, which is .00225. The result of this calculation is .008, which is the 6 sigma spread of our process.

The 6 sigma number is the spread I will expect to see over a long run of parts based on the 20 samples of 3 parts (subgroups) that we used in our calculations. This 6 sigma spread is equally spaced on both sides of our grand average ($\overline{\overline{X}}$). That is, 3 sigma (1/2 of 6 sigma) is on one side of $\overline{\overline{X}}$ and 3 sigma is on the other side.

Comparing the 6 sigma (process spread) to the print tolerance, we find that the process stays well within the print specs, therefore we expect that no nonconforming products will be produced. Keep in mind that what we are doing in this part of the work sheet, Limits for Individuals, is predicting how large the spread of our process will be over a long run and comparing it to our print specifications to see if it will fit. This 6 sigma number is our process capability.

Earlier in this chapter I mentioned that there are three important characteristics to any set of data. They were: (1) the point where the majority of our readings are gathered, which we now know to be our grand average ($\overline{\overline{X}}$); we also know how to find it; (2) the points where our readings start and stop (highest and lowest readings). This is our process spread or, as we just learned, the 6 sigma spread. The only characteristic left is (3) the shape of the distribution. This characteristic, shape, when explained will also help us gain a better understanding of the first two.

It is not necessarily part of the control charting techniques to check the shape of the distribution, but I have found that this extra step is helpful and oftentimes gives some valuable insight into the process. This step is often done before the plotting and calculations for the control limits.

To check the shape of our data, we simply plot it in the form of a histogram and visually compare its shape with some known distribution shapes. If we look back at Figure 18-3, we see the frequency distribution or histogram of our sample data. Figure 18-12 shows this same histogram with what we call a smoothing line drawn through it. This histogram has what we call a bell shape; this is the most frequent shape we find in industry. This bell shape is sometimes referred to as the *normal distribution.* The bell curve or normal distribution is the shape that much of statistical quality-control techniques are based on. It is for this reason that we should check to see that the shape our data histogram forms is somewhat similar to this bell curve. If the shape is much unlike a bell curve, we should investigate it further to see if we can find out why. One very important point to remember here is that it usually requires a rather large amount of data to form the bell curve, and that sometimes when we look at small samples they have very strange shapes. In this case, about all you can do is to obtain more data. There are some high-powered statistical techniques that can be employed to check for the normal distribution, but these types of techniques are far beyond the scope of this book.

Figure 18-13 shows some of the different shapes that might be encountered. Figure 18-13A shows the normal or bell curve. This is the one that we expect to find and the one that most of our control charting techniques are based on. If our shape is much different from this on a large number of readings—say, 200 or more—we may find that our predictability based on the results of our statistical formulas may be distorted. Figure 18-13B shows what we call a *bimodal distribution.* This type of distribution can be the result of data mixed from two machines, two different setups, or any circumstance that would result in two different distributions mixed together. In a situation like this you should identify what it was that caused the two different distributions, correct the problem, and rerun the study.

The other two shapes are what we call *skewed.* They may be skewed to either side. You will find many distributions have a slight amount of skew, but this will not matter if it is not too extreme, such as our examples 18-13C and 18-13D.

So far we have talked about several aspects of statistical quality control such as: histograms, averages, ranges, spread, shapes, 6 sigma limits, and so on, but maybe it would help if we could tie these all together.

Taking a close look at the theoretical normal distribution or bell curve (Figure 18-14), we see that at the highest point on the curve, the point where most of the readings are gathered, there is a line drawn representing the grand average ($\bar{\bar{X}}$). Also notice the 6 sigma limits. They extend nearly to both extremes of the curve, encompassing almost all the readings. This is true about all normal distributions. Notice, too, that the $\bar{\bar{X}}$ is located in the center, leaving 3 sigmas on either side.

The reason we stress the importance of this bell curve or normal distribution is that most of what we work with in industry shows this type of distribution or shape, and knowing much about this shape allows us to be

CHECKING FOR SHAPE

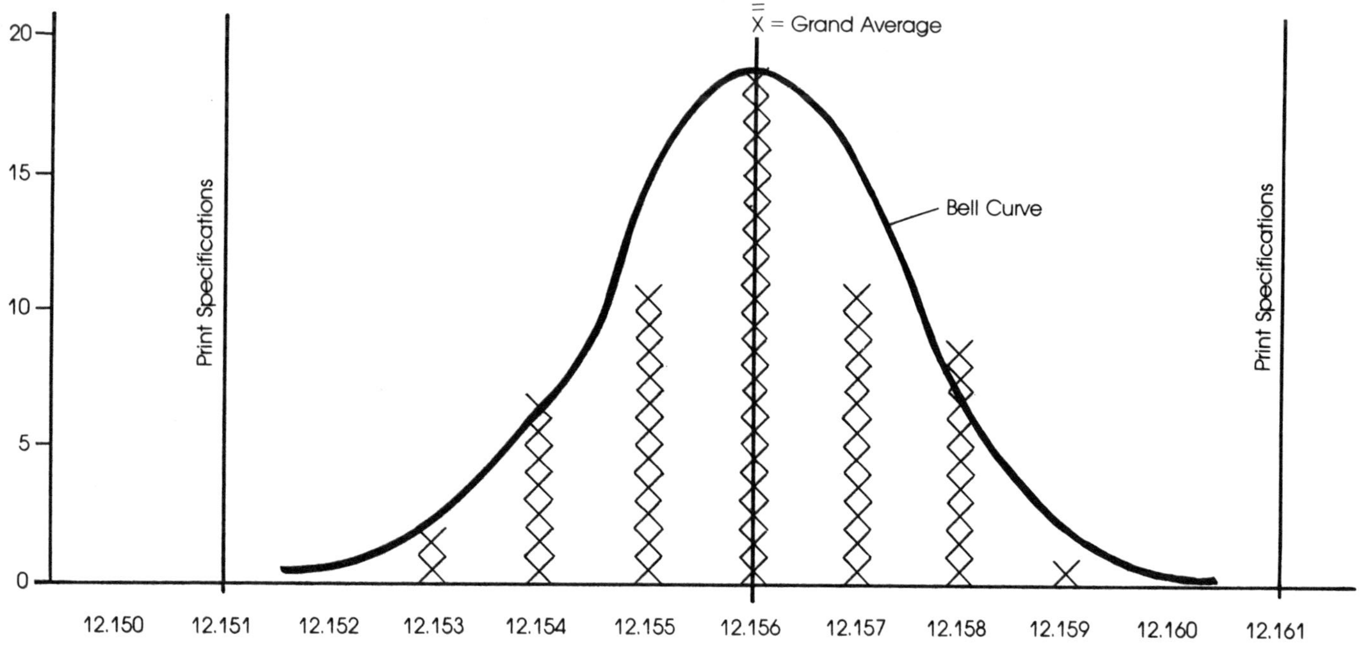

FIGURE 18-12

SHAPES

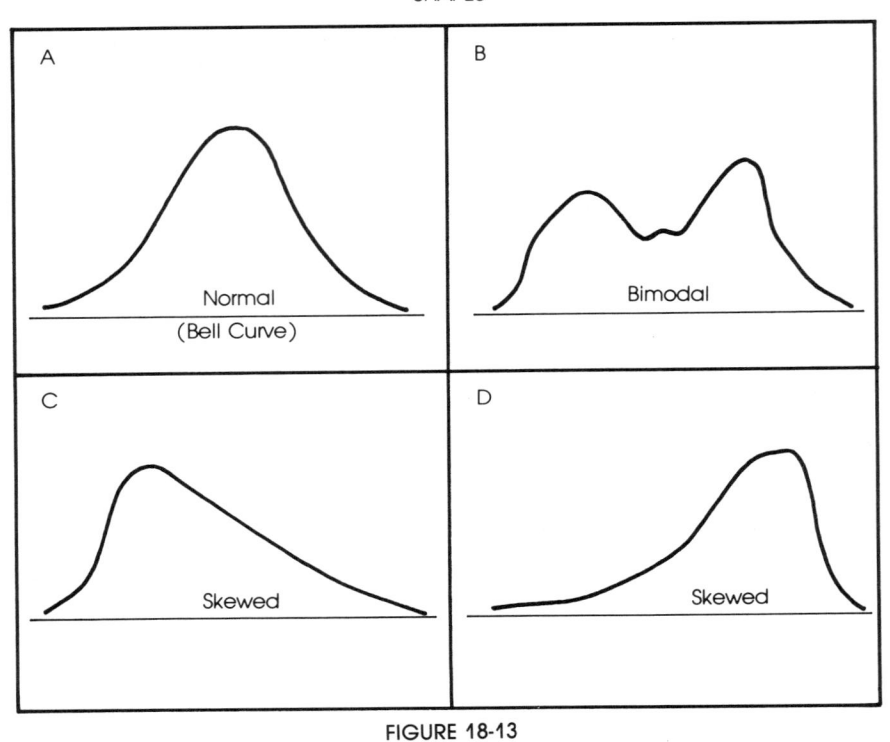

| A Normal (Bell Curve) | B Bimodal |
| C Skewed | D Skewed |

FIGURE 18-13

FIGURE 18-14

NORMAL DISTRIBUTION
(BELL CURVE)

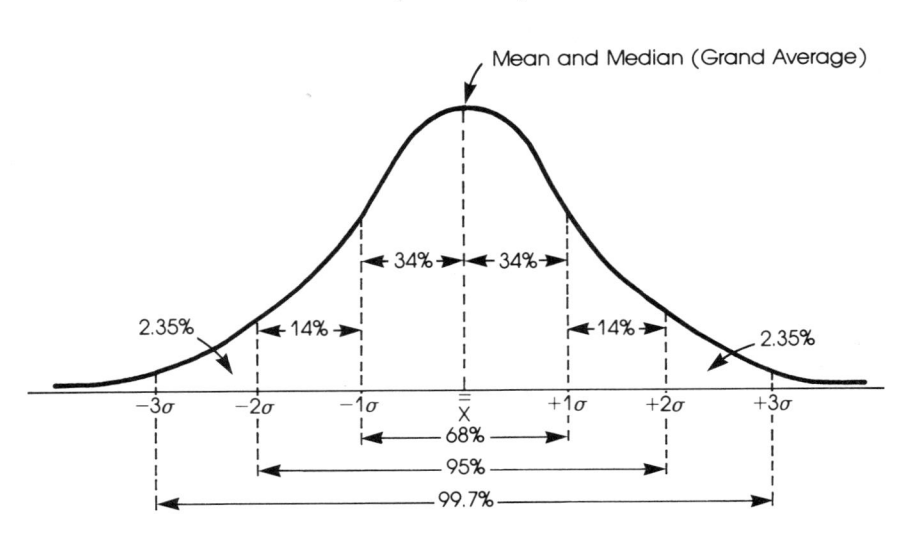

able to make predictions with a high degree of confidence. Figure 18-14 shows some of what we know about the distribution under this bell shape. We know, for instance, that about 68 percent of all our readings will fall within the $+-1$ sigma, and that 95 percent will be written $+-2$ sigma and 99.7 percent will be written $+-3$ sigma or 6 sigma.

We have talked about sigma (σ) and we know how to get 6 sigma ($6/d_2 \times \overline{R}$), but how do I find 1 sigma or 2 sigma? There are several ways to do this, but to keep it simple the best way is to simply divide the 6 sigma number by 6 to get 1 sigma, and then multiply that number by the number of sigmas you want. For instance, if I wanted to know what 1 sigma was from our sample data, I would take our 6 sigma formula, which was $6/d_2 \times \overline{R}$, and divide this by 6. This then looks like this:

$6 \sigma = (6/1.693) \times .00225 = .0079$

$6 \sigma = .008$ (rounded off)

$1 \sigma = .008/6$

$1 \sigma = .0013$

Therefore, if I wanted to know where 95 percent of my readings would fall, I would add and subtract 2 sigmas to the grand average ($\overline{\overline{X}}$). I chose $+-2$ sigmas because I know from Figure 18-14 that $+-2$ sigmas contains approximately 95 percent of all our readings on a normal or bell-shaped distribution.

One point that I mentioned earlier and would like to clarify because it is so important is the difference between individuals and averages. Remember that when you are working with an $\overline{X}$ and R chart, the points that you are plotting and the control limits (dotted lines) are all based on averages and not individuals of parts that were run on this process. Therefore, you cannot compare these plotted points or the control limits (UCL or LCL) with the specifications (print tolerances). To clarify this a bit more, when we say *individuals* we are referring to the readings from each part. In our sample data of Figure 18-10, we can see that we have 60 individual readings (20 subgroups of 3) and 20 averages. These 60 individual readings are but a sample of the entire lot of parts that were run on this process. The Limits for Individuals are limits to be applied to the entire lot of individual parts and compared directly to the print specifications. These individual limits (UL and LL) can be seen in Figure 18-15 with the print specs and the distribution of our 20 averages ($\overline{X}$'s). Notice that the average ($\overline{X}$) distribution is much narrower. This will always be the case. It is logical that averages will stay closer together than individuals. Think of bowling scores, for example. If you were to make a histogram of the individual scores for one season and then make up a histogram of each week's average score, wouldn't you expect to see the averages stay very consistent and the individual scores vary a great deal?

Now the worst is over. This is the basis of most all the work we do in statistical quality control, and if you can begin to understand some of these principles, you are well on your way. It might help to know at this point that of all the control charting techniques, the $\overline{X}$ and R (average and range) chart is the most complicated, but also the most effective.

Another very useful statistical charting technique that you should be aware of is the precontrol system. Precontrol, sometimes called stoplight control, is a charting system that uses the print specifications to derive the control limits. The chart itself is often colored red, yellow, and green, similar to a stoplight (traffic signal). Figure 18-16 shows a typical precontrol chart.

The precontrol system establishes three zones that serve to tell the user how to proceed based on the previous parts checked. The middle 50 percent of the print spec is shown as the green portion of the chart, with the outer two 25 percent areas shown as yellow. (Refer to Figure 18-16.) Anything outside the print spec on either side is shown in red. Notice in Figure 18-16 that we have used the specification limits of $12.156 + -.005$ from our printer bracket example. The green area is shown from 12.1535–12.1585, which is .005 and 50 percent of our .010 tolerance range. Then on either side of the green area is a yellow area of .0025, or 25 percent of our total tolerance.

Now, in order for this system to work properly for you, there is a set of rules that must be followed faithfully. The precontrol rules of operation are:

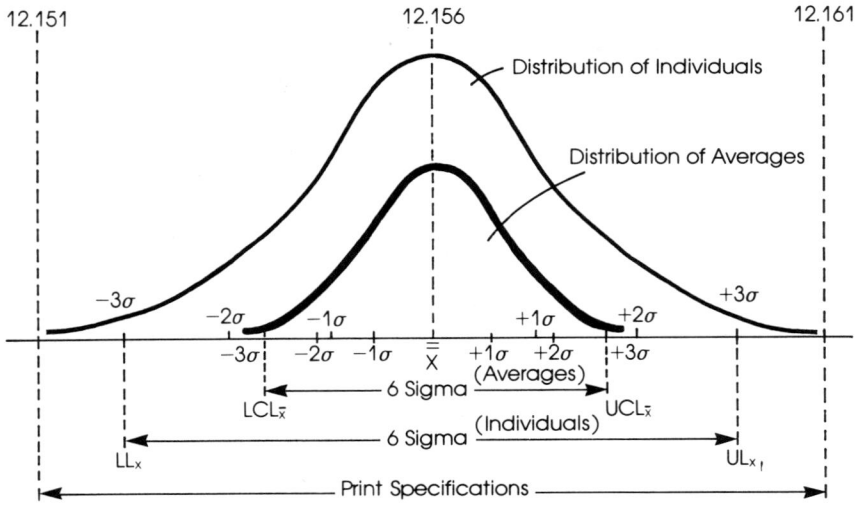

FIGURE 18-15

PART NO. 123-4560   OPER.# 30
PART NAME PRINTER BRACKET

.010 TOTAL TOLERANCE

EACH 2 DIVISION ON CHART = .001 TOLERANCE

- 12.161 U/Print Tolerance
- 12.1585 U/Control Tolerance
- 12.156 Mean Tolerance
- 12.1535 L/Control Tolerance
- 12.151 L/Print Tolerance

START 5/9
FINISH

PLOT EVERY 20TH PIECE

NOTE ALL TOOL CHANGES OR TOOL ADJUSTMENTS

FIGURE 18-16

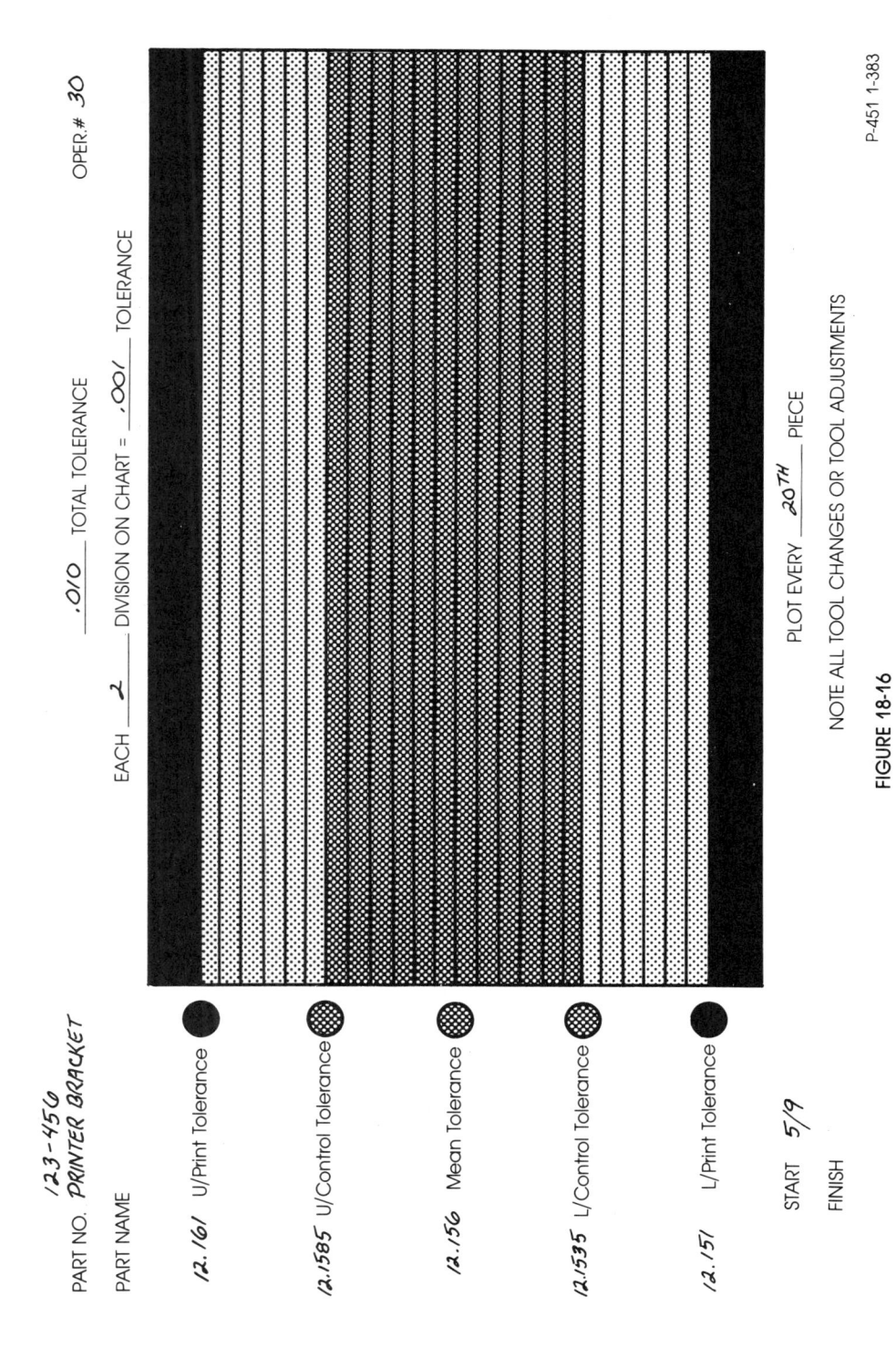

1. Establish that your process is capable of maintaining the print spec.
2. Set up a chart (red, green, yellow) as mentioned previously (Figure 18-16).
3. Start by checking and plotting every piece until you get five consecutive pieces in the green area.
4. Estimate the best you can an inspection frequency that allows about 25 checks per machine reset. For example, you estimate that you reset the machine about every 500 pieces, then your frequency of inspection should be 500/25, or 1 of every 20 pieces produced. This frequency should be adjusted as necessary to maintain this 25 checks per reset ratio. This is important for economics as well as for maintaining a prescribed level of quality output.
5. Start frequency inspection.
6. If a piece falls outside the spec limits (in red), stop and reset.
7. If a piece falls outside the control limits (in yellow) but within the spec limits, check another piece.
8. If the second piece is outside the same control limits, stop and reset.
9. If the second piece is inside the control limits, (in green), then continue the process.
10. If two consecutive pieces go outside opposite control limits (in yellow), stop and take corrective action.
11. Make no adjustments except when parts exceed the control limits.
12. Anytime a machine is reset, five consecutive pieces must fall within the green area before starting frequency gauging. Parts produced just prior to a reset should be screened for nonconformities.

This precontrol system has some very distinct advantages and disadvantages, which I have listed below:

Advantages

1. The precontrol system is much simpler than other comparable charting systems. Both implementation and training are minimal.
2. Fewer pieces are checked at each interval.
3. No calculations are required; just some simple plottings are needed.
4. A direct visual comparison of points plotted to print specs is constantly available.
5. The system can be modified to work with GO/NO GO gauging.

Disadvantages

1. The system assumes that your process is near normal and capable.
2. Your quality output is dependent on how capable your process is.

3. Does not serve as well as a problem-solving tool.
4. Is not as sensitive to process changes as the conventional control charts.
5. For the most part, it will not give you as much protection as other control charting techniques.

There is another helpful problem-solving tool that you might find very useful. It is called the multivary chart. When problems arise that you cannot readily solve, this chart can be of great help in identifying the problem. It is much like a run chart, but you just take small samples of consecutive parts, periodically, over a period of time—for example, three pieces each hour for two days (six shifts). Then, by plotting this data in time sequence, apparent trends and clues become more obvious. Such breakdowns are piece-to-piece variations, time-to-time variations, cyclical variations, and so on.

As you have probably already noticed, the statistical control techniques are simply tools that you as the user have to apply as required. There is no one tool that is best for all situations. The trick is to use the proper tool for the job.

Although there are many techniques available in statistical quality control, I have given you what I have experienced to be the most effective; they should prove to be sufficient for at least 75 percent of your process-control problems. Tools such as control charts, when applied properly, are some of the most powerful of all statistical tools we have.

I have given you enough information to get a good statistical control program started, but I highly recommend that you continue to study the use of these techniques. Below are listed some of the books you might refer to. Keep in mind that you don't have to read all these books cover to cover, but select an area of interest and dig into it. Believe it or not, it can be very entertaining even if you are not a math major. I do recommend, as I mentioned at the beginning of this chapter, that you stick with the simpler techniques, learn them well, and then start teaching others in your company. I can assure you that you will do more to improve quality this way than any other way we know. So get started, work hard, and happy charting!

Other Useful Techniques

1. Charting activities and processes: These methods help to follow the details of the processes and identify problem areas by using the activity analysis chart, the flow process chart, the man and machine chart, and the flow diagram (Figure 18-17).

2. Industrial statistics: One should learn more about other simple techniques such as multivary charts, scatter diagrams, stratification, and component search patterns (Figure 18-18).

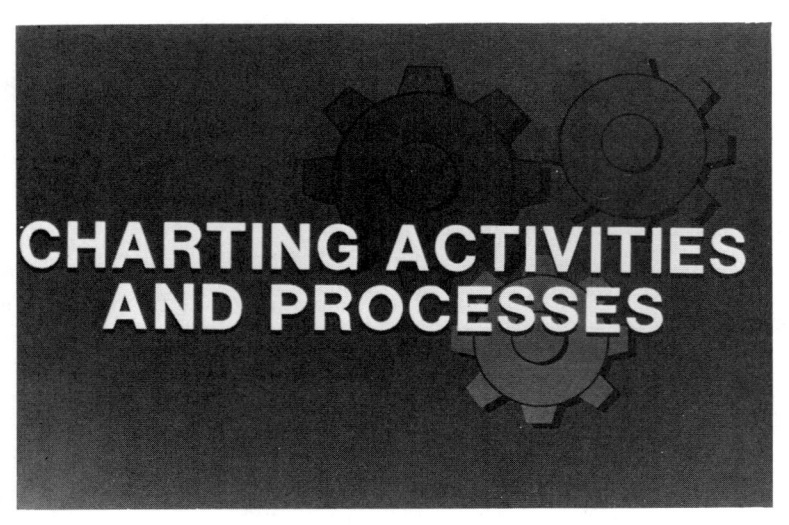

FIGURE 18-17

3. Looking at processes: One should learn, in this area, basic methods such as histograms and process capability studies. These methods help to identify whether a manufactured item is within specifications (Figure 18-19).

4. Control charts: We have already discussed the variable control chart and the precontrol method in detail in this chapter. There are other types of con-

FIGURE 18-18

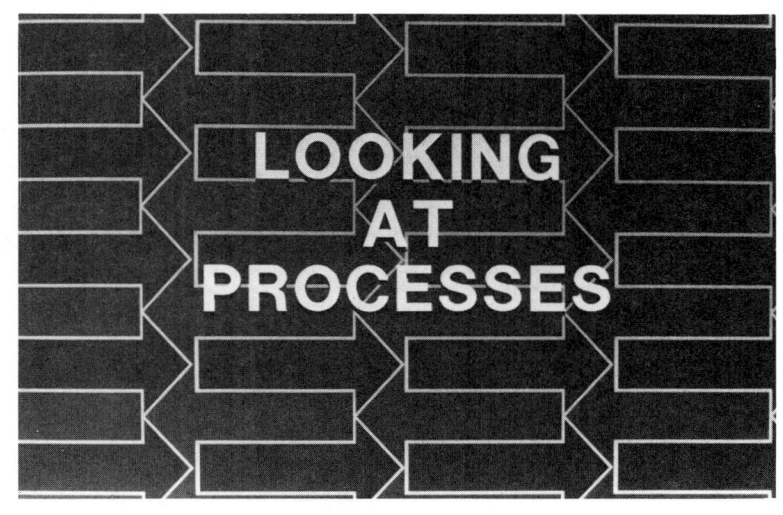

FIGURE 18-19

trol charts that should be used for analyzing defects or defective attributes (Figure 18-20).

5. Cost-Benefit analysis: This technique helps to determine the pros and cons of a quality-control proposal. It also explains the cost-benefit analysis using a force-field base (Figure 18-21).

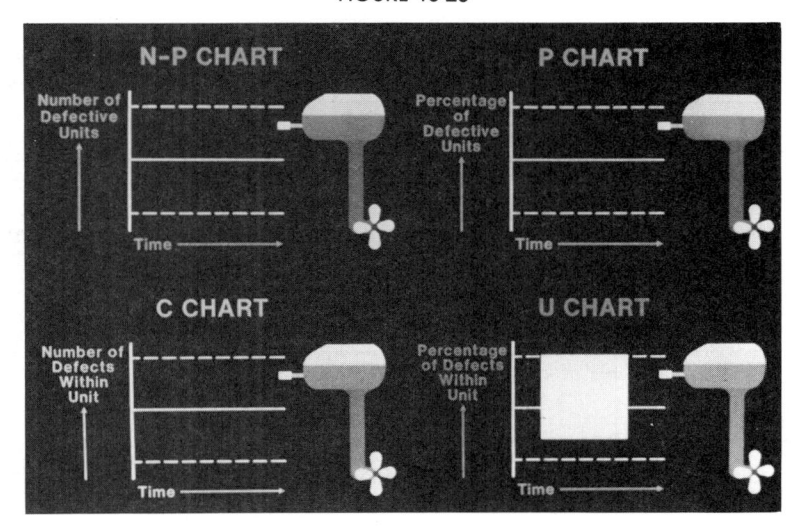

FIGURE 18-20

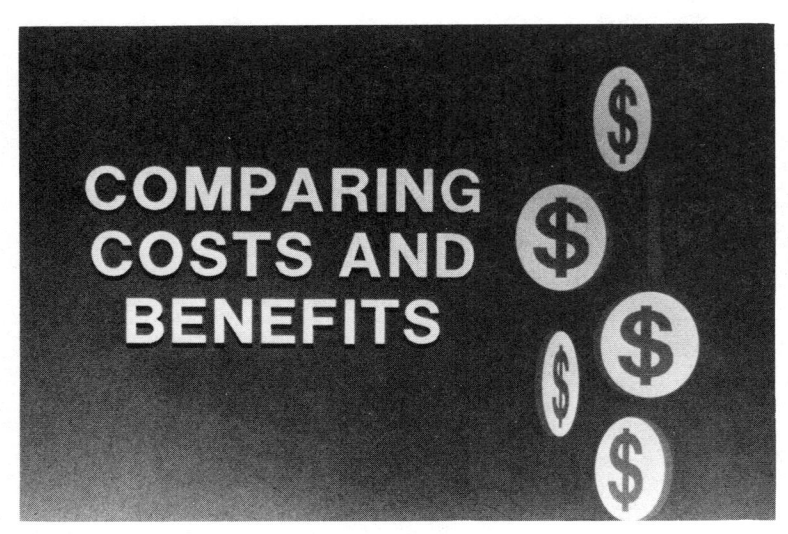

FIGURE 18-21

References

1. *Statistical Quality Control,* 5th ed., Eugene L. Grant and Richard S. Leavenworth, McGraw-Hill, 1980.
2. *Quality Control Handbook,* 3rd ed., J. M. Juran, McGraw-Hill, 1979.
3. *Quality Productivity and Competitive Position,* W. Edwards Deming, MIT Publishers, 1982.

Statistics may be described as the technology of the scientific method, consisting of a set of tools that are used to facilitate the making of decisions whenever conditions of uncertainty prevail. These tools have great utility in numerous fields of endeavor other than business, for example, biology, medicine, agriculture, psychology, and education. Statistics, in general, presents the decision-maker with relevant facts, and in many cases, provides an estimate of the probability of making a wrong decision.

Wayne David and James Terrell,
Business Statistics,
Boston: Houghton Mifflin Co., 1979

Note: This chapter was written by Tom Lewis, quality manager, Mercury Marine, Fond du Lac, Wisconsin, based on information provided by the author.

Part Three

Chapter Nineteen
CONCLUSION: WHO WILL SURVIVE?

It should be evident by this time that organizational quality improvement is not an easy task. It is easy to say that "quality is from womb to tomb" or "bust to dust," but in reality, it is very, very hard work. Customers are no longer happy with what was good for them yesterday. Quality expectations are raised by a tough worldwide competition that did not exist before, and it is going to be still tougher tomorrow!

In order to stay in this never-ending quality race, there are three types of activities that are necessary in any organization. These are as follows:

1. Activities that create quality
2. Activities that maintain quality
3. Activities that improve the present quality

Everyone has to get involved in one of these quality activities so that an organization can stay in business in the future. New products and services must be invented; ongoing improvement should be made; and processes must be constantly monitored so that the desired quality level can be maintained. We cannot talk anymore about a program or a campaign that operates like a Chinese calendar, which shows different festivals and activities as pictures; every month there is a new type of ceremony. Slogans will help, but they will not perform miracles. We need to change the total culture and management process in the organization. This takes time, energy, dedication, and persistence. It also requires good training and coaching. Any change must start with proper training and adequate planning. Participation and involvement from the top are musts. Training and involvement of all people must be carried out in all levels of management. Quality improvement, then, truly becomes institutionalized.

A Word About the Definition of Quality

The reader may have noticed that I have not given an exact definition of quality. One of the major reasons is the way emphasis is changing regarding various views on quality. American national standards define quality in Generic Guidelines in American National Standards for quality systems in this way:

> The word quality extends as applicable to the quality of design and/or the quality of conformance. It encompasses safety, performance, dependability and appearance, as well as specified quality attributes.

Today, many experts agree on only a part of this definition and suggest that quality is "fitness for use" or "conformance to the specification" or "zero defects." I believe that quality is a moving target, and customer satisfaction is going to play a very important role for the next twenty years. Hence, I would like to define quality as "the conformance to the requirements that is expected by the customer at a reasonable price." Quality encompasses more than just a few words. Hence, let us work at continual quality improvement and not be happy with what we did yesterday. Tomorrow's quality standards and requirements will be difficult and much stricter than yesterday's—and someone is going to meet them so that the customer is happy. So let us get going!

Who Will Survive?

It is not easy to answer this question, and there is no gimmick or panacea to avoid failures, either. Predictions have already been made that in the auto industry there will be only one manufacturer in the United States and similarly in a few other countries. Autos will be built on a worldwide basis. Blue-collar jobs in the United States are going to be fewer and fewer, with robots and more automation on the way, whether we like it or not. Hence, based on various observations and experiences, I feel that an organization that will try its best to institute some of the following changes will have a better chance to survive in the future. The organization must:

1. Realize that there is a problem and a need to improve the quality of products and services.
2. Understand and implement the Organizational Quality Improvement process (similar to that described in this book).
3. Understand the importance of the dynamic Quality Wheel.
4. Implement yearly self-analysis through quality teams in order to come up with new improvement projects.
5. Understand statistical methods and use them wisely.
6. Emphasize, involve, and follow up top-to-bottom quality commitment and involvements.
7. Start ongoing quality training programs.
8. Understand and plan use of robots and flexible manufacturing systems, computers, and automation (in the shop as well as in the office).
9. Have customer satisfaction and customer-oriented quality as prime goals in building products and offering services.
10. Recognize, monetarily or otherwise, the people in an organization who contribute to the improvement of quality.
11. Study all the jobs and eliminate waste through the use of techniques such as activity analysis and process analysis.
12. Demonstrate by activities that management is truly committed to the quality-improvement process.
13. Never stop the improvement process and strive for perfection (even though it is hard to achieve).
14. Take into consideration the global market and take action accordingly
15. Watch inventory closely through the use of JIT production and JIT purchasing.
16. Treat the vendors as a part of the family.
17. Thoroughly test new products and new services to assure quality.
18. Offer customers more for the price in terms of quality and/or service satisfaction.
19. Offer health improvement programs and stress management programs. Healthy people build quality.
20. Think about new technology, new quality methods, and new ways to improve processes.

IMPROVED QUALITY

REDUCED COSTS

HIGHER PRODUCTIVITY

REDUCTION OF WASTE

IMPROVED TECHNIQUES

BETTER EMPLOYEE RELATIONSHIPS

FIGURE 19-1

The list can go on, based on when each organization stands up in today's market, and the way it withstands competition. Organizations must realize and face the challenge of tomorrow to survive. That's why it is said, "Some organizations lead the way, some follow the way, and many organizations get the hell out of the others' way through obsolescence!"

What are your organization's plans for staying in business tomorrow?

It is a mistake to suppose that efficient production of products and service can, with certainty, keep an organization solvent and ahead of the competition. It is possible to go downhill and out of business, making the wrong product or offering the wrong type of service, even though everyone in the organization performs with devotion, employing statistical methods and every other aid that can boost efficiency.

W. Edwards Deming,
Quality, Productivity and Comprehension Position,
Boston: MIT Press, 1983

APPENDIX A: SOURCES FOR STATISTICAL AND OQI TRAINING

The Statistical Quality Control and Circle Institute, Inc. was established by me in 1980 to train people in quality management, an organizational quality-improvement process. The institute has worked with more than 500 different organizations in the United States, Mexico, Canada, England, and India. Many books and articles are also available about quality improvement.

Ingle's quality management system offers the following programs:

I. Ingle's Quality Improvement System

1. One-day quality-awareness program (for top management)
2. Implementing organizational quality improvement (five days)
3. Improving statistical thinking (three days)
4. Implementing Quality Circles (four days)
5. Advanced Quality Circle facilitator training (three days)
6. Developing a total quality system
7. Introduction to design of experiments
8. Evaluating your quality systems (one day)

9. Basic statistical control
10. Introduction to a quality-costs system
11. Vendor quality management
12. Managing for quality and productivity (for nonmanufacturing organizations)

II. Organizational Quality Improvement (your direct connection to organizational excellence)

A new spirit is pervading American business. You read about it in newspapers, hear about it on radio, and see it on television. It is the commitment to organizational excellence, and it is gaining new adherents every day.

What Is Organizational Excellence?

It is a total organizational commitment to achieve excellence in every area from product development and production through sales and service, to build high morale, to assure customer satisfaction, and to gain a competitive edge in today's area of accelerating change.

But achieving organizational excellence takes more than just a desire to achieve excellence. It requires plans, policies, dedication, and training—a lot of training.

That is where the brand-new Organizational Quality Improvement comes in. It is your direct connection to organizational excellence.

What Does Organizational Quality Improvement Do?

It provides the mechanism for implementing a system of excellence, identifies key personnel and details their training, presents quality-control tools, gives a systematic approach to problem solving, promotes teamwork and communication across organization levels, and shows how to incorporate Quality Circles into an organizationwide program for improvement.

It enables your organization to sharpen its insight into customer needs, develop salable products, improve production processes, reduce rejects, save time and money, improve teamwork and communication at all levels, improve morale, promote employee involvement, and gain a competitive edge.

Can It Be Used by Any Type of Organization?

Yes. Although manufacturing companies were the first to implement Organizational Quality Improvement, it is now being used effectively by organizations of many types.

Is It Restricted to Large Organizations?

Not at all. On one hand, it is being used by industry giants. On the other hand, it is achieving dramatic results for a company with 40 employees. Organization size is not a factor.

How Does It Work?

Your organization makes a total commitment to quality in every area at every echelon. Concentration is on special training for middle managers, those who make quality decisions on a daily basis.

Organizational Quality Improvement begins with product development and carries through production, sales, and marketing to product service, if required. It is customer oriented and is dedicated to providing the best possible product or service.

Beginning with how to organize your quality council, the policy-making segment, it will show you how to select and train quality-improvement teams, approach problem solving systematically, promote teamwork and communication, use statistical tools designed for nonmathematicians—everything from cost-benefit analysis to process capability and activity and process analysis. In brief, you get everything you need to implement a successful program for organizational excellence.

How Is Organizational Quality Improvement Different From Quality Circles?

In the Quality Circle process, volunteer employees solve problems related to their own work areas. Organizational Quality Improvement is entirely different. It is a management-controlled and -implemented system.

Ideas come down from the top, filter up from below, and move laterally at every level. It is a total organization effort. That is why it is so effective.

What Is the Program's Format?

Organizational Quality Improvement is a ten-module sound/slide program with pulsed and nonpulsed audiotapes, plus a leader's guide and ten workbooks—everything you need to implement your program for excellence.

What Is the Return on Investment?

According to the *Harvard Business Review,* companies with an inferior product have an average return on investment of 4.5 percent; those with an average product, 10.4 percent; and those with a superior product, 17.4 percent. This will give you a gauge on what Organizational Quality Improvement can do for you. Controlling quality is the most effective way to overcome competition from abroad and regain the benchmark of excellence.

See for yourself how Organizational Quality Improvement can help your organization meet its goal of excellence. It will certainly be worth your while.

III. Q. C. Trends (Quarterly Magazine)

The author publishes this quarterly journal to help organizations keep track of what's happening around the world in quality management and Quality Circles.

This self-instructive course includes the following material:

- Ten audio tapes (600 slides)
- Workbooks
- Leader's guidebook
- Many exercises

Module subjects:

1. Company-wide Q.C.
2. Getting started
3. Using industrial statistics
4. Looking at processes
5. Improving processes
6. Charting activities
7. Comparing costs and benefits
8. Quality Circles
9. Problem-solving process
10. Putting it all together

For details, write to:

Ingle's Quality Management System
P.O. Box 812
Fond du Lac, Wisconsin 54935

Generally, the following topics are dealt with in each issue:

1. Quality management
2. Statistical thinking
3. Quality Circles—projects
4. Design of experiments
5. What's America reading (nonfiction)?
6. Quality Circle management
7. Quality Circles training
8. Quality Circles and personal computers

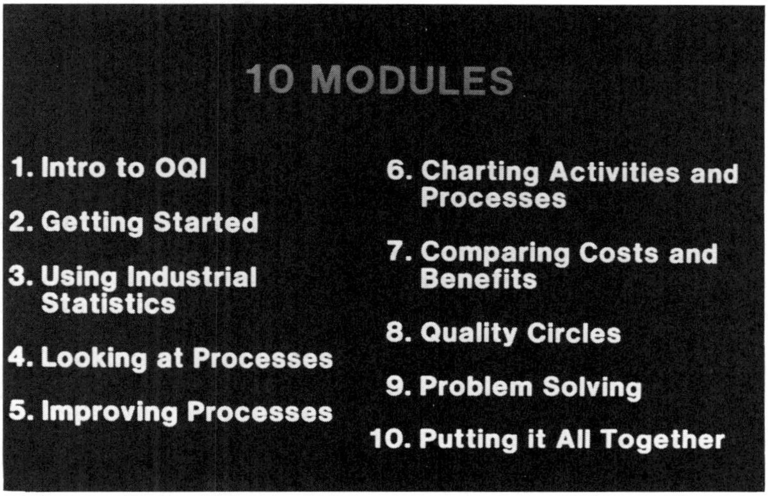

10 MODULES

1. Intro to OQI
2. Getting Started
3. Using Industrial Statistics
4. Looking at Processes
5. Improving Processes
6. Charting Activities and Processes
7. Comparing Costs and Benefits
8. Quality Circles
9. Problem Solving
10. Putting it All Together

FIGURE A-1

9. Q. C. and robotics
10. Q. C. and flexible manufacturing systems
11. Quality Control in education
12. Japanese manufacturing techniques
13. Quality Control in service industries
14. Quality Circles contest
15. Beyond Q.C., organizational quality improvement

For details on *Q. C. Trends* and several other magazines that discuss the quality-improvement process, please write to the author at the following address:

Ingle's Quality Management Systems
P.O. Box 812
Fond du Lac, Wisconsin 54935

BNA Communications

Thirty years ago, BNA Communications entered the training field by distributing motivational posters and placards. From this small beginning has emerged perhaps the world's largest pioneer and distributor of training materials—films, videos, and combined AV-printed programs covering the areas of management development, supervisory training, and many others listed below. In addition, BNAC conducts highly participative workshops for facilitator training, motivation, communication, discussion making, and problem solving at the managerial and executive levels.

With a clear understanding of the special problems encountered by trainers, BNAC pays close attention to training (the human resources development field) with each training package. BNAC not only provides a comprehensive leader's manual, but also makes its professional training staff available, free of charge, to counsel trainers on how to use and get the greatest possible benefits from the film or program they select. Moreover, BNAC's talented professional staff develops and produces customized programs, and its training staff conducts in-hours OQI training and other programs for clients.

BNAC has published audiovisual material in the following areas:

1. Safety—accident prevention
2. Quality improvement
3. Quality Circles
4. Communications
5. Computer literacy
6. EEO compliance/labor relations
7. Management development
8. Sales training/motivation
9. Negotiating
10. Supervisor training
11. Time management
12. Film/video-based courses
13. Employee health
14. Long-range planning
15. Delegation
16. Booklets, audiocassettes, and many other subjects

One can write to the following address for free information:

BNA Communication
9439 Key West Avenue
Rockville, Maryland 20850

APPENDIX B: QUALITY COSTS

For many years, manufacturing and service company executives have attempted to establish an industry standard for the ratio of the cost of quality to a measurable base. More and more companies are measuring the cost of quality as a percentage of sales. Due to inherent variations in types of manufacturing and service organizations, quality costs tend to vary considerably. For example, a company producing high-reliability semiconductors may be operating at a level where quality costs run as high as 20 percent of sales, while an average metal-working firm might comfortably achieve a level of 4 to 5 percent of sales.

Organizations that have not attempted to measure quality costs may be virtually throwing profits out the back door in waste, rework, and repairs. In the words of Philip Crosby, "Typical manufacturing and service companies spend in excess of 15 percent of their sales dollar for the cost of quality." Actually, this is the expense of doing things wrong: rework, repair, scrap, warranty, service after service, inspection, tests, and similar costs. A properly managed quality function can reduce this cost to 3–4 percent of the sales range. Thus, the words "quality cost" have become buzzwords in every organization.

The author has also used quality-cost terminology in other parts of this book. We will review the major areas of quality costs in this appendix and offer some guidelines in using quality-cost information in the organization.

Any organization that is interested in quality costs should first establish objectives and then follow a systematic procedure in collecting the quality costs through the financial department. (Generally, quality costs run between 10 and 25 percent of the sales of an organization.)

Elements of Quality Costs

Quality cost is the total cost involved in providing a product with quality acceptable to the customer, including the cost of failing to meet the customer's quality requirements.

Quality costs are usually divided into four categories which, when added together, represent the total quality costs. The elements that make up these costs are taken by and large from the ASQC publication, *Quality Costs—What and How*. All the elements in the following four categories may not be relevant to each business, but they are included here so that the pertinent ones may be chosen for use in the management of any specific quality system. Comparisons of quality costs between divisions will have no meaning because different elements will probably be used.

The four categories are:

1. Prevention. Costs incurred for planning, implementing, and maintaining a quality system that will assure conformance to quality requirements at economic levels. Specific prevention costs are:

- Planning the quality-control system
- Formulation of manufacturing controls
- Vendor evaluations
- Quality systems audits
- Allocated portion of divisional and group quality assurance
- CPSC, GMP, ASME, and so on—plan and develop
- Design and development of gauges
- Quality planning by other functions
- Quality training
- Quality-cost reporting
- Quality motivation programs
- Prototype testing

2. *Appraisal.* Costs incurred to determine the degree of conformance to quality requirements. Specific appraisal costs are:

- Receiving test and inspection
- Inspection and test
- Inspection and test materials
- Product quality audits
- Gauge maintenance and calibration
- Allocated portion of divisional and group quality audits
- Field performance testing
- Final test and inspection
- Data processing of inspection data
- Special product evaluations
- Outside agency product approval (UL, etc.)

3. *Internal failures.* Costs arising when products, components, and materials fail to meet quality requirements prior to transfer of ownership to customer. These costs are total costs and not variances from standard costs. Specific external failure costs are:

- Scrap, rework, and repair (burdened)
- Troubleshooting and failure analysis
- Reinspect; retest
- Material resource planning activity
- Inventory costs on held material
- Downgrading or seconds
- Allocation of divisional and group charges

4. *External failures.* Costs incurred when products fail to meet quality requirements after transfer of ownership to customer. These costs should be tabulated at factory cost. Specific external failure costs are:

- Warranty administration and expenses
- Returned material evaluation and repair
- Marketing specification error
- Product liability expense and insurance premiums
- Out-of-warranty expense

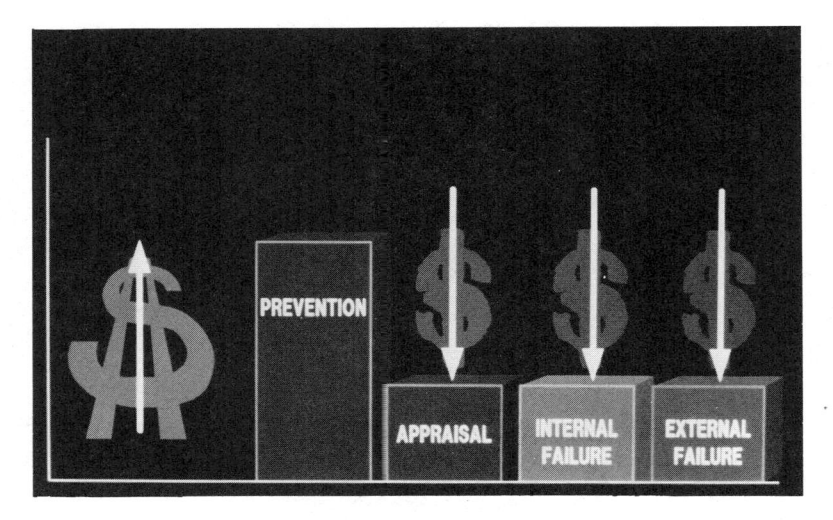

FIGURE B-1

- Engineering design error
- Complaint handling expense
- Allocation of divisional or group charges
- Installation failure
- Recalls for quality reasons
- Loss of business due to poor quality reputation

Guidelines to Establish and Cut Down Quality Costs

The following steps can be used in establishing the quality-cost system:

Step 1—team formulation. Before any quality-cost reporting begins, management approval and support must be obtained if there is to be an eventual impact on profits. Costs are associated with collecting the data, hence the management needs to be convinced that costs incurred in collecting the data and measuring quality costs has a high probability of being offset by real profit improvement. Once the approval is given by the management (quality council), a team should be formed to collect quality costs. Generally, quality control engineers, accountants, and manufacturing engineers are included in this team.

Step 2—cost collection. You should start by collecting information that is already available in the organization; don't reinvent the wheel. The accounting department will be the best source in this regard. In some cases estimates are necessary, since everything is not readily available. In some companies, a quality-costs steering committee is formed to review the details and to agree on the financial format. A lot of this data analysis can be done easily with the use of computers.

Step 3—establish a performance base. It is necessary to establish a performance base. Many organizations use a percentage of sales, a percentage of direct labor, or a percentage of total operating costs. This type of base helps to analyze the ongoing performance.

Step 4—cost reporting. Once the information is collected and agreed upon, the report should be prepared and should be released by the vice-president of finance. Many times organizations publish these reports through quality control; however, my experience is that they do not carry the same weight and many times are neglected. The report must be precise; you can use graphs and trend lines to make the information understandable. In general, quality-cost reports should be brief, concise, and clear.

Step 5—analysis. Once the report is issued it is the quality-control engineers' and the manufacturing engineers' job to analyze the details. Quality costs should be used effectively to identify key problems in the organization. One should use the famous Pareto analysis in this regard.

Step 6—communicating the details. Quality costs should be published periodically; it should be shown where dollars are lost. Proper inspiration as well as feedback must be provided in order for employees to do a quality job. If it is necessary to make changes in procedures, standards, or equipment, management should be ready to do that without hesitation.

Step 7—goal setting. Once quality costs are known and realized, it is advisable for management to set up goals for improvement. Goals should be attainable, but not too easy. Problems should be solved as soon as possible, and ongoing quality improvement should be the way to do business.

Step 8—employee involvement. Improve employee communications and involve all employees in the quality effort by encouraging their participation in decision-making processes. People like to get involved and see that their organization is successful. Quality Circles also help to do this job effectively. Organizations can reduce quality costs through effective communication.

Step 9—quality training. It is essential that the organization provide training for the employees. Properly trained employees can solve problems effectively and quickly. Complex products and services also require a well-trained, stable work force.

Step 10—establish proper procedures, standards, and field failure reporting. This has been discussed in detail in this book.

Step 11—ongoing follow-up. Periodic quality-cost reports should not only be issued, but also must be examined to analyze for any noticeable trends and changes. Without proper follow-up and corrective-action systems, many problems will reoccur since no one took time out to fix them and introduce preventive action.

Management of Quality Costs

One should remember the following key points in managing quality costs:

1. Quality costs mean more than just scrap and rework or warranty and complaints.
2. Quality costs serve as a guideline for showing trends.
3. Quality cost reports are not budgeted. They are not a measure of the quality audit department, but of the operation's quality system.
4. A person who is accountable for profit is the one who can be accountable for the level of quality costs.
5. A quality manager's job is to design the quality-cost system, but it must be approved by the quality council and must be implemented through the financial department to gain credibility.
6. Quality costs should not be compared with those of other organizations. Each organization should try to reach its own optimum level.
7. Quality costs provide for the quality council a business language everybody is familiar with and which deals with the intangibles of quality in dollars and cents.

In short, a manager should use quality costs:
   as a measurement tool
   as an analysis tool
   as a budgeting tool
   as a profit improvement tool
      and
   as a communication tool to improve quality and productivity.

Advantages of Using Quality Costs

1. They provide sensitive measurement of the effectiveness of the overall quality activities of the business.
2. They provide a measurement of the quality manager's effectiveness in integrating quality trends.
3. They can be used as a planning tool to establish long-range and short-range goals for quality improvement.
4. They are a decision-making tool to work on key problem areas.
5. They also determine the economically optimum effort of quality systems.
6. They help to translate quality achievements into dollars and cents.

A Sample Exercise

The ABC Shoe Company recently collected the data on the quality costs. The data is shown below:

Adjustments of customer's complaints	$ 5,000
Warranty	60,000
Rework	20,000
Scrap	15,000
Vendor certification	4,000
Engineering drawing review	5,000
New gauges	4,000
Inspection (in-process, final)	20,000
Preproduction testing	4,000

Questions:

1. Can you identify various quality costs?
2. Can you summarize the report and find the percentage of each category?
3. What can you conclude and recommend to management?

Sample Forms

Quality costs can be reported on various forms. Two sample forms are shown here.

A B C COMPANY PLANT QUALITY COST REPORT

_____ QUARTER, 19___   PLANT NO. _____

Performance Analysis

	Actual	Budget

1. Cost of quality/standard
   Cost of goods manufactured
   a. Prevention costs
   b. Appraisal costs
   c. Internal failure costs

2. Prevention and appraisal
   Hours (   )
   Direct and indirect
   Hours (   ) =

3. Internal failure costs/hour
   (Direct and indirect)

4. Returned material
   (In-plant)
   Returned material
   (Due to vendor)

5. % of returned material

COMMENTS:

Manager of Quality Control   Comptroller

QUALITY COST REPORT

_____ QUARTER, 19____   PLANT NO. _____

Description	Actual	Quarter Budget	% Var.	Y.T.D. Actual	Budget	% Var.
I. Prevention Costs						
1. Design review						
2. Supplier survey						
3. Plant 10 quality control						
4. Q.C. work for other plants						
5. Special studies						
6. Corrective action/ problem solving						
7. Other—See below						
TOTAL						
II. Appraisal Costs						
1. Quality testing						
2. Inspection: incoming In-process Excess: final						
3. Gauge maintenance and calibration						
4. Gauging						
5. Other						
TOTAL						
III. Internal Failure Costs						
1. Production scrap						
2. Rework						
3. Salvage						
4. Added operation						
5. Vendor rework (noncollect)						
6. Vendor scrap (noncollect)						
7. Other						
TOTAL QUALITY COSTS						

*Explanation of I-7

APPENDIX C: STATISTICAL PROCESS CONTROL (SPC)

I have discussed in Chapter 17 the use of statistical methods as shown by Edward Deming to Japan in 1946. Based on Dr. Deming's teachings, Japan developed the use of control charts in manufacturing as well as non-manufacturing areas. Once again, today many organizations in the United States are excited about implementing statistical process control (SPC) to improve quality and productivity.

My experience shows that SPC is being implemented at three different levels, as follows:

1. Traditional SPC. In this method control charts are manually plotted and used on the stop or other areas. Generally, standard graphs are used and control limits are calculated.

2. SPC using personal computers. At this level, the quality-control department is usually involved. The data is collected and plotted on a graph. However, the control limits and interpretation are done with the use of personal computers.

3. Automatic SPC. Many advanced-thinking organizations are using a completely automatic SPC system where data is collected using electronic gauging and can be seen on CRT tubes. Operators can view the data and can automatically stop the machine on process through electronic control using the calculated control limit as a stopping point.

Suggested Implementation Plan

The following implementation plan for SPC is suggested to implement it successfully in the organization.

Step 1—Introduction:
Top-Management Commitment

It is necessary for top management to understand the basic philosophy of statistical concepts and statistical thinking. Many times, management's approval is required when financial support is needed to improve quality. In order to obtain this support and commitment, a one-day quality awareness seminar is recommended for top management.

The following topics should be covered during the session:

1. Statistical thinking
2. Use of statistics and its advantages
3. What is happening around the world
4. New quality era
5. What is SPC?
6. Total quality system
7. Organizational quality improvement
8. Advantages of SPC, OQI, and Quality Circles

Step 2—Middle-Management Involvement

Once the top management approves the concept and quality council gives the green light, middle-management involvement is essential. This can be achieved through a one- or two-day training seminar.

Topics

1. Statistical methods
2. Variability, probability
3. Process-capability studies
4. Control charts (exercises)
5. Precontrol (exercises)
6. OQI, SPC, and Quality Circles
7. Advantages
8. Implementation plan

Step 3—Getting Ready (Foremen, Supervisors, and Lead Men Training)

Once the middle management is trained in the OQI and SPC systems, the next level of training is essential. This is where the organization is getting ready to implement SPC.

Training at this level can be precise and concentrated on SPC alone. The following outline can be used:

1. New quality era
2. Worldwide competition
3. Seven elegant quality tools
4. Variability and probability
5. Control charts interpretation
6. Precontrol
7. Advantages of SPC

Step 4—Employee Training

This is the basic training for employees (hourly employees as well as office workers). The following outline can be used:

1. What is SPC?
2. Problem-solving process
3. Data collection
4. Variation that exists in the process
5. What are control charts?
6. How to use control charts
7. How to plot control charts
8. What is precontrol?
9. Uses of control charts and precontrol
10. Advantages of SPC

Step 5—Preplanning

Once the training is completed, the quality council should receive the feedback on its progress and some idea about its acceptance. Many times, you will see improvement as you start the training. The next step is to determine and decide the answers to the following questions that are asked during SPC installation.

1. Where shall we start?
2. How shall we implement?
3. Who is responsible for the measurement?
4. Who should plot the charts?
5. Who should maintain the charts?
6. Who is responsible for interpreting the charts?
7. Who is responsible for corrective action?
8. Who is responsible for problem areas?
9. When should you use precontrol?
10. When should you stop using control charts?

Step 6—Using Statistical Techniques

Once the training is completed, the trained personnel can use SPC in two ways, as follows:

1. Formal use of SPC
2. Informal use of SPC

1. Formal Use of SPC

Even though SPC is a very effective tool, the results that are derived from its use in the shop or offices may not be appreciated. Many times processes or equipment may be out of control due to old equipment or poor processes; the organization may face problems in spending thousands of dollars for corrective measures. These could be long-range investments and sometimes may not seem to be successful. Hence, SPC needs to be continually implemented throughout the organization.

The author suggests the following procedures:

1. Select objectives—to reduce scrap, reduce rework, reduce inspection, and so on
2. Select the area in the organization where SPC is to be used
3. Discuss the concept with foremen and department heads
4. Training for supervisors and foremen
5. Training for operators
6. Select the area and processes or equipment (preferably two or three only) where SPC is to be used
7. Select the suitable control chart
8. Decide on characteristics and gauges

9. Check the blueprints and equipment
10. Determine sample size and frequency
11. Plot the chart and calculate control limits
12. Interpret the results
13. Decide on corrective action
14. Follow-up
15. Decide precontrol
16. Ongoing checks, as necessary

Sample Case Study

The following case study shows the successful use of SPC in one of the large companies in the United States[1]:

The Sealed Power Filter Division is located in Des Plaines, Illinois, and manufactures a line of lightweight, durable filters which combine metal with fabric and injection-molded plastic components. Rapid growth of sales and major original equipment manufacturer customers together contributed to a concern by division management that the issue of quality needed closer attention. In late summer and early fall of 1982, the general manager and several of his people began to explore different quality-improvement ideas through discussions with consultants and attendance at both a statistical process control (SPC) workshop and a customer-quality conference.

These experiences, together with recommendations from the quality-control manager, led to a management decision in January 1983 to begin quality improvement by upgrading the systems for quality measurement and administration.

Responsibilities Assigned

A group of 12 managers, including the general manager, was informally dubbed the quality-improvement team, and in January 1983 attended a week-long quality-improvement training workshop conducted by a consultant. The workshop covered a variety of quality topics such as using quality-cost systems, analyzing scrap, formalizing corrective action steps, error cause removal, building quality awareness through supervisory and hourly training, and preparing quality procedures. The workshop also included a self-audit of existing quality systems and procedures in the division.

Following the workshop, the quality-improvement team began meeting on a monthly basis.

[1] From Sealed Power Corporation, Des Plaines, Illinois. Used with permission.

Opportunities Identified, Master Plan Prepared

The quality-improvement team met late in January 1983, and based upon the results of the audit conducted during the consultant's workshop, defined a total of 11 projects spanning the next 18 months. Projects planned for the first six months included:

- Implementing a cost of quality system
- Conducting a quality awareness slogan contest
- Developing a new employee orientation program
- Developing and conducting statistical process control training for both supervisory and hourly people
- Implementing statistical process control on a pilot basis

Several team members were assigned to each project and a master plan was prepared.

Training and Development

While training began prior to implementation, it ran concurrently throughout implementation and became an ongoing activity.

Training courses were selected or developed for each level within the division based upon the training participants' intended role in quality improvement. Participation in training started at the top with division management and progressed downward, one layer at a time.

In January of 1983 the quality-improvement team attended a basic statistics course as well as the consultants' five-day quality-improvement workshop. Later, selected members of management from manufacturing, engineering, and quality control attended a three-day applied statistics course and a two-day course on control charts. The addition of a microcomputer expedited the utilization of the newly acquired statistical techniques. This later proved to be a major contribution to SPC implementation, as the number of quality engineering hours required to generate elaborate statistical equations was drastically reduced.

Continuing with the educational process, key personnel from manufacturing, production, and quality control attended several other multiday workshops and conferences. A strategy was developed whereby the context and depth of statistics training was proportioned to the individual's area of responsibility. Engineering and manufacturing department heads were primarily exposed to process capability, relationship of mean distributions to probability limits, and concepts of variation to process potential. The quality-control manager's training encompassed all aspects of statistics, with emphasis on capability studies, control chart interpretation, uniformity checks, and evaluation of variability within the measurement system itself (gauge repeatability and consistency between inspectors, and sensitivity of measuring equipment to tolerance zones).

It was at this time that the quality-control manager conducted a series of special courses for her own department, covering inspection methods and the use of inspection equipment. This "Metrology Series" was held all day Saturday, once a month, for four months (January through April 1983) and was aimed at building the skill and reliability of inspectors to lay the groundwork for SPC and the upgrading of inspection equipment and methods. This upgrading of quality control also included development of people. In early April two quality people (one a union member) attended a "train the trainer" workshop on statistical process control in order to create an SPC instructor cadre within the division.

In the production area, supervisory and lead people from across the plant were given a basic SPC course in February and then a three-day course in May covering statistical applications to manufacturing. This latter course covered not only statistical techniques, but also problem-solving methods. The course content was aimed at answering the question, "What do we do when the chart shows we are out of control?" While it repeated some of the February SPC content, the practical focus of the latter course produced a major attitude change in the most skeptical of participants. They now began to see SPC as more than just a curious technical subject. It was a practical tool for problem solving.

The final phase of training to support implementation was aimed at plant operators. In April 1983, prior to their training, operators were asked to fill out data sheets to assess the difficulty of the task and the points that training should cover. Other things were learned in this trial too: The operators needed a wall clock, a piece counter, and a place to keep the control charts at their work station. It was evident as well that there was a need to dispel their belief that SPC was just a disguise for another productivity check.

The following month, the project responsible for operator training prepared the training materials, including a statistical process control employee handbook printed in both English and Spanish. The hourly training course was developed to give operators a basic understanding of statistical variation. In June all production operators received training in a three-hour session covering the philosophy of SPC and how to fill out and interpret control charts.

At the end of June a plan was presented which would expand operator training to include new employee orientation. Using an audio-video presentation to introduce division department heads, the media enabled managers to project their personal message to employees, describing expectations relating to quality, productivity, and safety. This added assurance that employees would have a positive attitude and understanding of the importance of their function from the first day on the job.

Implementation

In March of 1983 the general manager upgraded the position of quality-control manager to quality-assurance manager and changed the position so that it reported directly to him rather than to production.

In April quality assurance consulted with production foremen and managers to select the test sites for SPC implementation. Control charting started on three test sites the same month with data supplied by production operators. It was at this time that the second microcomputer was installed to expand the use of statistics to other manufacturing areas.

In April a quality slogan content was run among all hourly employees. The response was enthusiastic, and in early May the winning slogan was prominently displayed on the wall over the time clock: "First in quality, foremost in production, always with pride."

In May the first cost-of-quality reports became available, using the newly available data from both production and accounting. The new data was summarized on a microcomputer and showed costs in three areas: prevention cost (cost of preventing defects in the design and procurement of deliverable products), appraisal costs (costs of determining whether purchased and manufactured products conform to specifications), and failure costs (costs due to failure to meet requirements—i.e., redesign, rework, scrap, and returns, among others.) These reports for the first time permitted isolation of specific quality problems and the effects of those problems in a wholly new and precise way.

But even more important than the new quality information was the new formal corrective-action system. This system also became operational in May and comprised monthly meetings for identifying problems, as well as special investigative procedures to isolate causes and follow-up action at three levels: shop floor, middle management, and general manager.

Problems such as customer complaints, returns, and internal failures were quickly flagged in the monthly meetings. From there they were entered in a log and tracked. Any problems not resolved at the shop-floor level (through action by supervisors and operators) progressed to the middle-management level for action (e.g., a tooling change, process change, drawing change, etc.). Problems not resolved at that level were next reviewed by the general manager.

The corrective-action system represented a new way of operating for management people in the division. The system pinpointed the high-cost quality problems and insured planning and investigation. Moreover, it was relentless. Some managers were beginning to question the burden placed upon departments outside of quality assurance by the system. Much discussion ensued: Did quality improvement require follow-up on each problem logged? Would the corrective action system continue in its present form? Division management decided: It did, and it would.

By the following month, corrective action had become the expected mode of operation. The corrective action system was incorporated into a standard operating procedure manual for quality, along with quality cost reporting, SPC, scrap analysis, and a number of other policies. By the end of June the newly codified operating procedures and measurement tools had been further reinforced by the training at all levels down through the plant operator. So by this time everyone had heard the same message about quality, and knew that management was serious. Quality *was* everyone's business.

Evaluation

The most immediate and visible result of the quality program was a 41 percent reduction in scrap plantwide for the month of July over the preceding month. Surprisingly, most of this reduction came neither from the SPC pilot projects nor from the formal corrective actions, but rather from the plantwide operator training. Operators became more aware of quality. Supervisors reported an increasing number of problems brought to their attention by concerned operators: The material wasn't correct, the parts didn't fit, or the product wasn't exactly right, and the supervisor simply had to do something about it.

Of the three SPC pilot test sites, one obtained a 90 percent reduction in quality rejects and another improved to the point where the customer lifted his requirement of 100 percent inspection and agreed to rely solely on the control charts. The situation at the third site proved to be more complex and, at this writing, the results are inconclusive.

The quality-cost reports, however, showed further evidence of improvement. Monthly total quality costs, either as a percentage of the total costs of sales or in terms of direct labor, have continued to decline each month since implementation began. And there is every indication that these costs will continue to follow a projected downward trend.

Further Evidence for Acceptance of SPC

Other signs point to the widespread acceptance of SPC in the division. It is now used as a preventive measure with new products and, in working with engineers, to fine tune the molding dies for existing plastic products and thereby reduce scrap and rework. At the request of accounting, supervisors now also use control charts to monitor material consumption in the molding area. Initially, these charts were implemented to monitor the consumption of plastic resin. However, when reviewed, an undeniable correlation was detected between the variation in part weight, problems at the assembly operation, and rise or fall of plastic component rework.

Charts are also being run on supplier materials to determine the supplier's process capabilities. In addition, purchasing has contacted suppliers regarding SPC, and several suppliers have indicated they are starting similar quality programs.

The demand for new SPC applications is steadily rising. Two new SPC test sites are currently being started and additional applications are being requested by engineering and production to solve specific problems. SPC is now not only accepted, but also used extensively as a problem-solving tool.

Data from capability studies now gives valuable process knowledge to filter division engineers. This knowledge enables division managers to determine with pinpoint exactness the manufacturing feasibility of proposed tolerance ranges on new and revised projects. Tooling and dies are being fine tuned to center a manufacturing operation on the most economic path.

Working relationships with customers are taking new depth as product engineers are utilizing capability studies to achieve a copious marriage of process potential and engineering specifications.

Presently the biggest challenge is to keep up with the requests for new applications, which exceed the capacity of quality assurance to provide the assistance. The solution to meeting this demand will lie in creating within production and engineering a strong base of knowledge in SPC. In the future, it is hoped that the quality-assurance department will take on more of a teaching and consulting role to other departments, leaving implementation to those who design and make the product.

To strengthen this teaching base, a series of videotapes, instructional guides, and workbooks has been added. Checklists are also being developed to aid the individual in using control charts as a problem-solving tool. Specialized to each manufacturing department, the checklists will direct the investigation to various process parameters indicative of the type pattern that develops on the control chart.

Working with several organizations around the world, the author has developed a "6 weeks—12 hours" SPC training course for the supervisors, foremen, and the grass-roots people who need to understand and use SPC effectively.

The following is a brief outline of the training course:

1. New Quality Era
2. Why and How to Use Statistics
3. Variability in the Process
4. Industrial Statistics (Slides)
5. Exercises (Basic)

6. SPC—What and Why?
7. Control Charts—Variables
8. Exercises
9. Successful Case Studies
10. Principles of Control Charts
11. How to Plot Control Charts
12. Exercises
13. Interpreting Control Charts
14. Attribute Control Chart (Videotape) C chart, P chart, np chart, U chart
15. Exercises
16. Project Through Brainstorming
17. Project Analysis and Solutions
18. Coding and Decoding
19. Implementation Plan for SUCCESSFUL SPC

More details can be obtained by writing to the author at the following address:

Sud INGLE
S.Q.C. (Ingle Quality Management Systems)
P.O. Box 812
Fond du Lac, WI 54935

APPENDIX D: DESIGN OF EXPERIMENT

Statistics can be categorized in different ways. One can divide it into two groups such as parametric and nonparametric statistics or practical versus theoretical statistics. One can also divide statistical methods into passive statistics versus active statistics. Most of the tools that we use, such as control charts, histograms, or process capabilities, are generally known as passive statistics. On the other hand, design of statistics is known as active statistics, where a systematic approach is needed in solving complex problems. Design of experiments not only helps to solve chronic problems but also helps to optimize the process conditions.

In the design of experiments one can apply the following steps:

1. Define the problem
2. List the factors and categorize them
3. Plan and design
4. Review and check
5. Run the experiment and collect the data
6. Analyze the data
7. Conclusion—recommend corrective action

Some of the key elements in the design of experiments are (a) factors, (b) levels, and (c) replications. Factors are those characteristics of a problem that the experiment wishes to study.

The level is generally associated with the setting of the factor or alter native under consideration. Finally, replication refers to the sample size within each combination. If we run an experiment without replication, this means that each combination is used only once.

There are different kinds of design of experiments that can be used in solving complex problems. Some of the common ones are as follows:

1. Single factor—multilevel model
2. Multifactor—multilevel model
3. Full factorial design with replication
4. Latin square model
5. Greco-Latin squares
6. Fractional factorial experiment
7. Other special designs

More details can be found in many statistical books.

Taguchi Method (Use of orthogonal arrays)

This information is taken from the book *Introduction to Off-Line Quality Control,* by G. Taguchi and Yuin Wu (Nagaya, Japan: Central Japan Quality Control Association, 1979, with permission from Yuin Wu).

Today once again Japan is showing to the rest of the world effective use of industrial design of experiments using orthogonal arrays (fractional factorial designs). This method is generally known as the Taguchi method or off-line quality control. One of the major goals of this experiment is to find combinations that will remove variability and reduce the impact of uneven distribution of the final characteristics.

The most significant R & D work Professor Taguchi developed is the cross-bar switching system, especially of the wire spring relay. As much as several million dollars were spent on designing the relay, a tiny component part that costs only a few dollars. The results brought a gain of more than several billion dollars to Japanese Telephone and Telegraph as well as to the nation. The performance of Japanese relays during testing was found better than the original despite the fact that the quality and material of most parts were poor compared to American relays.

Today it is reported that thousands of organizations in Japan conduct a number of experiments by using orthogonal tables. These types of experiments are used to improve quality of design and improve manufacturing processes.

In improving quality of design, experiments are listed in the following areas:

1. Primary design
2. Secondary design
3. Tertiary design

In manufacturing processes, the Taguchi method is used in the following areas.

1. Determining manufacturing process system using specialized techniques
2. Determining the optimum conditions of each elemental process, including the purchasing of materials and component parts
3. Determining the allowance ranges for changes in operating conditions and other variables

Many large organizations in the United States are taking interest in this approach and are actively checking the practical use of the Taguchi method. However, keep in mind that these types of experiments are time-consuming and not always successful. They require a lot of patience and understanding. Only time will tell whether we can use this approach effectively in America.

APPENDIX E: QUALITY ASSURANCE MANUAL

It is essential that every organization prepare and issue a quality-assurance manual. Quality assurance manuals serve the following purposes:

1. They standardize quality requirements.
2. They help to communicate quality information.
3. They help an organization to understand quality standards.

It is not easy to describe the detailed construction of a quality-assurance manual here. Booklets such as MIL-STD-9858 and others published by the United States Government Standards Committee are useful in this area. A suggested outline for preparing a quality-assurance manual is as follows:

Section	General Sections
	Topics
I	Total Organizational Quality System
II	Quality-Assurance Standards
III	Quality-Assurance Systems
IV	Quality Information
V	Quality-Costs Reporting and Improvement
VI	Quality Audits

VII	Quality Training
VIII	Customer Satisfaction
IX	Quality-Assurance Engineering (Statistical Thinking)
X	Special Quality Assurance Requirements
XI	Quality Assurance Bulletin—Update

The following sample for a manufacturing organization will give the reader a clear idea about the details that should be included in a quality-assurance manual.

Sample Manual

Quality Assurance Manual (Manufacturing)

I. Foreword
    Scope
    Table of Contents
    Holder's List
    Index

II. Quality Organization
    Purpose and Function
    Quality Policies
    Long-Range Objectives
    Annual Objectives
    Major Action Program
    Lab Description
    Responsibilities

III. Quality Administrative Procedures
    Interim—Standards
    Directives
    Guidelines

IV. Quality Information
    Quality Information System
    Assembly Procedure

Warranty
Parts in Process, Subcontracts
Purchased Parts
Periodic Reports

V. Inspection
Part Inspection
Assembly Inspection
Incoming Inspection
Subcontract Inspectors
Classification of Characteristics
Geometric Routings
Supplier Control Practices

VI. Equipment
Gauge Control and Instrumentation
Equipment and Numbering System
Calibration Standards
Equipment Inventory
Equipment Operating Instructions

VII. Quality Standards
Quality Control Standard #1
Quality Control Standard #2
Quality Control Standard #3
One can add other standards that are approved by the organization.

VIII. Q.A. Forms
Defective Material Reports
SIR—Simple Inspection Report
Inspection Approval Form
Inspection Audit Report Form
Material Withdrawal Form
Material Return Form
Corrective Action Form
Certificate of Calibration Form

IX. **Quality Training**
    Inspection
    Middle Management
    Vendors

X. **Statistical Concepts**
    Statistical Thinking
    Sampling
    Statistical Methods
    Control Charts
    Design of Experiment
    Statistical Quality Control

XI. **Manufacturing and Quality Planning**
    Material Identification and Routing
    Drawing and Specification Change Control
    Raw Material Control
    In-Process Inspection
    Testing and Shipping
    Packing and Shipping
    Production Processes and Fabrication
    Completed Internal Inspection

XII. **Service Requirements and Customer Satisfaction**
    Failure Analysis
    Early Warning System
    Customer Surveys
    Dealer Surveys

XIII. **Government, Customer, and Contractor Actions**
    Special Requirements
    Contract Conditions and Follow-Up
    Government Inspection of Audits

XIV. **Miscellaneous Issues**
    For more details, please write to Ingle's Quality Management Systems, P.O. Box 812, Fond du Lac, Wisconsin 54935.

We have discussed throughout many chapters of this book how to evaluate your organization. This method may not be perfect, but it has helped several organizations to locate weak areas for quality and productivity improvement.

One can summarize the results as shown below.

ORGANIZATIONAL QUALITY PROFILE

Area	Chapter Reference	Poor 0-25%	Below Average 25-50%	Above Average 50-75%	Good 75-90%	Excellent, Above Average 90-100%
Managing for OQI	3					
Quality Planning	5					
Quality Deployment	6					
New Product Introduction	7					
Vendor Quality Control	8					
Manufacturing Quality	9					
Computer-Aided Quality System	10					
Service Quality	8					
Quality Auditing	12					
Quality Circles	13					

Note: How to calculate percentage of performance

In each section I have given a number of questions and points based on your evaluation of the organization. Add up all the points you gave to your organization and also find out the total possible points. Dividing the total points of your organization by the total available points will give you an idea about the percentage to plot on this graph. More than 300-500 questions can be developed to find the weak areas in your organization.

APPENDIX F: ORGANIZATIONAL QUALITY PERFORMANCE EVALUATION

I have limited the following bibliography to some key books and periodicals. For additional information, refer to current periodical articles.

Books

1. American Society for Quality Control. "Annual Convention Transactions," 1951–1984. Published annually by ASQC, Milwaukee, Wisconsin.

2. Burr, I. W. *Engineering Statistics and Quality Control.* New York: McGraw-Hill Book Company, 1953.

3. Dixon, W. S., and F. J. Massey, Jr. *Introduction to Statistical Analysis.* 3rd ed. New York: McGraw-Hill, 1969.

4. Feigunbaum, A. V. *Total Quality Control.* New York: McGraw-Hill, 1961.

5. Grant, L. Eugene, and Richard S. Leavenworth. *Statistical Quality Control.* 5th ed. New York: McGraw-Hill, 1982.

6. International Association of Quality Circles. "Annual Convention Transaction," 1979–1984. Published annually by IAQC, Cincinnati, Ohio.

7. Juran, J. M. *Quality Control Handbook.* 3rd ed. New York: McGraw-Hill, 1974.

8. Kirkpatrick, E. G. *Quality Control for Managers and Engineers.* New York: John Wiley & Sons, Inc., 1970.

9. Peach, Paul. *Quality Control for Management.* Englewood Cliffs, N.J.: Prentice-Hall, Inc., 1964.

10. Shewhart, W. A. *Economic Control of Quality of Manufactured Products.* N.Y.: Van Nostrand Reinhold Co., Inc., 1931.

Periodicals

1. "Quality Progress." American Society for Quality Control, Milwaukee, Wisconsin 50103.

2. "Q.C. Trends." Statistical Quality Control & Circles Institute, Inc., P.O. Box 812, Fond du Lac, Wisconsin 54935.

3. "Quality." Hitchcock Publishing Company, Wheaton, Illinois 60188.

4. "Quality Circles Quarterly." International Association of Quality Circles, Cincinnati, Ohio 45203.

INDEX

Acceptable (average) quality level (AQL), 111, 120–21, 142
Activity analysis, 295
  by Quality Circles, 208
AGREE (Advisory Groups on Reliability of Electronic Equipment), 163–64
Air Force Systems Command, 93
Allis-Chalmers, 59
Althos, Anthony A., 265
American Insurance Association, 164
American National Standard Institute (ANSI), 59
American Society for Quality Control (ASQC), 173, 175, 283, 310, 337
Annual conventions, vendor-vendee, 119–20
Apelian, Derian, 109
Asahi, Joi, 257
Asaka, Tetsuichi, 170, 187
Audits, *see* Quality audits
Automation, 259
Availability analysis, 165
Average (acceptable) quality level (AQL), 111, 120–21, 142
Averages, 275–77
  average and range charts, 280–90

Bell curve, 286–88
BNA Communications, 307–8
Brainstorming, 207
Brunswick Corporation, *see* Mercury Marine
Burgess, John A., 91–101
Burnout, 15
Burr, I. W., 337
Business Week, 2, 10
BYTE (periodical), 154

California Institute of Technology, 5
California Medical Insurance Feasibility Study (California Medical Association/California Hospital Association), 236
Cambridge Corporation (Japan), 73
Carter administration, 4
Cause-and-effect analysis, 207
Central tendency, 275–77
Charting, *see* Statistical methods
Checklists in design review, 95–97
Chrysler Corporation, 124
Coding, 279–80
Companywide Quality Control (CWQC), 84, 255–56, 258
Competition, foreign, 3–4, 69–70
  See also specific countries
Complaints, *see* Customer complaints
Computer-aided design/manufacturing (CAD/CAM), 102–3, 155
Computer-Aided Inspection and Reporting Systems (CAIR), 160
Computer-aided quality systems, 21, 72, 77–78, 146–60
  elements of effective information systems, 146–48
  implementation of, 154–60
    key considerations, 159–60
  in new-product introduction, 102–3
  role of computers in, 148–54
  self-analysis on, 160
Consumer Reports, 77
Consumers Union of the United States, 77, 173
"Continual improvement," 142, 144
Control charts, *see under* Statistical methods

339

INDEX

Conventions, vendor-vendee, 119-20
Cost-benefit analysis, 295
Costs, see Quality costs
Cp/Cpk indices, 85, 131-32, 143
Crosby, Philip, 309
Customer complaints:
 closed-loop system for, 166
 in product deployment plan, 71, 72
Customer satisfaction:
 complacency about, 3, 69
 See also Quality deployment; Service quality

Data, see Statistical methods
Data-base management systems, 151
David, Edward E., Jr., 5
David, Wayne, 296
Deere and Company, 160
Defect-detection system, 125-27
Defect-prevention system, 127, 128
Deming, W. Edward, 40, 127, 136, 142, 250, 255, 256, 318
Deming Prize, 172, 186, 255
Deployment, see Quality deployment
Design of experiments, 329-31
Design quality, see New-product introduction
Direct Selling Education Foundation, 169
Dispersion of data, 276
Distribution, types of, 286-88
Dixon, W. S., 337
Drawings, lack of clarity of, 114-15
Drucker, Peter, 244

Educational system, 8, 14
 Japanese, 8, 256
Equipment:
 maintenance of quality of, 129
 new, evaluation of, 132-35
 See also Manufacturing quality control
Employee participation, see Worker/employee participation
Encyclopaedia Britannica, 11, 260, 264
"Engineering deviation," 111
Evaluation of organization, see Self-analysis
Experiments, design of, 329-39
Exxon Research and Engineering Company, 5

F-16 fighter plane, 101
Failure analysis, 97, 102, 103
 in Japan, 262
Failure mode effect analysis (FMEA), 167
Family parts purchasing, 118-19
Fault tree analysis (FTA), 167
Feigunbaum, A. V., 337
FEMA, 103
Field quality, see Service quality
Fishbone diagram, 207
Flow process analysis, 208-9
Ford Motor Company, 102, 124
Frank, Richard J., 31
Frequency distribution, 272-75, 286-88

Garrin, David A., 15
Gauge-control systems, 155-56
Gauging, integrated, 137
General Dynamics, 101
General Motors, 124

Germany, 4, 19
Grand average, 278, 279
Grant, L. Eugene, 337
Great Britain, 246
Grehner, W. S., 160
Grimmer, Ed, 80, 81

Harvard Business Review, 1, 15, 305
Hayes, Robert, 265
Histograms, frequency, 272-75, 286-88
Honeywell, 190
Hospitals, quality assurance in, 231-38
Hughes Aircraft Corporation, 190

IBM Corporation, 59
Illustrations, design-review, 98-99
India, 246
Industry Week, 217, 251
Information systems, see Computer-aided quality systems
Ingle, Anil, 148n
Ingle's Quality Management Systems, 306, 307
 programs offered by, 303-4
In-process quality control, see Manufacturing quality control
International Association of Quality Circles (IAQC), 173, 337
Introduction to Off-Line Quality Control (Taguchi and Wu), 330
Iron Age (magazine), 101, 138, 160, 225
Ishikawa, Kaoru, 207

Japan, 116, 254-65
 economic growth of, 2-4
 educational system in, 8, 256
 interest rates in, 247
 manufacturing methods in, 258-64
 quality control in, 1-2, 5, 8, 15, 19, 254-58
  national policies, 249, 257-58
  OQI, 32
  PPM, 120, 122
  quality audits, 170, 172-73, 186
  Quality Circles, 15, 85, 190, 201, 255-58
  training programs, 21, 256
  statistical methods, 8, 12, 22, 85, 131, 136, 250, 256, 261, 318, 330-31
 reading matter on, 264-65
Japan Economic Institute of America, 11
Japan Industry Specification (JIS), 762
 Mark auditing system of, 172-73, 186
Japan Productivity Center, 254
Japan Quality Control Prize, 172, 186, 255
Japanese management of U.S. companies, 11
JIT ("just-in-time") purchasing, 119, 258
JIT ("just-in-time") production, 6, 258-59
Joint Commission of Accreditation of Hospitals, quality-assurance standard of, 323-37
Juran, Joseph M., 171, 337
JUSE (Union of Japanese Scientists and Engineers), 122, 254-56

Kirkpatrick, E. G., 337
Koizumu, Mamory, 122
Kuma, Akira, 122

Labor, see Unions

Leavenworth, Richard S., 337
Lewis, Tom, 296
Lockheed (company), 190

Machinery, *see* Equipment
McClure, Edward, 101
Maintainability analysis, 165
Management:
  recommended training for, 221–22
  responsibilities of, listed, 11–13
Management by objective (MBO), 53
Management style, 7, 8
  See also Participative management
Managerial quality audit, 174–75
Manufacturing (in-process) quality control, 21, 125–45
  "continual improvement" approach to, 142, 144
  conventional (defect-detection) system of, 125–27
  machinery and equipment, 129
  material and components, 129–30, 166–68
  new-equipment evaluations, 132–35
  people and, 137–38
  PPM concept and, 142
  process capability studies, 131, 157, 294
  self-analysis on, 144–45
  standards in, 130–31
  statistical approach to, 127, 128 131, 136–37, 157, 166–68
    SPC, 132
  summary of factors in, 138–42
  training programs, 128–29, 137–38
  types of processes, 125
  vendor evaluation and, 131, 138
"Market-In" concept, 84
Massey, F. J., Jr., 337
Material, maintenance of quality of, 129–30
Material review board (MRB) system, 111–13
Matsushita, Masuharu, 265
Matsushita Ede. Component Company, 122
Mean, 275–77
Median, 275–77
Mercury Marine (Brunswick Corporation), 80, 81, 138, 190
MIL-Q-9858A standard, 146
MIL-STD-105D standard, 142
MIL-STD-9859 standard, 332
MODEM, 150, 153
Multivary charts, 293

Naguchi, Tunji, 254
Nelson, Lloyd, 145
New-product introduction, 3, 21, 82–109
  design-improvement methods in, 102–4
    off-line quality control, 103–5, 330
  design phases in, 12, 85–90
  design reviews in, 12, 90–101
    cost of, 92
    dry run, 99
    followup, 101
    how to conduct, 91, 99–101
    participants in, 91
    preparation for meeting, 94–96
    responsibility for, 92
    review package, 98–99
    technical aspects, 95–98
    time and place, 92–94
    types of, 101
  general system for, 105–10
    cost, 107–8
    process and manufacturing, 108
    product, 106–7
    schedule, 105–6
  problems in, 83–85
  self-analysis on, 108–9
New York Times, 2
Nissan Company, 138, 225
Noguchi, Junjo, 256

Off-line quality control, 103–5, 330
On-line computer failure analysis, 103
Organizational Quality Improvement (OQI), 12, 14, 19–41
  aims of, 23–24, 32
  case studies, 39–41
  definition of, 19–20, 32
  factors in success of, 38–39
  key features of, 20–23
  organization and responsibilities in, 26–29
  phases of, reviewed, 25–26, 33–38
  Quality Circles and, 24–25, 27, 190, 304, 305
  questions and answers on, 304–5
  in service industries, 238–43
    advantages, 242–43
    implementation, 240–41
    Quality Wheel, 239–40
    training, 241–42
  training for, *see* Training programs—recommended, for OQI
  See also Quality audits; Quality costs; Quality Wheel; Self-analysis; Statistical methods
Orthogonal arrays, 330–31
Ouchi, Bill, 264

Pareto analysis, 45, 207
Participative management, 8, 12, 13, 213
  See also Quality Circles; Worker/employee participation
Parts per billion (PPB), 122
Parts per million (PPM), 115, 120–23, 142
Pascale, Richard T., 265
Peach, Paul, 337
"People and Productivity" (film), 11, 260, 264
Planning:
  longterm, in U.S. industry, 4
  See also Quality planning and policy
Policy, *see* Quality planning and policy
Precision Metal (periodical), 116
Precontrol system, 290–93
Presentation skills, 210
Problem solving, *see* Statistical methods—in problem solving
Process analysis, 208–9, 294, 295
Process capability indices (Cp and Cpk), 85, 131–32, 143
Process capability studies, 131, 157, 294
Product audit, 174
Product deployment plan, 71–72
  See also Quality deployment
Product liability, 164–65
"Product-Out" concept, 84
Product testing, *see* Manufacturing quality control

Production Magazine, 137
Productivity improvement teams, *see* Quality improvement teams

Q.C. Trends (journal), 306-7, 338
Quality, definition of, 300
Quality (periodical), 338
Quality-action committee, 27, 28
Quality assurance in hospitals, 231-38
Quality-assurance manuals, 332-35
Quality audits, 20, 21, 23, 170-87
   advantages of, 186-87
   deficiencies in, 185-86
   purposes of, 170-72
   quality auditor, 175-77
   self-analysis on, 187
   steps in performance of, 177-78
   system and procedure for (case study), 178-85
   types of, 172-75
Quality Circle Services, 264
Quality Circles, 4, 8-10, 12, 13, 21, 190-217
   avoiding failures of, 211
   basic techniques for service industries, 206-11
   benefits of, 211
   definition of, 191
   future of, 213
   history of, 15, 190-91
   introduction of, 191-94
   in Japan, 15, 85, 190, 201, 255-58
   operation of, 201-5
   and OQI, 24-25, 27, 190, 304, 305
   organizational structure of, 190, 194-201
      executive committee, 194-95
      facilitators, 198-200
      leader, 196-97
      members, 197-98
      mini-coordinators, 201
   self-analysis on, 216-17
   successful, case studies of, 212-15
Quality Circles Master Guide, 167, 199*n*
Quality Circles Quarterly, 338
Quality control:
   in Japan, *see* Japan—quality control in statistics and, *see* Statistical methods traditional vs. off-line, 103-5, 330
   See also New-product introduction; Quality improvement; Quality Wheel
Quality-control department, 66-67, 138
   image of, 10
Quality Control Handbook (Juran), 171, 337
Quality costs, 20, 22, 136-37, 168, 309-17
   advantages of use of, 315
   attitudes toward, 5, 9, 309
   exercise on, 315
   forms for reporting of, 315-17
   four types of, 22, 310-12
   management of, 314
   setting up system, 312-14
Quality Costs—What and How (ASQC), 310
Quality council, 26, 27
Quality-council chairperson, 27-28
Quality deployment, 13, 69-81, 103, 261
   within closed-loop product deployment plan, 71-73
   customer-based quality measurement and, 77-80
   self-analysis on, 80-81
   use of quality tables in, 73-76

Quality improvement:
   Ingle's System for (programs offered), 303-4
   management responsibilities and, 11-13
   national, 245-53
      financial institutions and, 246-47
      government and, 5-6, 245-46, 251-53
      in Japan, 249, 257-58
      management and, 246, 252
      suggested programs for, 247-51
      unions and, 246, 252
   quiz on, 13-14
   roadblocks to, 53-54
   See also Organizational Quality Improvement (OQI)
Quality information systems, *see* Computer-aided quality systems
Quality measurement, 57-58
   customer-based, 77-81
   See also Statistical methods
Quality planning and policy, 5, 20-21, 51-68
   elements of total quality system, 55-57
   need for, 58-59
   objectives of, 54-55
   policy for "ABC Company," 60-61
   preparing plans, 61
   quality measurement in, 57-58
   and quality organization, 66-67
   roadblocks to improvement, 53-54
   sample plan, 62-66
   self-analysis on, 68
Quality Progress (periodical), 154, 338
Quality (*or* productivity) improvement teams, 27-29
   Quality Circles vs., 24-25
"Quality and reliability agreement" with vendors, 115-16
Quality standards:
   factors in low level of, 2-10, 53-54
   in hospitals, 232-37
   in manufacturing quality control, 130-31
   U.S. Government, 142, 146, 332
Quality Wheel, 13, 24, 26, 28, 48
   quiz, 29-31
   ten sections of, reviewed, 20-22
   for service industries, 239-40
   See also specific Wheel sections
Quantity vs. quality, 2

Range, 276-78
   average and range control charts, 280-90
Reagan administration, 4
Red X theory, 47-48
Reliability analysis, 163-64
Reports of Statistical Application Research (journal), 122
Research and development (R & D), 5, 7
Ricoh Company, 84
Roberts, John D., 5
Robotics, 259

Safety analysis, 164
St. Cloud (Minnesota) Hospital, 231*n*
Saka, Eij, 122
Salkevour, A. M., 231*n*
Schlitz Brewing Company, 59
Schonberger, Richard, 265
Schwinn, David R., 110, 124

INDEX

Sealed Power Corporation, 322-27
Self-analysis (evaluation of organization), 14, 19-20, 22, 32
  on computer-aided quality systems, 160
  on manufacturing quality control, 144-45
  on new-product introduction, 108-9
  on quality audits, 187
  on Quality Circles, 216
  on quality deployment, 80-81
  on quality planning, 68
  on vendor quality control, 124
  for service industries, 243-44
  on service quality, 169
  summary of results, 336
  See also Quality Wheel
Service industries, 229-44
  basic techniques for Quality Circles in, 206-11
  general operation of, 230-31
  hospital quality assurance (case study), 231-38
  implementation of OQI in, 239-43
  principal, listed, 229-30
  problems in, 238-39
  Quality Wheel for, 239-40
  self-analysis for, 243-44
Service quality, 21, 161-69
  how to analyze, 163-65
  how to improve, 166-69
  reasons for customer dissatisfaction with, 162-63
  self-analysis on, 168
Serviceability analysis, 165
Shainin, Dorian, 47
Shewhart, W. A., 337
SIGSTAT, 154
Specifications:
  lack of clarity in, 114-15
  quality deployment and, 72, 76-77
Solar energy, 4
Standards, see Quality standards
Statistical methods, 4, 8-9, 12-14, 22, 269-96
  advanced, 22, 44
  averages, 275-77
  basic, 22, 44
  basic training in, 219-20
  coding, 279-80
  computers and, 151-52, 157
  control charts, 280-93
    average and range ($\overline{X}$ and R), 280-90
    control limits, 281-85, 289
    multivary, 293
    precontrol (stoplight), 290-93
  data collection, 269-72
  data organization, 272-75
    frequency distribution (histogram), 272-75, 286-88
    run chart, 272, 273
  definition of, 42-43
  design of experiments, 329-31
  education system and, 8, 14
  grand averages, 278, 279
  intermediate, 22, 44
  Japan's use of, 8, 12, 22, 85, 131, 136, 250, 256, 261, 318, 330-31
  in problem solving, 42-50, 220
    basic steps, 43
    Red X theory, 47-48
    steps followed, 44-50

  types, 43-44
  range, 276-78
  and service quality, 166-67
  symbols used in, 209, 280-81
Statistical Process Control (SPC), 13, 60, 117, 118, 132, 280, 318-28
  continuing procedures in, 321-22
  implementation plan for, 319-21
  sample case study of, 322-27
  training course in, 327-28
Statistical quality control (SQC), 54, 280
  See also Statistical methods
Statistical Quality Control and Circle Institute, Inc., 303
Stiles, Edward, 41
Stoplight (precontrol) system, 290-93
Subgroups, 278, 279
Suppliers, see Vendor evaluation
Suzuki, Yukio, 254
Symbols, statistical, 209, 280-81
Systems audit, 173-74

Taguchi, Genichi, and Taguchi Method, 103-5, 330
Technological innovation, 4, 6-7
Terrell, James, 296
Time magazine, 148
Total Quality Assurance (TQA), 13
Total Quality Control, 12
Total quality system, elements of, 55-57
Trade-off studies, 97
Training programs, 10, 13, 15, 21, 32-37, 128-29, 218-28, 137-38
  in Japan, 21, 256
  national, 250-51
  OQI, for service organizations, 241-42
  recommended, for OQI, 218-28
    for all employees, 225-26
    for colleges, 226-27
    for engineers, 224
    for middle management, 221-22
    ongoing, 227-28
    for operators, 223-24
    in statistical methods, 219-20
    for supervisors and foremen, 222-23
    for top management, 221
    for vendors, 224-25
  See also Quality Circles; Statistical Process Control

Union of Japanese Scientists and Engineers (JUSE), 122, 254-56
Unions, 7
  and national quality, 246, 252
  and quality planning, 55
  in Japan, 261
United States of America Today (Japan Economic Institute of America), 11
U.S. Government:
  and national quality policies, 5-6, 246, 251-53
  quality standards of, 142, 146, 332
  and solar energy, 5

Vendor evaluation/quality control, 7-8, 21, 85, 110-24, 131, 138
  computers and, 156
  future needs and, 122-23

Vendor evaluation/quality control (*Continued*)
   in Japan, 261
   PPM use in, 115, 120-23
   problems in, 112-15
   procedures for, 115-22
   self-analysis on, 124
   traditional system of, 110-12
Vogel, Ezra, 265
Volkswagen Company, 21

Wachhiak, Robert, 175
Wall Street Journal, 2
Ward Reports, 173
Warranty costs, 168
Weibull distribution, 103, 167-68
West Germany, 4, 19
Westinghouse, 190
Wheelwright, Steven, 265
Williams, Vearl A., 137
Word processing, 150, 152-53
Worker/employee participation, 7-10
   approaches to, listed, 188-89
   and design quality, 102
   in Japan, 262
   See also Participative management; Quality Circles
Wu, Yuin, 76, 105, 330

$\overline{X}$ and R control charts, 280-90
Xerox Corporation, 116, 117